VOCATIONAL ADJUSTMENT OF DISABLED PERSONS

VOCATIONAL ADJUSTMENT OF DISABLED PERSONS

Edited by
Brian Bolton, Ph.D.
Professor
Arkansas Rehabilitation Research and Training Center
University of Arkansas—Fayetteville

University Park Press
Baltimore

UNIVERSITY PARK PRESS
International Publishers in Science, Medicine, and Education
300 North Charles Street
Baltimore, Maryland 21201

Copyright © 1982 by University Park Press

Typeset by Maryland Composition Co.
Manufactured in the United States of America by
The Maple Press Company

All rights, including that of translation into other languages, reserved. Photomechanical reproduction (photocopy, microcopy) of this book or parts thereof without special permission of the publisher is prohibited.

Library of Congress Cataloging in Publication Data

Main entry under title:

Vocational adjustment of disabled persons.

Bibliography: p. 231. Includes index.
Contents: Vocational adjustment and rehabilitation / Brian Bolton—The meaning of work / Mary Jo Schneider and Daniel E. Ferritor—Work motivation / Daniel W. Cook—[etc.]
1. Vocational rehabilitation—Addresses, essays, lectures. I. Bolton, Brian F.
HD7255.V58   362.4'0484   82-7058
ISBN 0-8391-1722-1   AACR2

CONTENTS

Editor vii
Contributors ix
Preface xi

Chapter 1
VOCATIONAL ADJUSTMENT AND REHABILITATION
Brian Bolton 1

Chapter 2
THE MEANING OF WORK
Mary Jo Schneider and Daniel E. Ferritor 21

Chapter 3
WORK MOTIVATION
Daniel W. Cook 39

Chapter 4
ASSESSMENT OF EMPLOYMENT POTENTIAL
Brian Bolton 53

Chapter 5
PRESCRIPTIVE VOCATIONAL EVALUATION
Michael Leland and B. Douglas Rice 71

Chapter 6
COMMERCIAL VOCATIONAL EVALUATION SYSTEMS
Karl F. Botterbusch 93

Chapter 7
BEHAVIORAL ANALYSIS OF WORK PROBLEMS
John N. Marr 127

Chapter 8
PSYCHOSOCIAL ADJUSTMENT SKILLS TRAINING
Robert L. Akridge and Bob L. Means 149

Chapter 9
VOCATIONAL PLANNING
Richard T. Roessler 167

Chapter 10
VOCATIONAL PLACEMENT STRATEGIES
Reed Greenwood 181

Chapter 11
EMPLOYMENT DECISIONS REGARDING HANDICAPPED PERSONS
Gerald L. Rose 195

Appendix A
REVISED SCALE OF EMPLOYABILITY 213

Appendix B
WORK ATTITUDES SCALE 225

REFERENCES 231

AUTHOR INDEX 245

SUBJECT INDEX 251

EDITOR

Brian Bolton, Ph.D., Professor, Arkansas Rehabilitation Research and Training Center (Fayetteville), is a Fellow of the American Psychological Association (Evaluation and Measurement and Rehabilitation Psychology), a Fellow of the Society for Personality Assessment, a past president of the Southwestern Multivariate Society, and the recipient of nine research awards from the American Rehabilitation Counseling Association. He is Editor of the *Rehabilitation Counseling Bulletin* and Consulting Editor in the field of rehabilitation for University Park Press.

CONTRIBUTORS

Robert L. Akridge
Associate Professor
Arkansas Rehabilitation Research
 and Training Center
University of Arkansas
 (Hot Springs)

Karl F. Botterbusch
Director of Development Services
Stout Vocational Rehabilitation
 Institute
University of Wisconsin-Stout

Daniel W. Cook
Associate Professor
Arkansas Rehabilitation Research
 and Training Center
University of Arkansas
 (Fayetteville)

Daniel E. Ferritor
Chairman
Department of Sociology
and Research Associate
Arkansas Rehabilitation Research
 and Training Center
University of Arkansas
 (Fayetteville)

Reed Greenwood
Coordinator of Rehabilitation
 Education
Arkansas Rehabilitation Research
 and Training Center
University of Arkansas
 (Fayetteville)

Michael Leland
Training Associate
Arkansas Rehabilitation Research
 and Training Center
University of Arkansas
 (Fayetteville)

John N. Marr
Director of Research
Arkansas Rehabilitation Research
 and Training Center
Professor of Psychology
University of Arkansas
 (Fayetteville)

Bob L. Means
Director of Training
Arkansas Rehabilitation Research
 and Training Center
University of Arkansas
 (Hot Springs)

B. Douglas Rice
Associate Professor
Arkansas Rehabilitation Research
 and Training Center
University of Arkansas
 (Hot Springs)

Richard T. Roessler
Professor
Arkansas Rehabilitation Research
 and Training Center
University of Arkansas
 (Fayetteville)

Gerald L. Rose
Associate Professor
Department of Management
   Sciences
College of Business
   Administration
University of Iowa

Mary Jo Schneider
Professor of Anthropology
   and Research Associate
Arkansas Rehabilitation Research
   and Training Center
University of Arkansas
   (Fayetteville)

PREFACE

The state-federal vocational rehabilitation program recognizes the critical importance of the work role in American society. Successful vocational adjustment is the goal of vocational rehabilitation services for all clients, because it is believed that vocational adjustment enhances the prospects for successful adjustment in other life areas. This operational assumption was given academic credence by Super (1957) when he hypothesized that by "...helping attain success, and developing a feeling of competence in one important area of adjustment, the vocational, it is possible to release the individual's ability to cope more adequately with other aspects of living..." (p. 300).

Vocational Adjustment of Disabled Persons is an introduction to the conceptual issues and service strategies that focus on the vocational preparation of handicapped persons. The volume consists of 11 chapters that address three primary aspects of the vocational adjustment process. The first three chapters establish a conceptual foundation for the subject by reviewing key areas in the vocational, sociological, and motivational literature. Chapters 4 through 6 are concerned with methods and procedures for assessing the handicapped person's vocational potential, and Chapters 7 through 11 outline strategies and techniques for facilitating the vocational adjustment of rehabilitation clients.

Vocational Adjustment of Disabled Persons was designed as a companion volume to the earlier *Psychosocial Adjustment to Disability* (1978). The rationale for the separation of vocational and psychosocial adjustment is important and merits brief comment. The available research evidence indicates that vocational adjustment and psychosocial adjustment are relatively independent *outcomes* of rehabilitation services (see Bolton, 1979, pp. 102–107, and Roessler & Bolton, 1978, pp. 7–10). However, this statistical justification for treating the two major domains of client functioning in separate volumes should *not* be misconstrued to suggest that vocational adjustment and psychosocial adjustment are independent developmental processes. In fact, considerable clinical experience and rehabilitation theory indicate that just the opposite is true: successful vocational adjustment depends upon the acquisition of minimum essential levels of interpersonal skills and facilitative social attitudes, but the attainment of adequate psychosocial skills does *not* guarantee successful vocational adjustment. Hence the relative independence of vocational and psychosocial outcomes. The models of vocational adjustment outlined in Chapter 1 are based on the principle of the *inter*dependence of vocational and psychosocial developmental processes.

The organization and emphasis of this volume reflect to a substantial degree the model of work adjustment developed at the Chicago Jewish Vocational Service (CJVS), where the editor was employed from 1968 through 1971. The formative influence of William Gellman, former Executive Director of CJVS and now at DePaul University, and Asher Soloff, Research Director at CJVS, is gratefully acknowledged. The now-classic CJVS monograph *Adjusting People to Work* (1957) is the source of material for one section in Chapter 1, and its indirect impact is evident in several other chapters.

A third person who greatly influenced the contents of *Vocational Adjustment of Disabled Persons* is Walter Neff, whose book *Work and Human Behavior* (1977) reflects strongly his 10 years in conducting research at CJVS. In addition to his pervasive impact on several chapters, Dr. Neff generously gave permission to reprint the *Work Attitudes Scale* in Appendix B.

Grateful appreciation is also expressed to Frank Lewis for preparing the indexes for this book.

Vocational Adjustment of Disabled Persons was written with the support of a research and training center grant (16-P-56812, RT-13) from the National Institute of Handicapped Research to the Arkansas Rehabilitation Research and Training Center. The book is dedicated to the International Year of Disabled Persons, with all royalties assigned to the Arkansas Rehabilitation Research and Training Center for research on the adjustment problems of handicapped persons.

Brian Bolton

This volume is dedicated to the International Year of Disabled Persons.

VOCATIONAL ADJUSTMENT OF DISABLED PERSONS

chapter 1
VOCATIONAL ADJUSTMENT AND REHABILITATION

Brian Bolton

For 60 years the fundamental premise underlying the state-federal vocational rehabilitation program has been that successful vocational adjustment is the basis for satisfactory adjustment in all areas of life. This assumption, which has been supported by research evidence as well as extensive clinical experience, reflects the central importance of the work role in American society. Having a job not only provides the means for financial independence, it confers on the employee the benefits of meaningful participation and enhanced self-respect. In other words, the vocational rehabilitation philosophy and service program view work as a therapeutic activity that serves to integrate handicapped persons into American society.

The employment goal of the vocational rehabilitation program is appropriate job placement of the handicapped client in the competitive labor market. For some severely disabled clients, however, competitive employment is not a realistic objective, and placement in a sheltered workshop or homebound program is the only feasible alternative. Hence, it becomes important to de-emphasize the economic rationale for employment in the vocational rehabilitation program and stress the interpersonal and intrapsychic aspects of work activity. For the purposes of this volume, successful vocational adjustment results from a) participation in some form of productive activity that b) contributes to the common good and c) enhances the individual's self-esteem and general life adjustment.

It should be noted that employment is not a necessary goal of vocational rehabilitation services for all clients; the 1978 Amendments to the 1973 Rehabilitation Act authorize the provision of comprehensive services designed to prepare severely disabled persons for living independently, without any explicit vocational goal (see Rice and Roessler (1980) for a discussion of independent living legislation).

This chapter consists of four major sections that establish the foundation for all subsequent chapters in the book. The first section includes brief overviews of three models of the vocational adjustment process in vocational rehabilitation. Next, the rehabilitation technique known as the therapeutic workshop, which evolved concurrently with the Chicago model of vocational adjustment at the Chicago Jewish Vocational Service in the late 1940s and early 1950s, is described in some detail. The third section summarizes the nature and correlates of the long-term vocational adjustment of 225 former clients of a comprehensive rehabilitation center 12 years after their discharge from the center. Thje final section documents the impact of vocational rehabilitation programs on the vocational adjustment of handicapped persons 2-5 years after services were rendered, and outlines the implications of the results for the improvement of vocational rehabilitation service programs.

MODELS OF VOCATIONAL ADJUSTMENT

In this section three conceptual models of the vocational adjustment process that have clear implications for the vocational rehabilitation of disabled persons are briefly described. These three models are the Chicago Jewish Vocational Service model (Gellman, 1953), the Minnesota Theory of Work Adjustment model (Dawis, 1976), and Hershenson's (1981) developmental model of vocational adjustment. There are at least three other models that have their origins in rehabilitation, namely, the models of Goldberg (see Goldberg & Satow, 1972), McMahon (1979), and Neff (1977). Goldberg's model is implicit in a series of studies of the vocational development of persons with various disabilities; McMahon's model is a synthesis of concepts from several sources, primarily the Minnesota Theory of Work Adjustment; and Neff's model derives substantially from the Chicago model, reflecting his 10-year tenure as research director at the Chicago Jewish Vocational Service. However, the three models presented here are especially significant in that they all have a substantial history of development and refinement, they have been the subject of numerous empirical evaluations, and they have been translated into procedures and techniques for use in vocational rehabilitation counseling.

Although the three models outlined here each have different emphases— the Chicago model relies on psychodynamic mechanisms and concepts, the Minnesota model is basically a person-environment correspondence system, and Hershenson's model is premised on a developmental sequence—the three models actually have much in common. Foremost among the similarities is their focus on vocational adjustment as the cornerstone of the rehabilitation process, an emphasis that is consistent with the history and legislative justification for the rehabilitation movement in the United States. Other similarities are delineated in the summary section that follows the descriptions of the three models.

Why are these models of vocational adjustment important? What functions can they serve for the rehabilitation practitioner? First, they provide conceptual frameworks for thinking about the vocational adjustment problems of disabled persons. Second, they indicate which characteristics and response capabilities should be the focus of client assessment programs. Third, they suggest what the optimal treatment approaches might be and provide guidelines for the planning and provision of services. Fourth, they have implications for preparing the client for placement in employment, which is the ultimate goal of the vocational rehabilitation process.

The Chicago Model

Gellman (1953) outlined a model of vocational adjustment that served as the framework for the pioneering vocational adjustment research carried out at the Chicago Jewish Vocational Service during the 1950s and 1960s. The Chicago model is premised on two major components: a) use of situational techniques to analyze and modify vocational attitudes and behavior, and b) focus upon the vocational patterns and psychosocial factors influencing vocational adjustment.

Vocational adjustment in the Chicago model is defined as the balance between the satisfaction that the individual requires from work and that individual's ability to derive satisfaction from work. The underlying assumption is that vocational adjustment is achieved through satisfying personal and emotional needs in the work situation. Motivation and the meaning of work to the individual are considered to be the primary determinants of vocational adjustment.

The Chicago model can be summarized in five basic propositions:

1. Each individual has a characteristic vocational pattern that reflects that individual's personality structure and the manner in which his or her needs are incorporated in work situations. The vocational pattern is comprised of six elements: a) the meaning of work to the individual, b) ability to derive satisfaction from work (motivation), c) mobilization of energy in the work situation, d) interpersonal relations on the job, e) positive and negative work identifications, and f) ability to adjust to work pressures. The most important aspects of the vocational pattern are the meaning of work, which expresses the goals and aspirations of the individual,

and motivation and ability to use energy constructively in the work situation.
2. Vocational adjustment is *not* a direct function of personal adjustment. Satisfactory vocational adjustment may or may not occur as a result of improved psychosocial adjustment, and adequate psychosocial adjustment does not necessarily lead to successful vocational adjustment. The relationship between these two areas of adjustment is a complex function of the individual's vocational pattern and underlying personality dynamics. Either vocational or psychosocial adjustment may help or hinder the other type of adjustment.
3. Individual vocational goals and patterns reflect cultural forces. Vocational patterns, including attitudes toward work and characteristic work methods, result from the unique interaction of cultural goals and individual life experiences. Level of aspiration, anticipated job satisfaction, and meaning of work are individual variations of a subcultural occupational value system.
4. Learning to work is a complex developmental process. Ability to work is a learned capability with its roots in the developing vocational pattern of the individual. Mature work attitudes and behaviors are based upon expectations of the satisfaction and values to be derived from work. It follows, then, that vocational adjustment is the result of a learning process that can be taught and developed.
5. Adequate job performance is dependent upon the individual's vocational pattern and possession of sufficient ability to meet minimal job requirements. Extensive research by the United States Employment Service indicates that there are job families or clusters of occupations that have minimum critical ability requirements; that is, a certain minimum level of skill or knowledge is necessary (but not sufficient) for successful job performance. The Chicago model postulates that successful vocational adjustment is determined by the individual's personality and motivational characteristics, assuming that the minimal ability requirements are met.

Within the conceptual framework of the Chicago model, it is apparent that the vocational rehabilitation process should focus on the client's psychosocial and interpersonal adjustment in the work environment. Instruments to assess the individual's work habits, attitudes, and motivation, as well as the meaning of work, were developed at the Chicago Jewish Vocational Service. At the same time, a rehabilitation strategy evolved that centered on the use of the workshop as a therapeutic technique to prepare handicapped persons for employment.

The therapeutic workshop is discussed later in this chapter, and the instruments for assessing employment potential and meaning of work are described in Chapter 4 and reproduced in the Appendices.

The Minnesota Model

The Minnesota Theory of Work Adjustment (Dawis, 1976) begins with the basic assumption that individuals seek to achieve and maintain correspondence with the environment. Correspondence between the individual and his or her environment implies conditions that can be described as a harmonious and suitable relationship. Vocational adjustment is the process by which the individual seeks to achieve and maintain correspondence with the work environment.

Tenure, or length of sustained employment, is the ultimate indicator of vocational adjustment. Tenure is hypothesized to be a complex function of the correspondence between the individual and the work environment. The primary determinants of tenure, and the most direct measures of individual-environment correspondence, are job satisfaction and job satisfactoriness.

Satisfaction with work reflects the extent to which the individual's work needs are satisfied by reinforcers in the work environment. For example, persons whose work needs include a preference for working alone rather than with other people, or who prefer situations that require decision making, will be more satisfied in jobs that provide opportunities for these types of activities. The similarity between vocational needs and job reinforcers leads to job satisfaction.

Satisfactoriness, on the other hand, is a function of the correspondence between the individual's abilities and the essential skills required by the job. For example, some individuals are good with their hands, others may have exceptional arithmetic skills, whereas still others are adept in social situations. These persons with different abilities will perform more successfully in jobs that involve primarily manual skills, bookkeeping or numerical tasks, and interpersonal relationships, respectively. In other words, matching the individual's abilities with the ability requirements of the job leads to job satisfactoriness.

The pattern of work needs and work-related abilities is referred to as the individual's work personality. Reinforcers and ability requirements are characteristics of the work environment. The degree of correspondence or similarity between needs and reinforcers determines job satisfaction, whereas the correspondence between abilities and ability requirements determines job satisfactoriness. Furthermore, satisfaction with the job helps to determine satisfactoriness and vice versa. Finally, the use of the concept of correspondence depends on the assumption that the relevant characteristics of the person and of the work environment are relatively stable.

The Minnesota model can be summarized in five basic propositions:

1. An individual's vocational adjustment is indicated by his or her concurrent levels of satisfaction and satisfactoriness.
2. Satisfaction is a function of the correspondence between the individual's needs and the reinforcement system of the work environment (assuming that the minimal ability requirements of the job are met).
3. Satisfactoriness is a function of the correspondence between the individual's abilities and the ability requirements of the work environment (assuming that a reasonable degree of job satisfaction is achieved).
4. Tenure is a joint function of satisfaction and satisfactoriness, concepts which are operationalized as need-reinforcer and ability-ability requirement similarity.
5. Work personality-work environment correspondence increases as a function of tenure.

The last proposition is known as the "work adjustment principle." It provides the foundation for the applications of the Minnesota model to problems of work adjustment of disabled persons that are discussed in the chapter on motivation.

Hershenson's Model

Hershenson (1981) has progressively refined his developmental model of vocational adjustment during the past 15 years, incorporating the results of a series of empirical studies of the vocational adjustment of disabled persons. The model postulates that vocational adjustment is a function of three basic domains:

1. Work personality: self-concept as a worker and a personal system of motivation for work
2. Work competencies: work habits, physical and mental skills applicable to jobs, and work-related interpersonal skills
3. Work goals: appropriate, well defined career goals.

Hershenson's formulation is premised on a) a sequence of hierarchical development that follows the order listed above, and b) a reciprocal influence process in which each domain affects the other two. For example, although the basic work personality is fairly well established before the development of work competencies assumes major importance, the acquisition of work habits and skills influences the individual's self-concept and motivational system, as well as his or her career goals. In other words, the development of vocational adjustment involves a dynamic balance among the three domains; it follows that the occurrence of disability causes a disruption of this vocational equilibrium.

The impact of disablement on vocational adjustment can be summarized in three propositions:

1. The onset of a disability has its initial impact on the individual's work competencies through the loss of essential skills.
2. The impairment of work skills then has a deterimental effect on the work personality, e.g., through damage to one's self-concept as a worker, and also on the individual's work goals.
3. The extent to which the disability becomes a vocational handicap depends on the extent to which the achievement of career goals is modified, as well as on the degree of maturity of the work personality. In general, the greater the impact of disability on the person's work motivation, the more handicapping will be its effect on work goals.

Consistent with this hypothesized pattern of impact of disablement on vocational adjustment, Hershenson has organized the vocational rehabilitation process into "the three R's of vocational rehabilitation."

1. *R*estoration (and/or replacement) of work-related skills to ameliorate the effects of disability on the client's work competencies
2. *R*emotivation of the client to work and to the worker role to deal with the impact of disability on the work personality
3. *R*estructuring of the client's career goals to alleviate the effects of handicap on work goals.

Hershenson recommends that the vocational rehabilitation process begin with both restoration of skills and remotivation to work. Restructuring of work goals should be undertaken after the client is motivated for work and has acquired some new work skills. Finally, because of the interdependence of the three domains, Hershenson believes that the vocational rehabilitation process should be initiated as soon as possible after the occurrence of disability in order to minimize deterioration of existing vocational adjustment.

Summary

The three models of vocational adjustment share several assumptions and concepts. Three primary elements are either explicitly formulated, or at least indirectly implied, as essential to each of the models:

1. The centrality of the work personality to successful vocational adjustment, including work motivation, abilities, habits, attitudes, and values
2. The importance of preparing or adjusting the individual to the requirements of the work environment
3. The necessity for in-depth assessment of the individual's work personality as a basis for service planning and eventual job placement.

The Chicago model is the most inclusive of the three vocational adjustment models, encompassing both the developmental premise of Hershenson's model and the person-environment correspondence concept of the Minnesota model (see propositions 1, 4, and 5 of the Chicago model). However, Hershenson's model and the Minnesota model expand considerably more than does the Chicago model on these points.

Five of the six models of vocational adjustment that originated in rehabilitation (Chicago, Hershenson, McMahon, Minnesota, and Neff) are used as organizing frameworks in subsequent chapters. The Chicago model underlies the vocational adjustment workshop in the following section, as well as the Scale of Employability described in the chapter on assessment of employment potential. Hershenson's model provides a scheme for job placement strategies in the chapter on that topic. McMahon's model is used in the chapter on vocational planning. The Minnesota model illustrates one approach to work motivation in the chapter devoted to that topic. Finally, Neff's extensive contributions are incorporated in the chapters on meaning of work, work motivation, and assessment of employment potential.

THE THERAPEUTIC WORKSHOP

The vocational rehabilitation process is a comprehensive program of services that includes medical, psychological, social, and vocational components (see Wright, 1980). Within the vocational component are several phases, including work evaluation, work adjustment, skill training, and job placement. On the basis of the models of vocational adjustment outlined in the previous section, it can be argued that the development of an adequate work personality is the most fundamental aspect of the vocational preparation process; in fact, it is essential to successful vocational adjustment.

This section describes the historical background and conceptual basis of the primary technique for the development of the work personality, the therapeutic workshop. The concept of the therapeutic workshop emerged at the Chicago Jewish Vocational Service in the early 1950s as a result of a unique employment problem—that of vocationally disabled immigrants. This description of the emergence and evolution of the therapeutic workshop as a procedure for fostering vocational maturity in disabled workers is adapted from the now-classic monograph *Adjusting People to Work* (Gellman, Gendel, Glaser, Friedman, & Neff, 1957).

Historical Background

The concept of the therapeutic workshop originated in response to the vocational problems of "apparently unemployable" immigrants who were referred to the Chicago Jewish Vocational Service in the late 1940s. Most had not had any regular work experience for 6 years preceding their entry into the United States. Although many of the immigrants were assisted in attaining employment, a small but significant subgroup (the "apparently unemployable" clients) seemed to be impervious to traditional vocational guidance, even when supplemented with casework and counseling services.

These "apparently unemployable" immigrants seemed to be physically capable of working to some extent, despite physical, mental, social, or emotional problems. However, all members of this group displayed difficulty in dealing with employers and appeared to be unable to conduct themselves appropriately during interviews. When a position was obtained, it was seldom held for more than a day or two because of difficulties in functioning productively or in dealing with supervisors or co-workers. Employers characterized these persons as unable to work or to assume the role of a worker. Their vocational handicaps seemed to reside in a negative attitude toward work and an inappropriate vocational pattern rather than in the disabilities themselves.

The rehabilitation techniques attempted with the "apparently unemployable" clients included skill training, on-the-job training, group counseling, role playing, and selective job placement. When these traditional approaches to employment preparation failed, it was decided to use a "work trial" technique in which employers sympathetic to the difficulties faced by immigrants would provide them with a structured work experience. It was hoped that the work trial experience would provide a sympathetic environment in which the client could become acclimated to American industrial practices. The overall results were not satisfactory, although the technique was successful with a few individuals.

Experience with the work trial program suggested the possibility of a situational technique that could overcome the defects evidenced in the work trial approach. It was felt that it would be feasible to devise a controlled work situation that would permit direct observation of client work behavior, and would provide for manipulating and varying the work environment to help guide clients toward the formation of acceptable work patterns. Such a work setting could meet these needs and also serve as an adjunct to the vocational counseling process. The workshop would have to be sufficiently rigid to simulate true working conditions, and yet flexible enough to emphasize or de-emphasize selected aspects of the work situation in accordance with client needs.

The prototypic therapeutic workshop, the Vocational Adjustment Center, was established in 1951 to help "apparently unemployable" immigrants become employable. The Vocational Adjustment Center concept slowly evolved to encompass work with other types of vocationally handicapped persons. The result was a structured, situational approach to the resolution of vocational adjustment problems of physically, mentally, and emotionally disabled persons.

The Vocational Adjustment Workshop

The primary objective of the therapeutic workshop is to facilitate the transition to employment of vocationally handicapped persons suffering from physical, mental, emotional, or social disabilities. Its vocational treatment goals may either be an improvement in the capacity to function productively, or in the ability to secure appropriate employment, or in the capacity to adapt on the job. The therapeutic workshop aims to stimulate the formation of an adequate work personality through training in habituation to work, adaption to supervision, accommodation to routine, and adjustment to fellow workers. Emphasis is placed upon work habits, desire to work, the development of work satisfaction, and the application of these traits in gainful employment.

The therapeutic work program is based on six assumptions or hypotheses about the relationship between the work personality and employment:

1. The majority of unskilled and semiskilled positions require an adequate work personality rather than specific experience, and job turnover is more often due to inadequate vocational adjustment than to lack of skill.
2. Each individual reacts in a characteristic manner to the entire range of vocational situations, and when work acquires a positive value for an individual, job seeking efforts, job performance, and job satisfaction will increase.
3. A successful work experience that generates job satisfaction will help an individual to identify with and strive to attain the work personality stressed in our culture.

4. A satisfying work experience will enhance an individual's confidence in his or her working ability and enable the individual to accept realistic vocational goals.
5. When resistance to work is primarily cultural, a satisfying and successful work experience will help to stimulate the growth of an adequate work personality and promote vocational adjustment.
6. If an individual's resistance to work is primarily the result of personality maladjustment, but there is a strong drive to accept authority or to conform to recognized cultural and social standards, a guided work experience will help to promote vocational adjustment.

It follows from these assumptions and hypotheses that the workshop program focuses on vocational adjustment problems, primarily those concerned with the effective use of abilities, motivation, attitudes, and adaptive techniques, and does not attempt to train clients in specific vocational skills. Furthermore, the atmosphere, climate, and functioning of the Vocational Adjustment Center simulates, as much as possible, a true industrial situation. Clients perform simple assembly and clerical tasks under conditions that approximate an industrial work setting. Every attempt is made in terms of physical arrangements, work activities, and the behavior of shop supervisors to create a situation that communicates an accurate picture of work to the clients. The tasks performed consist of subcontract work which must meet industrial specifications.

The workshop supervisors are professionally trained counselors who function both as foremen and as observers. Discussions with clients, when appropriate, deal with work behavior, work attitudes, and the problems encountered in the workshop. As observers, supervisors provide reports on client behavior at biweekly staffings, and prepare reports for the use of vocational counselors. In addition, shop supervisors are expected to be able to assume a variety of roles toward the client. The role or roles that the foreman adopts with respect to a particular client are determined at a staff conference and may be benign, authoritative, matter-of-fact, or supporting. The role will vary in accordance with client needs.

Client needs may be manifested in a variety of vocational problems that impair adjustment to work. In general, these vocational problems can be organized into three types of primary problems, although a client may exhibit more than one class of adjustment problem.

Issues of Occupational Acculturation These are problems concerned with adaptation to the pressures and demands of a work environment, the level and type of functioning ability, and the use of capacities in a work setting. Problems of occupational acculturation tend to be exhibited by persons who either have never worked or have been out of the labor market for extended periods. Such problems may be found among the mentally retarded, among discharged psychiatric patients, or in young people with severe physical handicaps, who have not had the opportunity to learn how to work through the experience of chores, part-time work, or summer work.

Interpersonal Relations on the Job These problems are concerned with adaptation to supervision, relations with co-workers, and the acceptance of appropriate norms of behavior in dealing with interpersonal job relationships. In general, such problems may be exhibited by persons who have negative identifications in a work situation, or who fear supervision, or who are unable to work in a group. Characteristically, such persons manifest behavior patterns that clash with those of the work group.

Inappropriate Vocational Patterns This category of problems is concerned with vocational behavior or attitudes exhibited in a work situation and the sociodynamic aspects of work. Among the problems subsumed in this category are the concept of self as a worker, the meaning of work, the relationship of the handicap to work behavior, psychosocial barriers to the use of abilities, and the derivation of work satisfaction. In practice these problems are found in individuals whose vocational behavior or attitudes are inappropriate and do not conform to the stereotype of a good worker.

The therapeutic work program actually operates at two levels. On the overt level, clients work at assembly tasks secured on a subcontract basis from private industrial firms. On the covert level, the work program is individualized for each client. It is based upon a counseling plan developed at a pre-entry conference which collates vocational, physical, social, and personality data secured through interviewing and psychological testing, and medical reports and case material secured from the referring agency. The work plan for the client is built around the following variables: a) supervisory attitude, which may be benign, matter-of-fact, or authoritative; b) co-worker relationships, which may involve working alone, or as a leader, or as a group member; c) work pressures, which vary from nominal to strong; d) type and level of work; e) emphasis upon qualitative or quantitative aspects of production; and f) work rewards such as praise or disapproval.

During the course of the program, the work plan is revised in accordance with the progress of the client. Observations of shop supervisors and interview material secured by the vocational counselor determine the nature of such modification. In implementing the plan, shop supervisors are careful to maintain their role as foremen. For example, even when suprvision is benign, the shop supervisor will confine discussions with the client to vocational behavior and workshop activities. Other matters are referred to the vocational counselor.

Finally, the design of the workshop setting should include three considerations: a) to simulate as closely as possible the typical physical setting to be found in the actual labor market (attempting to duplicate the environment of such functions as simple manufacturing, simple assembly, stock shipping, and clerical work); b) to provide space for line assembly operations as well as work performed individually; and c) to arrange for the possibility of physically isolating a client at work or incorporating him or her in a working group, as the situation might demand.

Summary

The therapeutic workshop is a psychological technique for preparing vocationally disabled persons to assume and retain employment in the competitive labor market. It is the fundamental rehabilitation procedure for helping the client to acquire an adequate work personality, that is, a set of attitudes and values that are recognized to be essential to successful vocational adjustment. The clinical experience of rehabilitation practitioners, as well as a variety of research evidence (e.g., Gellman et al., 1957; Shulman, 1967; Soloff, 1967), attests to the efficacy of the therapeutic workshop as an important rehabilitation technique. As a result of the accumulated successful experience with the rehabilitation workshop with numerous populations of disabled clients, an entire professional subspecialty has evolved. The Vocational Evaluation and Work Adjustment Association is a division of the National Rehabilitation Association that publishes its own journal and is organized into regional and state chapters. Interested readers are referred to the comprehensive text by Wright (1980) for further information.

VOCATIONAL ADJUSTMENT 12 YEARS LATER

The ultimate objective of vocational rehabilitation services is the lifelong vocational and psychosocial adjustment of handicapped persons. The success of the rehabilitation program in restoring handicapped individuals to optimal functioning can only be ascertained through follow-up studies. Follow-up studies involve contacting former clients some time after rehabilitation services are completed and assessing the ex-clients' vocational and personal circumstances. The specific findings from a long-term follow-up of former clients of the Hot Springs (Arkansas) Rehabilitation Center are presented below, and the general results of the major follow-up investigations in vocational rehabilitation are summarized in the next section.

The Hot Springs Rehabilitation Center (HSRC) is a comprehensive facility offering diagnostic, medical, residential, and vocational services. The fundamental premise on which the Center was founded is that successful rehabilitation requires an intensive, integrated program of medical, psychological, social, and vocational services. Although vocational preparation is emphasized in the work evaluation and vocational adjustment services, and in specialized vocational training in more than 30 occupational areas, a comprehensive, individualized program of services is planned with every client that will prepare him or her for a satisfying and productive life.

To evaluate the long-term benefits of HSRC services, 225 former clients were located 12 years after discharge from the facility. The ex-clients received services between 1965 and 1968, and the follow-up contact occurred in spring 1979. Information about their vocational and psychosocial adjustment was obtained through telephone interviews and a mailed survey questionnaire. The data were analyzed by dividing the sample into three age groups (younger, 27–34 years; middle, 35–58 years; and older, 60–86 years) and into males and females within each age group.

The vocational adjustment of the 225 former HSRC clients 12 years after rehabilitation services were received is summarized in the sections that follow; Readers interested in a more detailed report of the methodology and results of the investigation are referred to Bolton, Rowland, Brookings, Cook, Taperek, and Short (1980).

Characteristics of the Research Sample

All *disabilities were represented* in the research sample; younger clients were more likely to have intellectual, behavioral, or developmental disabilities, whereas clients in the middle and older groups were more likely to have suffered amputations, hemiplegia, arthritis, and cardiovascular disorders.

The *severity of the clients' disabilities* was indicated by the following: one-third (31%) had secondary disabilities, the prognosis for one-half (50%) was significant or severe loss, and two-thirds (64%) had received rehabilitation services prior to admission to HSRC.

One-third (36%) of the clients had not worked during the 5-year period prior to admission; the usual occupations of the majority of clients who were not students (40%) were at the unskilled (43%) and semiskilled (12%) levels, suggesting that *few clients had developed vocational skills*.

Although two-thirds (64%) of the clients completed their rehabilitation programs, one-third did not, indicating that many clients *did not receive all prescribed services*.

The overall adjustment ratings of the clients at HSRC discharge were: excellent (18%), good (30%), average (26%), below average (14%), and poor (12%), indicating *extensive variability in the clients' rehabilitation outcomes.*

Vocational Adjustment at Follow-up

Although slightly more than one-half (56%) of the exclients were *working at follow-up*, employment status was a function of age and sex; the proportions of males working in the three age groups were 80%, 44%, and 10%, respectively; the corresponding proportions for females were 55%, 24%, and 0%.

An analysis of the employment histories of the ex-clients for the 12-year period indicated that the majority (73%) had held *some employment* since leaving HSRC.

Almost all (95%) of the ex-clients who were working at follow-up were employed *full-time*; the average weekly salary was $198.

One-half (49%) of the working ex-clients had been employed on the same job for 5 years or more, indicating considerable *job stability.*

Most (81%) of the working ex-clients like their jobs, whereas very few (7%) disliked their jobs, suggesting high *job satisfaction.*

Nevertheless, more than one-half (59%) would exchange their present jobs for a better job, reflecting a *realistic attitude* toward employment.

The vast majority (84%) of the working ex-clients had received some *encouragement from their families* in their efforts to become employed.

Very few (6%) of the employed ex-clients were receiving any type of *public assistance* support.

The primary categories of employment for *males* were: machine trades (22%), structural work (22%), clerical and sales (15%), and professional, technical, and managerial (11%).

The major categories of employment for *females* were: service occupations (29%), clerical and sales (19%), and professional, technical, and managerial (19%).

The majority (73%) of former clients were *not* employed in occupations directly related to the vocational training that they received at HSRC, suggesting that it is the acquisition of some type of *occupation identity*, rather than specific skill training, that facilitates future employment.

Two-thirds (66%) of the nonworking ex-clients stated that their *disabilities* were preventing them from obtaining employment.

Two-thirds (69%) of the unemployed ex-clients believed that their chances of getting a job were poor, and three-fourths (76%) stated they would probably be unemployed 1 year later, indicating a *pessimistic or hopeless attitude*.

Almost one-half (47%) of the nonworking ex-clients indicated that they had received *no encouragement* from their families in their efforts to become employed.

More than one-half (60%) of the unemployed ex-clients were receiving some form of *public assistance*.

Counselors' ratings of psychosocial and vocational goal attainment and overall adjustment at HSRC were *significant predictors* of work status at follow-up and 12-year employment history.

Prognosis at acceptance, whether or not evaluation, medical, or vocational services were received, and completion of rehabilitation program or vocational training were not predictive of vocational adjustment at follow-up.

For *male* ex-clients, working at follow-up and better employment histories were associated with greater mobility, better health and family relationships, and greater social participation, suggesting that vocational adjustment and psychosocial adjustment are *interdependent processes* for males.

For *female* ex-clients, working at follow-up and better employment histories were associated with greater encouragement from families, indicating that *family support* may enhance females' employability.

In general, the correlations between vocational and psychosocial criteria of adjustment at follow-up were modest, supporting the conclusion that they are relatively *independent domains* of rehabilitation outcome.

Summary

Disabled clients referred to workshops and comprehensive facilities are typically the more difficult rehabilitation cases, and they usually require more intensive services. The description of the 12-year follow-up sample is consistent with this general rule. Yet despite their greater case difficulty, a substantial proportion of these ex-clients achieved employment, with younger persons and males evidencing more successful vocational adjustment. The typical employed ex-client seemed to be a stable and satisfied worker. However, the employment prospects for those ex-clients who were not working at follow-up were poor, as reflected in several factors, including defeatist attitudes, lack of family support, and disincentives associated with public assistance receipt. Finally, the pattern of results suggests that it is not the type of services received or whether or not the program is completed that leads to successful vocational adjustment, but rather it is the combination of facilitative personal, family, and community resources that enhances the probability of success.

FOLLOW-UP STUDIES IN REHABILITATION

The long-term adjustment of former vocational rehabilitation clients has been assessed in more than 100 follow-up studies conducted during the last 25 years. Most of the earlier rehabilitation follow-up studies were located and summarized by Bailey (1965) and Overs (1971), whereas the results of more recent investigations are reviewed in the chapter by Bolton (1981).

Summaries of Earlier Studies

Bailey (1965) reviewed 32 follow-up studies in rehabilitation, of which 26 were concerned with former general caseload clients of the state vocational rehabilitation agencies. Employment rates at follow-up for the general caseload rehabilitants approached 80%, whereas nonrehabilitants and severely disabled clients who received special services had much lower employment rates. Only 41% of severely disabled workshop graduates were working at follow-up.

Overs (1971) summarized the results of 76 follow-up studies *not* included in Bailey's review. The studies covered all types of rehabilitation programs, for example, medical, psychiatric, alcoholic, institutional, workshop, and state vocational rehabilitation agencies, and were typically carried out in conjunction with a research and demonstration project. The individual investigations were not examined critically; rather, the outcome statistics were simply averaged for 72 of the studies: 61% of the ex-clients were employed at follow-up, 6% were in training, and 33% were unemployed. The follow-up interval for most studies was between 1 and 3 years, with very few exceeding 5 years.

Hamilton and Muthard (1973) reviewed seven follow-up studies of public assistance recipients who had received vocational rehabilitation services. The employment rates of rehabilitants 1 to 2 years after closure ranged from 49% to 85%. However, it should be noted that the proportion of public assistance/vocational rehabilitation referrals accepted for services is substantially lower than that of referrals generally accepted for vocational rehabilitation services.

Conclusions from Recent Studies

Bolton (1981) limited his review to studies that met three criteria: a) they were surveys of former clients of the state/federal vocational rehabilitation program; b) they were published in journals, books, or widely circulated reports; and c) they were described in sufficient detail to permit a critical examination of the research methodology and results.

Eight general conclusions concerning the vocational and psychosocial adjustment of former vocational rehabilitation clients were drawn from the results of the studies examined:

1. Approximately two-thirds of general caseload rehabilitants are employed at follow-up, between 2 and 4 years after case closure. This finding, based on a fairly consistent pattern of results across a variety of studies, indicates that the benefits of vocational rehabilitation services are sustained by the majority of former rehabilitants.
2. About one-half of nonrehabilitated former clients eventually obtain employment, suggesting that unsuccessful case closure should not be equated with rehabilitation failure. It is clear that nonrehabilitated clients derive considerable benefit from the provision of vocational rehabilitation services.
3. Approximately one-half of the former clients of workshops and comprehensive centers are employed at follow-up, from 1 to 12 years after discharge from the facility. However, employment rates vary considerably, depending upon the nature of the program and the average difficulty of the caseload. It can be concluded that a substantial proportion of severely disabled, hard-to-place clients benefit from intensive rehabilitation service programs.
4. Three studies examined the relationship between time elapsed since closure or facility discharge and employment rates. No differences were observed between recently closed or discharged ex-clients and those who had received services 2, 3, or 4 years earlier. This finding suggests that employment success (or failure) occurs within the first year after closure or discharge for most ex-clients, and emphasizes the importance of careful job placement and periodic supportive contacts with former vocational rehabilitation clients.
5. It can be inferred from the unemployment rates at follow-up that many ex-clients could benefit from additional vocational rehabilitation services. This conclusion received direct support from the Michigan studies, in which one-third of the former clients indicated that they desired further assistance. The nature of the needed additional services are suggested in the ex-clients' perceived barriers to employment, e.g., employer resistance, lack of training, and lack of self-confidence.
6. Three studies found a relationship between family support and encouragement for the client, and successful vocational adjustment

at follow-up. The implication of this finding for the vocational rehabilitation practitioner is obvious: the client's family should be actively involved in the rehabilitation program from planning through case closure and in any subsequent services.
7. Other than severity of disability and general case difficulty, no client characteristics seem to be consistently predictive of successful adjustment at follow-up. In various programs and facilities, selected prognostic variables may be useful in planning the program of vocational rehabilitation services, but these variables must be identified in the particular settings.
8. Successful vocational adjustment at follow-up seems to be related to better psychosocial adjustment, but the magnitude of the relationship is modest. The appropriate conclusion, which is supported by other research (see Bolton, 1979, Chapter 5), is that improved psychosocial adjustment should be regarded as an outcome of major importance in vocational rehabilitation rather than simply assumed to be an invariant function of employment success.

Implications of Follow-up Studies

The Vocational Rehabilitation Act of 1973 authorized state vocational rehabilitation agencies to provide necessary supportive services to rehabilitated former clients to enable them to maintain employment (Taylor & Rice, 1976). If one accepts as accurate the previously stated conclusion that two-thirds of vocational rehabilitants sustain employment benefits, then approximately one-third of this group needs some type of postemployment services. Furthermore, because approximately one-half of nonrehabilitants are able to achieve employment, it is not unreasonable to believe that many unemployed nonrehabilitants could benefit from additional services. In other words, there is some justification for proposing that state vocational rehabilitation agencies provide lifelong supportive services to all former clients.

In addition to the requirement that the agencies provide postemployment services to former clients, the Vocational Rehabilitation Act of 1973 mandates that agencies evaluate the effectiveness of their programs. Two of the standards are focused on ex-clients' status at follow-up, to determine whether the benefits of vocational rehabilitation services were sustained, and if they were not, to document the reason(s) why they were not sustained. The merger of the postemployment service requirement with the follow-up evaluation mandate into a comprehensive service and evaluation follow-up system would seem to be an obvious step. Periodic contact with ex-clients throughout the remainder of their lives, to assess levels of adjustment and service needs, would represent an optimal program.

A comprehensive follow-up system for clients of state vocational rehabilitation agencies would serve two major functions: a) it would provide the basis for a continuous service program giving needed assistance to disabled persons, and b) it would serve as a foundation for accountability that would generate long-term evidence of the benefits that accrue to disabled individuals and to society. Some specific uses of the results of the longitudinal follow-up studies include: c) to yield a data base for legislators, administrators, and program planners regarding the relative effectiveness of service units and procedures, d) to give a long-term perspective for vocational rehabilitation counselors to enable them to examine the results of their work beyond case closure, e) to provide a framework for predicting long-term adjustment of ex-clients in order to identify high-risk clients at the time of acceptance, and f) to afford a unique opportunity to extend our knowledge about the vocational and psychosocial adjustment of disabled persons in American society.

chapter 2
THE MEANING OF WORK

Mary Jo Schneider and Daniel E. Ferritor

WEST COST, BORNEO, 1,000 B.C.
   Dilatn, age 35, stretches as he wakes up. It is dawn and he shivers in the dank chill of the tropical virgin forest. He goes from his lean-to made of bamboo covered with palm leaves to a nearby mountain stream where he dives in to take a bath. Wearing a loincloth made from the inner bark of a palm tree which he has hammered until it is as soft as cloth, he brushes his teeth with a twig, and then returns to the camp. He lives with his wife, Rani, and their four children. Dilatn's family lives with about 30 other individuals who are bound together loosely by kinship ties.
   Today, like most other days, when Dilatn returns to camp, he joins the other men to make plans for the day. He and his friend Kimut, a man of about his age, decide that they will go the nearby mountains to hunt wild pigs. They will take Dilatn's 14-year-old son, Kilon, who is already an excellent marksman. Other men in the camp are not so ambitious. Tikal and Raum will stay in camp, repairing their blowpipes and spears. Garupm, who is generally considered to be lazy, doesn't enter into the conversation, since he has decided that he will pass the day dozing under his lean-to. The men talk about Nanti. Since his arm has withered as a result of a fall several months ago, his wife has left him, and he has retreated to the edge of the camp. Others must feed him, and they do so willingly because they appreciate the problems that accidents cause.
   Early this morning, Dilatn's wife, Rani, joins several of the other women who, with their babies and small children, move slowly through the jungle in a circular route that takes them less than a mile from camp. The women's gathering activities provide the bulk of the daily diet for the members of the band. They gather edible leaves, roots, and nuts. Much of what they gather is eaten on the spot, but some is taken back to camp in string bags. Most of the women leave camp each day to forage, although sometimes older children and older women stay in camp to care for small children.

When Rani returns to camp she is met by Dilatn and Kimut, who have killed a 40-pound wild pig with a fire-hardened bamboo spear. While they were still in the mountains, they divided the animal into parcels which they would later give to kinsmen according to culturally prescribed rules. The pig will provide sufficient meat for the entire camp for at least two days. Dilatn begins to roast his pig on the family fire; other familes do likewise. It is the men's responsibility to roast the meat while the women prepare the vegetables by boiling or encasing them in bamboo leaves and placing them on the fire. By early afternoon the meal is ready. Families share food with other members of the camp, but cooking and eating are done within the family unit.

By mid-afternoon the heat is bothersome. It is time to relax, nap, and visit. Some of the camp members are amused by the loud fighting between Lanum and Sarih, a married couple who will probably get divorced soon. Divorce is not uncommon, and carries with it little social stigma.

In the evening, there is a simple meal consisting mainly of leftovers. Some drink an alcholic beverage made by fermenting palm sap, but it is rare that anyone drinks to excess. Visiting must soon come to an end because darkness comes early. So to sleep for a long night, lulled by the sounds of the jungle.

NEW YORK, NEW YORK, 1981 A.D.

Robert Beckworth, age 36, awakens at 6:00 a.m. to the clock radio's message that it's going to be another scorcher in Fun City. "Hot and humid, what's new?" mumbles Robert as he wonders what people did before air conditioning.

Robert takes a quick shower and fixes breakfast. Dry toast and Instant Breakfast is not his idea of a satisfying meal, but with his son at science camp, his wife at a fashion designer's seminar in the mountains, and his ulcer throwing a fit, it's quick, serves the purpose, and, at least according to the TV ads, is nutritious.

Robert leaves the house at 6:45, picks up a Wall Street Journal at the corner newstand, and heads for the subway to his office in midtown Manhattan. As always, the subway is packed, but Robert finds a place to stand and opens the paper to the stock market listings. Since completing the night course in finance at Columbia University, he has shifted all his investment money to Genetics, Inc. Even with his college degree in engineering and physics and his M.B.A. from Harvard, he can't keep up with the modern scientific advances.

Robert enters the elevator in his office building at 7:20 and pushes the button for the 85th floor. Even though the work day doesn't officially start at Omega Electronics until 8:30, as the youngest vice president he has more than enough work and has to set an example for the other employees. Once in his office, Robert checks his calendar and finds that he has several meetings scheduled, a mountainous pile of correspondence to answer, and a report for the board of directors due next week.

So much of Robert's day is spent in meetings that he has to cancel his 12:00 squash game and instead sends out for a sandwich, which he hurriedly eats between meetings. With the correspondence half answered and the report unfinished, he leaves the office at 5:45 and rushes to a dinner with a prospective client. After dinner he stops by the Young Executives Professional Association to catch the end of the weekly meeting. Since he became president-elect, the association is draining more and more of his time, but the presidency should provide an immeasurable boost to his career.

After the meeting Robert hails a cab and returns to his apartment. He arrives home at 11:05 and begins laying out his clothes for the next day. Robert feels a momentary guilt pang as he sees his wife's clothes. This is the first time all day he has thought of her or his son. The guilt quickly eases as he realizes that she also has a career and probably hasn't had time to think of him either. His son is another matter! But if he does well at science camp, it will almost guarantee his admission at MIT in three years.

Robert gets ready for bed, turns on the TV, and begins looking at his appointment book for the next day's work schedule. His head nods a couple of times and the last thing he remembers is a voice on the TV saying "Here's . . . Johnny!"

The preceding narratives describe typical days in the lives of two men who hold extremely different views of work. For Robert Beckworth, work is so important that his whole life is structured around it. Dilatn, on the other hand, like others in his society has no concept of work as we know it. In a sense, Robert lives to work; Dilatn works to live.

Even though Robert's work habits are not typical of all Americans, few would have difficulty understanding his life and work. Moreover, many Americans might feel that he is a "success" and perhaps assume that he balances his work with one or more carefully selected hobbies, occasional highly satisfying leisure time activities, and at least one well planned vacation each year. These same Americans would feel very differently about an American whose work pattern resembled Dilatn's.

He might be judged a failure, a lazy "no-account" who will never amount to anything. People of Dilatn's Borneo would probably find Robert's behavior totally inexplicable.

What would be at issue between Americans and the people of Borneo would be the meaning that each has for the concept of *work*. It would be as difficult to explain American notions of "work," "vacation," "hobby," and "leisure time activities" to a person living in an isolated hunting and gathering society in Borneo as it would be to convince a modern American that one ought to work only as much as is necessary to satisfy basic human needs (Schwimmer, 1979).

It may seem at first that Robert's modern society with its huge cities and space-age technology has little in common with a level of life in the earliest societies, where the most complex tools were hand-manufactured animal snares and traps, and where the political and social relationships were determined primarily by kinship. Yet in the time perspective of human existence (some 5 million years), we are not so far removed from the earliest societies—those where the principal routine was hunting and gathering. Until approximately 10,000 years ago, all human societies subsisted through hunting and gathering. Other methods of subsistence are by contrast recent history.

The meaning that each of us attaches to the concept of work is profoundly influenced by a particular set of cultural norms and values, a set that varies greatly from society to society as well as over time within one society. Different cultural meanings of work are not simply reflections of the type of work that is done but rather indicate basic differences in people's social, political, and religious beliefs and values. C. Wright Mills (1951) captured the difficulty in defining work when he said:

> Work may be a mere source of livelihood or the most significant part of one's inner life; it may be experienced as . . . an expression of self, as duty or as the development of man's universal nature. Neither love nor hatred of work is inherent in man . . . for work has no intrinsic meaning (p. 215).

The fundamental purpose of work is to extract a living from nature (Wallman, 1979). This simple definition permits a longitudinal and cross-cultural examination of work, but it does not convey the varied meanings of work. Work has psychological meaning, because it profoundly affects an individual's allocation of energy, time, and self-identity. Work also has sociological significance, because the very fabric of social relationships is determined primarily by the division of labor in society. Finally, work has cultural and subcultural meaning and differs significantly across societies, as was seen in the opening vignettes. Different academic disciplines approach the meaning of work in varied ways, and because the authors of this chapter are trained in anthropology and sociology, the social and cultural meanings of work are emphasized in this chapter.

To understand work and the meaning that work has for disabled Americans, it is helpful to examine more carefully the concept of work, how it evolved, and how its meaning has differed through time and across societies. In the following section, the history of work is examined in the context of three types of societies: hunting and gathering, agricultural and pastoral, and early industrial.

HISTORY OF WORK

Hunting-Gathering Societies

Hunting-gathering societies in contemporary times as well as in the past are characterized by low population density, lack of social class differentiation, little or no occupational specialization, and dependence on kinship as an integrating mechanism. Life is carried on in relatively nonspecialized groups. Political, legal, religious, and economic activities all occur through kinship groups.

Relationships such as kinsman, neighbor, co-worker, co-worshiper, and so forth exist simultaneously among members of society. When differences take place between members of modern society, they generally affect only one type of role or relationship. In a primitive society, however, the disruption of one relationship may seriously disturb the entire community, and perhaps the entire cosmic order.

In hunting-gathering societies there are no social classes, no full-time specialists, and no significant wealth differences. Members are known primarily by their kinship connections, not by the jobs that they perform. Of course, some are known as good hunters, others as knowledgeable in the ways of animals and spirits, and some, called shamans, are believed to have supernatural powers. Individual personality differences are recognized, but these do not stratify the society. In fact, many societies have elaborate "leveling mechanisms," which ensure that those with special abilities do not become too haughty and arrogant. For example, among the Kalahari Bushmen, no one thanks another for a gift, for to do so would make the recipient beholden to the giver. Instead of praising the virtues of a hunter's prey, the animal is ridiculed so that the hunter will not get a swollen head and believe himself to be above the rest of the group.

Economic exchanges within the hunting and gathering band are conducted largely through reciprocity. That is, although services and products are to be paid back eventually, no definite set of rules specifies time or quantity. When !Kung Bushmen hunters return to camp, they share whatever they have found regardless of whether the recipients have spent the day sleeping or hunting (Lee, 1979). Certainly, examples of reciprocal exchange (Christmas and birthdays) can be found in modern societies, but most exchanges take place in the formal marketplace.

No one individual or group of individuals has the power to compel obedience in hunting-gathering societies. What political control exists is exercised by leaders, almost invariably male leaders traditonally called headmen, but even they lack the power to enforce their commands and often control by conciliation rather than by coercion. In the words of one anthropologist, the headman is "more a spokesman for public opinion than a molder of it" (Dentan, 1968, p. 68).

Although it is commonly believed that life in a hunting and gathering society is severe, in actuality the opposite is true. Harris (1980) and Sahlins (1972) have documented the easygoing pace of most hunting-gathering existences. The !Kung average fewer than 16 hours per week in their food quest, and the average day of hunting or collecting is about 6 hours long. Of course, when people are not hunting and gathering, they are not necessarily idle or sleeping. Time is spent preparing food; manufacturing essential items such as clothing, tools, and shelter; performing household tasks; and engaging in child care activities. When illness, disability, or personality factors prevent persons from working, others increase their workload to sustain the group.

In hunting and gathering societies, there seldom exists any distinction between work and other "natural" activities. The concept of work simply has little meaning. Like breathing, it is a part of life. In many societies, the language does not even contain a word that means "work" (Sahlins, 1972).

Agricultural and Pastoral Societies

A major limitation of the hunting-gathering economy is that, in all but the richest environments, a large amount of land is needed to support a very few people. If populations grow too quickly and cannot easily expand to surrounding areas, new methods of subsistence as well as new social structures must emerge to accommodate the larger number of people. As societies develop new economic systems, they move from a particularistic to a universalistic ethic (Peacock & Kirsch, 1970). This means that, as societies become larger and more technologically complex, the importance of statuses ascribed at birth (sex, race, kinship) gives way to statuses acquired through achievement, merit, and skill. As societies develop, then, one finds that they utilize new methods of subsistence needing different types of social organization, which often result in new conceptions and organization of work.

Leaders become necessary for organizing and coordinating diverse activities, and in all but the most lush environments, hunting and gathering must be supplemented with horticulture and animal husbandry. There are three major subsistence modes based on food production in nonindustrial societies: horticulture, agriculture, and pastoralism. No society uses one of these modes exclusively. Pastoralists, for example, who rely mainly on the meat, milk, blood, and by-products of animals, commonly cultivate some grains. Food producers often gather and hunt as well as husband livestock to supplement their diet and to serve as draft animals.

The distinction between horticulture and agriculture is one of degree. Horticulturists do not intensively use either land or labor. Plots are often cultivated only until the richness of the soil is depleted. Agricultural systems, on the other hand, require greater labor input and a continuous and intensive use and modification (e.g., terracing, irrigation) of land.

As hunting-gathering evolves into horticulture, certain basic social changes can be found. Headmen give way to leaders called big men. Like headmen, big men (who are almost always male) achieve status through hard work and a winning personality. Their wealth and charisma attract others and give them influence. To be sure, big men work hard in subsistence activities, but because they often give away their wealth in exchange for prestige and gratitude, their individual wealth and life styles are not dramatically different from those of other villagers.

The seeds for social ranking are apparent in horticultural societies. As the number of people in regular interaction increases, interpersonal conflicts increase, and leaders are necessary to regulate conflicts and arbitrate disputes. Cultivating economies often require community-wide activities, such as building drainage ditches or monuments, which demand the coordinating efforts of leaders. Leadership positions gradually evolve into social classes, which become more evident in agricultural societies.

As in the hunting-gathering society, the division of labor in a horticultural society is based primarily on age and sex. Although both sexes are involved in cultivation, men typically clear the land and plant the gardens, whereas weeding and picking are the responsibilities of women.

The time and effort required to make a living in horticultural societies are not, however, greatly different from hunting-gathering societies, unless population pressures stress resource availability. Roy Rappaport's (1968) study of the Tsembaga Maring, a village people living in the central highlands of New Guinea, showed that essential subsistence tasks averaged 7.3 hours per week for each food producer.

The major change in horticultural societies is an emerging social differentiation. With differentiation, it becomes possible to distinguish between workers and nonworkers, a distinction that ultimately allows for social evaluations of people and gives meaning to the concept of work.

These distinctions among types of people become clearer as agricultural economies develop. Most, if not all, agricultural people live in sociopolitical systems possessing governments and marked contrasts in prestige, wealth, and power. Anthropologists label these societies "chiefdoms" and "states," with the chiefdom regulating the society solely through kinship mechanisms, whereas the state is regulated through both kinship and government.

In the chiefdom, economies based on reciprocity are replaced by ones based on redistribution. In societies where leadership rests with headmen or big men, persons trade directly with one another, goods and services flowing through reciprocity. In redistributive societies, an individual's products are brought to a central location, sorted, counted, and then given away. Redistributive exchange marks the beginning of class and power distinctions, because it becomes possible for leaders, called chiefs, to take a portion of the society's wealth to use for the government of the group. Chiefs, who unlike big men do not contribute directly to the subsistence effort, commonly administer ecologically diverse regions where different sorts of crops are grown. Through redistribution, the chief can make specialized products available to the entire society, and can maintain a central storehouse to guard against times of shortage.

With ecological specialization and power distinctions, occupational specialization also emerges. No longer do all people of the same age and sex do the same work. Some specialize in growing wheat, others in making baskets, and still others in producing ritual paraphernalia. Inevitably, some of these occupations are considered more prestigious than others. At this point work assumes a clear, shared meaning among people in society; it is an activity separate from "living," an activity that can be valued greatly or perhaps not at all.

A number of other significant contrasts can be made between chiefdoms and states. Perhaps most relevant for this discussion, states, unlike chiefdoms, are not organized principally by kinship or descent. Rather, populations are divided into socioeconomic classes which separate the commoners from the elite. The separation between elite and commoners is associated with specialization of labor. In the primitive society, all adults of the same sex perform the same tasks. In the state society, however, the specialization of labor is based on the premise that some people are innately better qualified than others to pursue certain tasks. The elite specialize in religious and political duties, the masses in manual labor.

Occupational positions increase in number in moving from hunting-gathering to state-level organization and agricultural societies. However, most of the new positions created in the state are available only to the elite. Manual labor remains the mode of livelihood for the great majority of the population. Leisure time does not increase for the masses. Rather, the slow pace of the hunting-gathering society gives way to forced labor demanded by the ruling class. In contrast with hunter-gatherers, who can decide whether or not they want to work for the day, superiors decide the time and place of work for the commoner in an agricultural society.

Work available to persons with disabilities is extremely limited in all preindustrial societies, although the disabled member of the elite group in a state-level society may fare better than his or her counterparts in a kin-based group. In all preindustrial groups, those with mild mental retardation may effectively assist with subsistence efforts, and some with minimal physically handicapping conditions, as for example, arthritis or missing limbs, may do more than their share of artisan work or child care. The elderly infirm will be cared for by the rest of the group as long as food supplies are adequate. In times of stress, however, these persons are often victims of neglect. Throughout preindustrial societies, babies who are born with severe or obvious disabling conditions are generally killed at birth (infanticide) or abandoned.

In some groups, however, certain types of emotional handicaps are turned into positive assets. For example, schizophrenics may be revered for their special ability to communicate with the spirit world. Deviant behavior among hunter-gatherers is usually tolerated, but if it becomes so severe that it threatens group or individual welfare, the offender is physically punished or expelled from the group. As society becomes larger and more bureaucratic, deviant behavior due to emotional disorder is more likely to be subject to strict and autocratic punishment. The concept of rehabilitation is not well formed in preindustrial societies, and what efforts are made fall within the jurisdiction of shamans, priests, and healers.

Because the occupations of highest prestige in early agricultural and pastoral economies were held by the elite, manual labor seldom acquired a highly positive meaning. Most laborers had little if any control over the type, place, or hours of work, and work was not highly valued. Rather than providing satisfaction and reward, work came to be viewed as a curse or punishment.

Strongly negative views of work can be found throughout much of recorded history. Most familiar to Americans is the early Judaic view of work as never-ending earthly punishment for the sins of Adam and Eve (Tilgher, 1930). A similar view of work can be found in the early Greco-Roman cultures. At the height of city-state development, virtually all manual labor was performed by slaves and other noncitizens. Technical expertise was less valued than philosophizing, and the work of peasants had a social meaning different from that of tradespeople. From the writings of the great philosophers, Arendt (1958) concluded that in early Greek society manual labor was thought inherently degrading, forcing people to behave "as animals do."

The early Christians shared this negative view of work. The pursuit of material goods was incompatible with contemplative preparation for the next life. Christians, like their counterparts in hunting and gathering societies, felt they needed work only to sustain the most basic human needs. The rest of the day, then, could be spent preparing for the next life.

This negative conception of manual labor characterized most of our early Christian heritage. Somewhat more positive views can be first found in the prescriptions of St. Benedict and later in the precepts of other monastic orders as they developed into large productive enterprises. During the Renaissance, artistic work and some skilled crafts came to be valued insofar as they allowed humans to creatively fulfill their destiny. For the most part, however, work was not highly valued in societies with primarily agricultural economies.

Industrializing Societies

The Protestant Reformation and the Industrial Revolution were crucial in changing the meaning of work. As a result of these two events, work was transformed from toil and burden to "something intrinsically good in itself" (Neff, 1977, p. 87).[1]

Martin Luther fully legitimated a positive view of work. Luther argued that work was not only acceptable but was the will of God— whether carried out by monks as a supplement to a contemplative life or in the secular world as a life mission. This acceptance of work culminated in Calvinistic doctrine. Work assumed for John Calvin an almost religious fervor; it was the will of God. Work and the fruits of one's work—wealth, power, and prestige—became signs that a person was among the elect, predestined for a heavenly reward.

Max Weber, in a penetrating sociological analysis, argued that the religious beliefs inspired by Luther and Calvin supported the rise of

---

[1] In this section and in succeeding sections the authors often utilized ideas and themes which were found in various writings of Walter S. Neff. Although Neff is not always directly cited, we acknowledge the importance of his work as background for an examination of the meaning of work.

the capitalist entrepreneur by providing a positive work ideology. Weber termed the new work doctrine the Protestant Ethic. Scholars today generally feel that Weber overstated his argument and that the new Protestant belief system did not directly produce capitalism or even the wholesale changes in work ideology. It is agreed, however, that the new religious conceptions of work were almost totally compatible with the economic changes of the Industrial Revolution. At the very least, the new beliefs strongly legitimated a new conception of work, one in which work was no longer a necessary evil but rather an important, even central, aspect of human existence. Whatever the causal chain, the new orientation to work flourished in societies where agricultural feudalism was supplanted by rapid industrialization (e.g., France, England, Germany, Belgium).

With the growth of factories and other centralized work places, wholesale migration changed rural agricultural residence patterns to urban industrial life. Concurrently, there was a growth of the nuclear family and a loss of the influence and importance of extended family and kin relationships. In the new urban industrial system, work and home were separated and families experienced a new role: that of the parent as breadwinner. Instead of the entire family working as a single economic unit, one member left the home to earn a livelihood. This separation of work and home, in and of itself, highlighted the importance of work as a separate, highly valued activity.

Because of these changes, families developed a different internal division of labor. As the male role changed, the female role became less valued. Women lost much of the productive economic role they had earlier shared with their husbands and took on more of the role of homemaker and socializer. Children also became further removed from economic production and assumed a more subservient role in the family. Increasingly complex technological requirements in the workplace required children to spend more time in formal education. For male children this meant occupational preparations; for female children this often meant formal preparation to assume the roles of wife, mother, and homemaker.

Changes in the organization of work, then, produced changes in the structure of the family. These structural changes in basic family role relationships served to reinforce further the growing importance of work in people's lives.

Finally, businesses and communities experienced a force that further strengthened the status of work: job specialization. Important social distinctions were made between manual and nonmanual laborers, between skilled and nonskilled laborers, between managers and workers, and between highly valued and less important products. Work became the basis for community growth and development. Some have argued that work became the very foundation upon which all social relationships, social class systems, and culture rested (Anthony, 1980).

Whether or not work actually assumed this total sociological dominance, it is clear that by the end of the 19th century work was highly important to the individual and to societies. Individual social value was being assigned primarily by the kind of work performed (Neff, 1977).

MEANING OF WORK IN AMERICAN SOCIETY

To this point we have focused on the changing meaning of work over time. As has been seen, with industrialization, community prestige and individual self-worth came to be intimately linked with work. Nowhere in the industrial world, however, was this more true than in America. From our earliest history, work was highly valued. Americans seldom asked "Who are you?" Rather they asked, "What do you do?" The Horatio Alger stories of the early 20th century have long been a part of the American ideology.

The advancing technology of the 19th century was accompanied by rapid work specialization and increased labor force participation. In 1850, the U.S. Census recorded approximately 350 separate occupations; today the Census lists over 35,000. By 1975 a majority of both men and women aged 18–55 were employed in the labor force. Although many women leave the labor force briefly during their childbearing years, the Advisory Committee on the Status of Women (1969) estimated that over 90% of all American females work outside the home at some time in their lives.

Americans willingly accept and even personally endorse the importance of work. When a sample of male Americans was asked whether they would continue to work even if they inherited enough money to live comfortably without doing so, 80% said they would (Morse & Weiss, 1955). In a more recent study (U.S. Senate Committee on Labor and Public Welfare, 1973), professionals overwhelmingly said that they would choose similar work again if they could start over, and approximately 50% of white collar and skilled laborers would choose similar work again. Robert Kahn (1980), in a study of unemployment concluded, "a job has to be pretty bad before it is worse than no job at all."

To understand why even the rich in America prefer to work, it is necessary to examine the cultural significance of work. According to Yankelovich (1974), work means being a breadwinner, and breadwinners can positively evaluate their contribution in providing for themselves and their families. Work also means independence or autonomy—work allows workers to "stand on their own two feet." Work also means success: hard work pays off; it permits people from all social stations to achieve life goals. Occupation has become the most important determinant of an individual's position in the stratification system. Finally, work means self-respect, because it establishes the mechanism through which individuals demonstrate their worth. If people work hard at their jobs, they can feel good at the end of the day.

For the individual, work provides economic, social, and personal benefits. In addition to money for the necessities and luxuries of life, work provides a setting for individuals to develop new friends and to socialize with old ones. The work atmosphere is a focus for personal evaluation, a mechanism for shaping a sense of identity, and a way of bringing order into one's life. Although work is not the only source of economic survival, sociability, or self-esteem, it is an easily recognizable, often quantifiable, public indicator of the results of an individual's life.

Although a classic study of American values (Williams, 1959) found work to be among our most highly valued activities, there is a line of research that suggests that it may have lost some of its positive connotations. As early as the mid-1950s, Dubin (1956) concluded that the primacy of work was beginning to recede. At least for industrial workers, work was valued almost solely for its material and economic functions.

By the mid-1960s there were further indications that significant proportions of Americans were becoming skeptical about work as the focus for their lives. Some observers suggested that the questions, "How do you play?" and "What are you into?" were replacing the traditional question, "What do you do?" A prospering economy freed many Americans from the anxieties of material success. The belief that hard work, self-denial, and moral restraint were their own rewards was replaced by the notion that self-actualization was an all-important pursuit. Author Tom Wolfe called the new ethic the "me" generation, and social observer Christopher Lasch used the phrase "culture of narcissism" to describe the phenomenon. Terence Carroll (1965) argued that American society had overemphasized the importance of work, saying that the fact that work was highly valued "does not mean that all people should share it, or that it is even a healthy attitude for those who do" (p. 26). Others echoed Carroll's theme.

During the early 1970s workers continued to question the meaning of their own work, while researchers paid renewed attention to the writings of Karl Marx. Popular as well as academic literature was filled with references to work alienation, the meaninglessness of work to the workers. The automotive assembly line, where one car passed each worker every 36 seconds, typified the repetitive, personally unsatisfying work setting. Terkel (1974) reported the following conversation among automobile workers:

> "It pays good," said one, "but it's driving me crazy." "I don't want more money," said another, "none of us do." "I do," said his friend. "So I can quit quicker."

There is recent evidence, however, that a more positive meaning of work is returning to American society. It may be that the critical evaluation of the 1960s and early 1970s reflected the social turbulence of the time and the questioning of many of society's central mores and values.

As a result of the rise of OPEC, a decline in American productivity, inflation, and the huge cost of maintaining federally funded programs, many Americans found themselves in more austere economic circumstances by 1980. The realities of a tightening job market and a sluggish economy prompted 77% of entering college freshmen in 1980 to view their college career primarily as preparation for the work world (Astin, 1980). Yankelovich (1981), a student of the American psyche, has recently suggested that a new era is dawning that will emphasize the "ethic of commitment." Americans facing harsh marketplace realities, according to Yankelovich, are returning to conservative, old-fashioned moral values, including the value of work.

MEANING OF WORK FOR PERSONS WITH DISABILITIES

As we have seen, people interpret their work experiences in the light of the meanings their culture offers. The meaning work has in any given culture, therefore, can greatly influence the lives of disabled members of society.

As work assumes greater importance to a society, the consequences of the inability to work become more severe. In 1978 almost 300,000 persons were rehabilitated in the United States through public vocational programs (Caseload Statistics, 1978). Of more importance than the number, which is impressive indeed, is the meaning of the term "rehabilitated." In the Arkansas Rehabilitation Services Operating Procedures Manual (1981), a "closed rehabilitated" case was defined as a person who was a) declared eligible, b) provided an evaluation, c) provided appropriate rehabilitation services, and d) *determined to have achieved a suitable employment objective that had been maintained for at least 60 days.*

From this definition of "closed rehabilitated" we get an important insight into the contemporary meaning of work as it relates to persons with disabilities. The relationship is clear. To be rehabilitated is to be employed. The employment may be competitive employment or it may be sheltered employment. The key, however, is that work is inextricably tied to the concept of rehabilitation.

Carroll (1965), however, decried the tendency to equate rehabilitation with work. He said:

> The objective of rehabilitation is the enlargement of the individual human personality and the realization of individual human potential. It is the paradox of our time that while we have embraced this concept we have at the same time imposed a strait-jacket resulting from the values of an acquisitive society (p. 26).

Most others, however, are considerably less critical of the close identification of work and rehabilitation. It is generally agreed, among vocational counselors and among many persons with disabilities as well, that work is the principal mediator of life chances.

Several studies indicate that disabled workers not only accept the high value placed on work in this society but, perhaps because of their disability, hold work in even higher esteem than the nondisabled worker. Goodyear and Stude (1975) compared severely disabled and nondisabled workers in an Internal Revenue Service Center along several dimensions including job performance and job satisfaction. They found virtually no difference between the two groups regarding job performance. They did, however, find the sample of disabled workers to have significantly higher general job satisfaction than the nondisabled sample.

Studies of worker absenteeism underscore the importance of work for the disabled. In a review of research on worker absenteeism, Wessman (1965) found that disabled workers averaged significantly lower rates of absenteeism because of illness. Wessman's conclusion is especially noteworthy because many impairments might predispose persons to higher absenteeism.

In general, then, the evidence seems to suggest that the person with a disability not only values work highly but perhaps values it more highly than does the able-bodied worker. Wilkinson (1975) summed up this thought by saying, ". . . the client has been conditioned . . . to believe that work is the central force of life" (p. 73). More important than the conditioning process, according to Wilkinson, "the client believes he is what he does" (p. 73).

Not all persons with disabilities share the same work values, however. Safilios-Rothschild (1970) concluded that the work experiences of some occupational groups are so negative that they suffer vocational handicaps even with a relatively nonsevere physical disability. This pattern seems to be particularly prevalent among unskilled or semiskilled workers. To understand adequately the meaning of work to the disabled one must examine it in terms of broad occupational categories, which provide different intrinsic and extrinsic satisfactions.

Work for the unskilled does not hold the same value as for other occupational groups. For these workers, it provides little if any intrinsic satisfaction. When faced with a disability, lower class workers may react with several strategies, ranging from denial of the disability through turning the disability into an asset by receiving compensation with no attempt to return to work. Safilios-Rothschild (1970) reported that when unskilled lower class disabled workers are referred to rehabilitation facilities they are often rejected before being "closed rehabilitated," because they are unmotivated or uncooperative.

Among working class males in skilled blue collar occupations, work seems to have a more positive meaning. Perhaps because their work is more highly valued than that of unskilled workers, work serves to some extent to provide self-respect. Skilled blue collar workers often return to some type of competitive employment after the onset of a disabling impairment.

Finally, work is most highly valued among professional and white collar workers. For people in these occupations, work often provides both intrinsic and extrinsic satisfaction, and in the extreme case of successful professionals, work may be the most important life interest. The reader may remember the extent to which the hypothetical 20th century worker, Robert Beckworth, organized his entire life around his profession. Disabilities among professionals, Safilios-Rothschild concluded, do not seem to affect their self-concept seriously, and for the most part they are eager to return to competitive employment.

CONCLUSION

At the present time work in America is probably valued higher than at any other time in human history. It is valued not only for its economic substance but also in many cases for its ability to convey identity, prestige, and self-respect. The particular value that individuals place on their work is directly influenced by the general social value placed on work.

Not all individuals value work to the same extent, but similarities across occupational categories do seem to exist. Work is often considered a central life interest among professionals but becomes successively less central and more instrumental as one moves through white collar occupations to skilled laborers and finally to unskilled laborers and service workers.

The particular value and importance a disabled person places on work will to a large degree determine the extent to which a rehabilitation program will be successful. By considering an individual's work orientation and work valuation, the counselor can gain important information that can be used in developing individual rehabilitation goals.

chapter 3
WORK MOTIVATION

Daniel W. Cook

Understanding rehabilitation clients' motivation, and especially their motivation to work, has been cited as one of the most pressing problems faced by rehabilitation counselors (Thoreson, Smits, Butler, & Wright, 1968; Zadny & James, 1979). Part of the problem is that motivation is a relatively abstract concept that has important practical implications. For example, Safilios-Rothschild (1970) suggested that clients will be labeled as "unmotivated" when they "refuse to follow prescribed tasks, try a task but give up quickly, or do not accept professional definitions of solutions to their problems" (p. 318). On the other hand, according to Safilios-Rothschild, clients who have "the utility and willingness to mobilize psychological resources to cope with disability" and who cooperate in obtaining "the prescribed goals which must be realized in order to be successfully rehabilitated" (p. 318) would be considered to be "motivated." Unfortunately, work motivation is much more complicated than a simple ordering of persons on a motivated–unmotivated continuum.

The work motivation literature draws from the more general motivational literature which spans the field of psychology. Consequently, an authoritative synthesis of that literature is beyond the scope of this chapter. Rather, this chapter reviews work motivation models developed by industrial psychologists that have direct applicability to vocational rehabilitation, presents models developed by rehabilitationists specifically for vocational rehabilitation purposes, summarizes work motivation problems associated with economic disincentives, and concludes with a summary of the main themes in the work motivation literature.

WORK MOTIVATION MODELS

Industrial and personnel psychologists have long been concerned with the question of why people work. Obvious answers such as the work ethic, to earn money, security, co-worker affiliations, status, and identity, although important, provided only part of the answer. Researchers quickly discovered that what was needed was a definition of work motivation as well as models or frameworks by which those things and processes making up work motivation could be described. Industrial psychologists generally accept Vinacke's (1962) definition of motivation: the condition responsible for variations in the intensity, quality, and directions of ongoing behavior. More specifically, industrial psychologists have suggested that work motivation consists of those things or processes that are independent of, but interact with, a worker's level of aptitude, skill, and understanding of the job task (Campbell & Pritchard, 1976). In industry the primary interest is in learning how worker motivation relates to job performance and employee satisfaction.

Landy and Trumbo (1980) pointed out that most managers probably view worker motivation in one of two ways. Some managers subscribe to a trait approach and consider workers to have different amounts of motivation. Persons low in motivation would be labeled as lazy, and persons high in motivation as "eager beavers." Other managers subscribe to an environmental approach and view motivation as something that can be manipulated or done to workers, for example, by increasing or decreasing pay. Both views are oversimplifications, but as Landy and Trumbo (1980) suggested, neither one is entirely incorrect. Individual differences and environmental rewards do affect worker motivation. Many work motivation models focus on managerial behavior (e.g., McGregor's (1960) Theory Y and Likert's (1961) System 4) or industrial performance (e.g., Adams' (1963) equity theory) and are less appropriate for use in vocational rehabilitation. However, two work motivation approaches, Maslow's (1970) need hierarchy model and Vroom's (1964) cognitive model are popular with rehabilitationists.

Maslow's Need Hierarchy Model

Maslow (1970) developed a general motivational theory based on the proposition that people strive to meet basic needs. Maslow proposed a linear, ordered hierarchy of five needs: a) physiological, b) safety, c) belongingness, d) esteem, and e) self-actualization. Work motivation theorists study how workers satisfy these needs in the workplace. According to Maslow, human beings are proactive and self-determining. Because Maslow's need structure is hierarchical, lower order needs are more pressing than higher order needs. Physiological needs are more pressing than safety needs, and so on. Satisfaction of needs at one level does not return one to an unmotivated state, however. Rather, need satisfaction at one level allows the unfolding of higher level needs. Also, it is not necessary to fulfill a need completely at one level before striving to meet a need at the next level. Physiological needs may be, for example, 85% fulfilled and safety needs 70% fulfilled, allowing the emergence of some belongingness needs.

Maslow's theory has been immensely popular in the work motivation literature. In the workplace, application of the theory consists of determining what needs an individual is trying to satisfy and structuring the work environment to satisfy those needs. Maslow's theory has been equally popular in rehabilitation. In fact, Barry and Malinovsky (1965) used Maslow's needs theory as a classification scheme in their extensive review of rehabilitation motivation studies. Also, the Human Service Scale (Reagles & Butler, 1976), one of the few inventories developed specifically for use with vocational rehabilitation clients, is partly based on Maslow's hierarchy of needs. No doubt the popularity of the theory among rehabilitation professionals stems from its commonsense approach to motivation. It seems quite reasonable to assume that newly disabled persons will be more concerned about physiological and safety needs than they will be with meeting self-actualization needs. Consequently, Maslow's hierarchy parallels the rehabilitation intervention philosophy (Fink, Fantz, & Zinker, 1963).

Vroom's Cognitive Model

Because people make decisions to expend effort at least partly on the basis of expected rewards resulting from that effort, it is not surprising that one of the most popular work motivation models combines elements of cognitive decision making. Vroom's (1964) valence-instrumentality-expectancy (VIE) model is perhaps the best known using that approach. Vroom suggested that people attach valence (V) to objects and conditions they encounter. Valence is defined as positive or negative values that attract or repel. According to Vroom, certain outcomes, such as earning money, have a positive valence. Other outcomes, such as dealing with an employer's prejudicial attitudes toward disability, have negative valence. Instrumentality (I) refers to the perceived link between an outcome, such as getting a job, and other outcomes such as being independent. The assumption is that before electing to seek a job, or to expend more effort in a job, a person must perceive a link to a related and valued outcome, for example, becoming independent or earning money. The third component of Vroom's model, expectancy (E), concerns the person's subjective estimate of achieving a valued and instrumental outcome. All three components—expectancy, instrumentality, and valence—suggest that we a) judge that a given effort has a high probability of leading to b) an outcome such as satisfactory performance which leads to other outcomes such as earning money and c) that earning money is positively valued. Two theorists, McDaniel (1976) and Wright (1960) have applied elements of Vroom's model to rehabilitation concerns. Their approaches are reviewed in subsequent sections.

REHABILITATION MODELS OF MOTIVATION

Some rehabilitation experts (Barry & Malinovsky, 1965; Poor, 1975) have suggested that motivation is too broad and vague a construct to be applied to rehabilitation concerns. Most rehabilitationists view the motivational problem as "how to get people to do what they are supposed to do and learn what they are supposed to learn." This pragmatic approach has led counselors to view lack of client motivation as a primary reason for client failure. Specifically, Thoreson et al. (1968) surveyed rehabilitation counselors and found four problem areas that counselors believed reflected lack of client motivation for vocational rehabilitation. They were:

1. Client disability-related feelings of hopelessness and depression
2. A passive role in the counseling relationship
3. Unrealistic vocational goals
4. Financial aid that was a disincentive to rehabilitation.

The last problem, economic disincentive, is mostly outside the control of the counselor and is considered at the end of this chapter. The other three problem areas suggest a need for understanding the dynamics of client work motivation.

Neff's Work Personality Model

Walter Neff (1971, 1977) has developed a model suggesting that work motivation can be studied by analyzing the work personality in interaction with the environmental demands of the job setting. Neff's position is that work is a time-structured activity that requires performance of some task. Because the work environment is a social situation, the worker is required to adapt to interpersonal demands. These demands include the ability to respond to supervision in an appropriate manner and the ability to relate effectively with peers. In learning to meet these demands, one adapts the worker role. Neff suggested that in assuming the worker role, certain requirements must be met.

> First, the individual must have some motivation to work, although the precise nature and source of his motivation may vary widely from person to person. Second, he must have some necessary minimum of aptitude and skill. Third, he must be able to conform to certain work-rules. Fourth, he must be able to meet certain minimal standards for productivity and quality. Fifth, he must "look" like a worker, i.e., he

must meet certain conventional standards for dress, demeanor, and deportment, with the additional proviso that he must have awareness of what is expected from him in different occupations and workplaces. Sixth, he must be able to relate appropriately to various kinds of people on the job, showing the required amount of respect to his superiors and the required amount of camaraderie with his peers. Seventh, he must be able to shift his emotional and cognitive gears well enough so that he can "turn on" all those behaviors appropriate to work and "turn off" all those affects and needs which are mobilized and gratified by other settings (Neff, 1977, pp. 157–158).

Neff sees the work personality developing through internalization of cultural demands for activity, productivity, and achievement. The process by which cultural demands are internalized is psychodynamic in nature and includes developing a work attitude complex. Formation of the work personality determines each person's idiosyncratic work style—those defenses, coping behaviors, and work attitudes exhibited in the workplace.

According to Neff (1977), motivation to work stems from the following five kinds of needs:

1. Material needs are probably the most basic and obvious reason people work. Although there may be many motives for working, monetary rewards are the basis for material existence. Because in industrial societies work is *the* instrumental activity for obtaining money, and because the amount of money earned is the easiest way to judge one's work performance, people work for money.
2. Activity needs reflect the importance of the workplace in setting time limits and having a definite place to go. Relative to the specific work task, working can be a method to meet the human need for activity and stimulation.
3. Self-esteem needs refer to feelings of self-worth resulting from working. Persons who can work, and want to work, but remain unemployed are said to suffer reduced feelings of self-worth. Feelings of self-worth can vary according to the status associated with different occupations, and by position within occupations. Most employed persons are unaware of the degree of self-worth they associate with work. Unemployment brings out those feelings.
4. A need for respect from others differs from the need for self-esteem in that self-esteem refers to personal evaluations whereas the need for respect from others refers to evaluations of others. The two needs are said to be interrelated but to represent different value systems. It is, for example, possible to have high self-esteem as a person, but little respect for the job one performs. Individuals can gain respect from others by virtue of the kind of work they perform, or through the way they perform their work.

5. The need for creativity concerns satisfaction not only with those idiosyncratic activities associated with scholars and artists, but also activities of rearranging and putting together common objects. The latter case refers to the feeling of accomplishment from creating some tangible product. The need for creativity is less universal than the other four, but is thought to be significant for persons in such jobs where it can be fulfilled.

Neff's approach is conceptual in nature and can help professionals gain an understanding of the unique work personality of an individual. In fact, Neff has developed the Work Attitude Scale (see Chapter 4) to aid that understanding. Given the meaning that work holds for the individual, in conjunction with assessment of worker abilities and job requirements, rehabilitation professionals can assist their clients in meeting vocational objectives.

Shontz's Trait Model

A common conception is that motivation is a global factor measured on a single continuum. Persons high in motivation could be expected to exert more effort and show more persistence than persons low in motivation. Franklin Shontz (1957) rejected the idea that there is such a thing as a general motivational factor, and that persons with so many "motivational units" were more likely to complete rehabilitation tasks. Rather, he suggested that motivation may best be understood and measured when treated as a group of interrelated dimensions. To Shontz, it is the pattern of and position on different dimensions that describes a person's overall motivation.

From his clinical analysis of seven rehabilitation clients, Shontz (1957) isolated five factors he thought were necessary, but not sufficient, to describe rehabilitation client motivation. Those five dimensions are:

1. *Reality orientation:* a quantitative factor that represents acceptance of the limitations imposed by disability
2. *Energy level:* a second quantitative factor reflecting the degree of effort expended
3. *Cooperativeness:* a third quantitative factor that incorporates client willingness to follow treatment plans
4. *Breadth of motivation:* a qualitative factor referring to the degree of motivation for different types of activities
5. *Ultimate social requirement:* another qualitative motivational factor that connotes the effect of realistic goal choice.

In a later study, Nadler and Shontz (1959) empirically described the patterns of work motivation exhibited by rehabilitation clients enrolled in a sheltered workshop. They isolated six motivational dimensions on which each workshop client could be ordered. The three most important dimensions were Drivenness Toward Work, Intellectual Deficit, and Laissez-Faire-Realism. Drivenness Toward Work and Laissez-Faire-Realism were postulated to resemble the earlier clinically determined factors of energy level and reality orientation.

The importance of Shontz's approach does not rest primarily in the specific motivational dimensions isolated. Those dimensions may be limited to the underlying measurement scheme used and the populations studied. Rather, Shontz's approach points out that motivation does not occupy a single continuum from motivated to unmotivated but rather is multidimensional and interactive. The major advantage of a trait approach is that it objectively describes and defines motivation.

McDaniel's Decision-Making Model

McDaniel (1976) has modified Vroom's (1964) expectancy theory into a motivational model that has direct applicability to rehabilitation. According to McDaniel, client participation in rehabilitation tasks, whether attending physical therapy or seeking a job, will depend upon a) the client's subjective appraisal of the costs or effort involved, b) the utility or personal value of task performance and outcome, and c) the estimated probability of a favorable outcome or chance of success. Using these three factors, McDaniel devised an equation whereby motivation equals the estimated probability of favorable outcome multiplied by task utility divided by perceived costs. Because the three factors concern the client's subjective estimates, McDaniel suggested that counselors can gauge the level of client motivation by assisting clients to estimate costs, utility, and probability of success regarding various rehabilitation tasks. He also noted that "professional decisions, too, are subject to the same rules. A counselor's decision to accept for services any particular applicant could be predicted by knowing the estimate of the costs of providing the necessary services, his judgment as to the likelihood of a favorable outcome to the case, and the utility he attaches to serving this person, whether moral or practical" (McDaniel, 1976, p. 128-129). Finally, McDaniel pointed out that in using his model, or any other motivational model for that matter, it is important to remember that motivation for task performance interacts with aptitude, and what people hope they can do may be quite different from what they think they can do. In the latter case, determining what is probable, rather than what is possible, may be a crucial distinction in estimating rehabilitation client motivation.

Wright's Goal-Setting Model

Beatrice Wright (1960) is an advocate of the somatopsychological point of view. Somatopsychologists believe that what is important in understanding psychological adjustment to disability is the perception of the disability held by the person and the stimulus value of the disability to others in the person's environment. To Wright, adjustment to disability occurs when one limits the importance of physique, holds a wide range of values, limits disability to the impact of the actual impairment, and emphasizes personal intrinsic values while limiting external comparative values.

Wright's (1960) motivational model stresses the importance of personal goals, and incentive conditions, values, rewards, and punishment linked to those goals. Because of the common influence of Lewin's (1935) ideas, Wright's position is close to Vroom's (1964) expectancy theory. The emphasis on goals as an important motivational variable remains popular in vocational rehabilitation (Cook, 1981) and in the more general motivation literature (e.g., see Locke, Shaw, Saari and Latham (1981)).

Like Vroom (1964), somatopsychologists view goals, such as seeking or avoiding a specific job, as having valence, or positive and/or negative values. Goals with a positive value attract; goals with a negative value repel. Goals can be enhanced by associating incentive conditions, such as money, with the goal.

Motivational analysis considers the importance the person attaches to goals and incentive conditions, and the existence and strength of barriers that impede movement toward a goal. Barriers may be physical, such as functional limitations associated with a physical impairment, or psychological, such as prejudicial attitudes of employers toward persons with a disability. In some cases the barrier to a goal is impermeable and the person must choose a new goal. For example, it is unlikely that a deaf person would ever find employment as an air traffic controller. Other times the motivational situation is much more complex, as when a goal has both negative and positive valence. The classic approach-avoidance conflict represents such a situation. Assume that an individual is positively attracted to a job, but also assume that the individual fears being rejected by the employer. If these driving and restraining forces are roughly equal, the individual reaches equilibrium somewhere short of goal attainment. That is, the further the person is from the goal, the weaker the restraining forces (rejection) and the stronger the driving forces (employment). The closer the person is to employment, the stronger the restraining forces and the weaker the driving forces. The conflict might be resolved by modifying the client's fear of rejection or increasing the incentive conditions associated with the job.

Finally, Wright (1960) suggested a number of strategies to enhance task motivation:

1. Break a big goal, such as employment, into subgoals such as learning specific work behaviors.
2. Make sure the person has the ability to accomplish the goal.
3. Build incentive conditions into negative or neutral tasks.
4. Reward effort toward task accomplishment.
5. Help the person to experience a number of successes before experiencing failure.

Fordyce's Behavioral Model

Wilbert Fordyce has long been a spokesman for the behavioral approach in rehabilitation. The behavioral approach (sometimes referred to as behaviorism, behavior modification, or behavior analysis) is based on the learning model developed by Skinner (1953). Basically, Skinner has been concerned with responses, reinforcement contingencies, and functional analysis. Any observable, quantifiable, voluntary action a person makes is called a response. The number and rate of responses emitted depend upon reinforcement contingencies. Reinforcement is defined as something that follows a response and increases the probability that the response will recur. Reinforcement is thus defined by its functional effect on a response. Therefore, to predict the occurrence of a response, one must analyze the reinforcement (or lack thereof) to which the response is linked, or contingent.

The timing of the reinforcement is also important. For example, gamblers who play slot machines often play for hours, losing more than they win, because the reinforcement (money) is linked to a variable-ratio payoff. In essence, the slot machine controls the lever pull because the reinforcement comes at unknown intervals spaced just enough apart (on the average) to maintain the behavior. To Skinner, the direction and regulation of behavior is determined by the responses the individual makes and the environmental consequences of those responses. The rate of reinforcement, by definition, determines whether or not a response will recur.

Fordyce (1976) has succinctly pointed out the differences between traditional models of motivation and the behavioral viewpoint. According to Fordyce, the traditional way of conceptualizing motivation is as a sometimes hidden, internal structure. The job of the rehabilitation professional becomes one of determining how much of this internalized motivation anyone has. Motivational change occurs when the internal structure is reorganized. According to Fordyce, a major drawback of the traditional approach is that, because motivation is thought to be internal, the responsibility for rehabilitation is placed on the client, not on the treatment environment.

Approaching motivation from the behavioral perspective, Fordyce (1976) pointed out that, although behaviorists might recognize such internal factors as motivational traits and genetic endowment, they are more likely to view motivation simply as responses governed by environmental contingencies. Changing, or motivating behavior thus becomes the application of behavioral principles (see Chapter 7 for an overview of these techniques) to decreasing, increasing, and/or teaching and maintaining new behaviors. For example, Fordyce proposed that physical disability can be viewed as punishment. That is, by virtue of the disability, one suffers the loss of some of those things that were previously reinforcing, for example, work. Expected reactions to the immediate effects of disability are avoidance or withdrawal. The behavioral strategy of choice is to ignore withdrawal behaviors, thereby removing their reinforcing properties and setting the stage for learning more appropriate work-related behaviors.

Behavioral techniques have been widely applied in rehabilitation, and thinking of client motivation in behavioral terms is somewhat advantageous because:

1. Considering client motivation as environmental contingency management directly addresses the question, "How to get clients to do what they are supposed to do?"
2. Focusing on motivation as extrinsic to the person places responsibility for client performance within treatment systems.
3. Motivation is conceptualized simply as those things a person will work to obtain.
4. Behavior is never labeled as bad or good, merely as effective or ineffective.
5. The basic principles of the behavioral approach are easily learned, although application of the principles (e.g., determining what things are reinforcers) can be difficult.
6. Work motivation can be enhanced by selectively modifying client goals, effort, and/or persistence.

The Minnesota Work Adjustment Model

Perhaps the best application of a work motivation approach to rehabilitation is the Minnesota Theory of Work Adjustment (MTWA;

Dawis, Lofquist, & Weiss, 1968). According to the MTWA, a person is most likely to stay in a job when the person's abilities match the requirements of the job and when the person's needs or work-related preferences match needs-satisfying conditions in the job. The potential applicability of the MTWA has been enhanced by the development of different instruments to measure the ability requirements and need reinforcers inherent in different classes of jobs as well as instruments to measure an individual's specific needs and abilities. Prediction of work success or tenure follows the degree of match between how well a person with a given ability level meets the ability requirements of the job in conjunction with the reinforcers within the job available to meet the individual's unique work-related needs. Because worker needs are defined as those things an individual found previously to be reinforcing, and because the theory makes use of specific inventories to measure work-related needs and abilities, the Minnesota approach combines behavioral and trait models of work motivation.

Dawis (1976) outlined the implications of the MTWA for rehabilitation. He pointed out that work adjustment problems result when workers lack job-related satisfaction, and when employers find their workers' abilities unsatisfactory. Therefore, such undesirable rehabilitation outcomes stem from a lack of correspondence between the individual and the work environment. Rehabilitationists could intervene by teaching new work-related skills, by modifying work attitudes, or by modifying the ability requirements and reinforcers in work environments. Dawis (1976) suggested that the latter strategy is an example of job redesign. The MTWA defines work adjustment as maximum correspondence between workers and work environments.

Economic Disincentives as Motivational Barriers

Most, if not all, work motivation models are just as applicable to able-bodied persons as they are to disabled persons. There are, however, differences between how the industrial psychologist and the rehabilitation psychologist approach the problem of work motivation. For example, industrial psychologists focus on maintaining and increasing job task performance. In industrial settings, workers are prescreened and are assumed to have adequate task-related abilities and to be motivated enough to have applied for the job in the first place. Rehabilitationists often start at a much lower level and must help the disabled person reach a number of prework goals such as learning to adapt to the functional limitations associated with the impairment, relearning basic activities of daily living, and learning to live independently. Once these goals are reached, then work-related tasks such as learning new occupational skills, work behaviors, and methods to deal with prejudice are considered. Throughout the entire process the overriding goal is employment. Although there are numerous benefits associated with employment, rehabilitation clients are often faced with powerful economic disincentives to achieve this final goal.

The problem of work disincentives is often cited by rehabilitation counselors as a primary reason for client failure (Thoresen et al., 1968). The following interchange between a counselor and a potential client graphically illustrates the problem.

> "Hi, Mr. Smith, I got your name from the United Mine Workers, and I'd like to take a few minutes to explain a variety of services available to help you. Vocational Rehabilitation can help you learn a skill and find a job, even though you have a disability. Can I tell you about them?"
> I had driven up a snowy back road in the dead of winter to see a new referral. He was a coal miner who had sustained a permanent leg injury in a mine accident. We were sitting in his living room by the fireplace. He was staring thoughtfully at the flames and sipping a cup of coffee.
> "Son," he asked, "how much money do you make?"
> "About $800 a month."
> "Son, I make $900 a month on this leg of mine. Now if you can get me a job where I can make more money than that without paining this leg, I'll listen to what you have to say. If not, why don't you just have a cup of coffee and we'll talk about football." (Walls, Masson, & Werner, 1977, p. 143).

As Neff (1977) pointed out, money is an obvious and powerful motivator. It is equally obvious why Mr. Smith would make a completely rational decision not to accept vocational rehabilitation services. The degree to which financial disincentives act as a motivational barrier to work directly depends on the amount of non–work-contingent income associated with the disability.

Besides receiving income from such programs such as Social Security Disability Insurance (SSDI), Supplemental Security Income (SSI), and Workman's Compensation, rehabilitation clients may also be eligible for in-kind subsidies for food (food stamps), housing (low-rent public housing) and health care (Medicare and Medicaid). Indeed, Walls et al. (1977) noted that vocational rehabilitation clients might be eligible for one or more of 76 federal assistance programs. As might be expected, most severely disabled clients qualify for assistance. Cook, Bolton, and Taperek (1980) found that 83% of former spinal cord injured rehabilitation clients received some financial support from SSDI and SSI.

Transfer payments can become disincentives depending on the amount and type of guaranteed benefits and the benefit-loss ratio, or that point at which earnings from work are subtracted from benefits paid. In some cases, guaranteed benefits provide more income than could reasonably be expected to be earned from working. In other cases, persons who work reach an earned income ceiling that reduces transfer benefits to the extent that, by working, people have actual income equal to or even less than they would have by not working. Consequently, even if a person wants to work and is able to work, economic disincentives may suggest that the rational decision would be not to work. In fact, Better (1979), in a study on the importance of economic disincentives, found that beneficiaries closed as successfully rehabilitated were more likely to be either homemakers or sheltered workshop employees, who thereby retained SSDI and SSI benefits.

Economic disincentives to vocational rehabilitation are of great concern to rehabilitation professionals. However, Congress has addressed the problem through recent changes in the Social Security Act (PL 96-265). Specifically, such changes as a) providing automatic reentitlement to SSDI and SSI benefits if an attempt to return to work fails within 15 months following the trial work period, b) continuing health benefits for up to 3 years after benefits stop, and c) deducting impairment-related work expenses from earnings, thereby stabilizing the benefit-loss ratio (Social Security Administration, 1981), should increase client motivation for gainful activities.

Besides influencing national policy, there is relatively little rehabilitationists can do to lessen the effect of legally mandated economic assistance programs. Counselors should be aware, however, that employed disabled persons may be eligible to claim tax credits for medical expenses and low income jobs; that motivation for work may be greatest for persons who had a moderate or severe loss of income following disability (Nagi & Hadley, 1972); and that, among benefit recipients, younger educated males who have dependents are the best bet for vocational rehabilitation (Treitel, 1979).

SUMMARY

There are dozens of work motivational models and theories; no one approach, however, is all-inclusive for all people in all situations. Given the complexity of human motivation, it is unlikely that any one approach will achieve dominance in the foreseeable future. There are, however, several primary themes in the work motivation literature.

1. People work to meet basic needs, such as to earn money to provide food and security. People also work to satisfy higher ordered needs such as self-esteem.
2. People will work to achieve idiosyncratic rewards. It is important that these rewards be contingent on work behavior.

3. Workers develop strategies to achieve what they want from working. They will set goals and act on those goals they think they can achieve.
4. There is no such thing as an unmotivated client, nor are there such things as innate "motivational units." Rather, different people strive to achieve different things. The direction, effort, and persistence of striving will vary by situation.
5. Work motivation interacts with worker ability and the demands of the workplace. Work success depends on the degree to which a worker's ability level matches the ability requirements of the job and the degree to which the job satisfies the worker's needs.

chapter 4
ASSESSMENT OF EMPLOYMENT POTENTIAL

Brian Bolton

A fundamental assumption of the vocational rehabilitation process is that comprehensive diagnostic assessment of the handicapped client is essential to the effective provision of services. In no area of assessment in the vocational rehabilitation program has more progress been made than the area of vocational evaluation. This progress reflects accurately the critical role of the results of vocational evaluation in planning the individualized rehabilitation program with the client. Because of the primary importance of the topic, three chapters in this volume outline the strategies and techniques of vocational assessment in rehabilitation. The two chapters that follow this one outline the vocational evaluation process and describe available vocational evaluation systems.

    The present chapter consists of four sections. The first provides an operational definition of employment potential in terms of seven categories of employment-related behaviors. The second section includes capsule descriptions of 10 instruments that measure most of the relevant aspects of behavior that lead to successful vocational adjustment. The third section describes a comprehensive assessment model (RIDAC) that can be used in field offices or facilities and illustrates the RIDAC assessment process with four case summaries. The last section contains brief descriptions of two instruments, the Revised Scale of Employability and the Work Attitude Scale; both are reproduced in the Appendices.

THE CONCEPT OF EMPLOYMENT POTENTIAL

Employment potential (or employability) refers to the skills, attitudes, and work behaviors that are necessary to job placement and successful vocational adjustment. An operational definition of employment potential is provided by the seven areas of employment-related competence assessed by the Vocational Behavior Checklist (VBC; Walls, Zane, & Werner, 1978):

1. *Prevocational skills* include knowledge about the need for work and about what a job is, and the trainee's own vocational interests and potential. Also included are generally applicable skills such as folding, sorting, functional reading and math, and the like.
2. *Job-seeking skills* refer to those behaviors involved in locating and applying for employment, such as interpreting ads, matching skills to jobs, completing applications, and preparing a resume.
3. *Interview skills* are the behaviors involved in preparing to be interviewed and in presenting a favorable and accurate impression of oneself in a job interview. Such skills include knowing what to expect, how to respond, and how to gain additional information from a prospective employer.
4. *Job-related skills* refer to the skills that each worker must have to "get around," locate particular areas, conform to rules, and adapt to the physical characteristics of the work setting.
5. *Work performance skills* include such behaviors as setting up the work station, starting work on time, following instructions and models, sorting and using materials, using and caring for tools, working safely, seeking help, and so on.
6. *On-the-job social skills* include being friendly to others, following accepted communication procedures, being able to deal constructively with criticism, refraining from socially destructive or annoying behaviors, talking, answering, and touching others appropriately, and the like.
7. *Union and financial security skills* are concerned with economic considerations, such as company policies, withholding and payroll deductions, obtaining pay, overtime, union functions, insurance and benefits, and budgeting.

It should be noted that the concept of employability includes various pre-employment and ancillary work behaviors, in addition to those performance skills that are usually associated with successful vocational adjustment. The 10 instruments described in the next section were designed to measure different aspects of employment potential of handicapped persons.

VOCATIONAL MEASUREMENT IN REHABILITATION

Because the primary focus of the state/federal vocational rehabilitation program has traditionally been the enhancement of the vocational adjustment of handicapped clients, a substantial investment has been made in the development of measures of work-relevant attitudes, behaviors, and skills. In this section 10 instruments that were judged to meet minimal standards of psychometric development are described and their potential applications in client assessment are briefly outlined. The 10 instruments are divided into two categories: a) vocational adjustment scales and b) psychosocial adjustment instruments with vocational subscales. Each capsule description includes information about the rationale, primary purpose, item format, and scoreable scales. Information about the technical characteristics and relevant supporting research is contained in Bolton (1982).

Vocational Adjustment Scales

This section includes descriptions of four observer rating instruments (Functional Assessment Inventory, Vocational Behavior Checklist, Work Adjustment Rating Form, and Workshop Scale of Employability), a self-report measure of vocational information (Social and Prevocational Information Battery), and a self-report measure of vocational needs (Minnesota Importance Questionnaire).

Functional Assessment Inventory The Functional Assessment Inventory (FAI; Crewe & Athelstan, 1978) is a diagnostic instrument designed to assess the client's capacity for work or other productive activity. The FAI originated with a list of problems recorded as barriers to employment in a sample of client case files. The inventory consists of 30 items that denote behavioral characteristics relevant to employment, each one consisting of four response alternatives beginning with "no significant impairment" and progressing through three levels of increasing limitations. The FAI also includes nine supplementary items that focus on the client's specific vocational strengths. The FAI is scored on eight factor-analytically derived subscales: Motor Function, Medical Condition, Cognitive Function, Personality and Behavior, Vocational Qualifications, Economic Disincentives, Vision, and Hearing (Crewe & Athelstan, 1980).

Vocational Behavior Checklist The Vocational Behavior Checklist (VBC; Walls, Zane, & Werner, 1978) contains 339 vocationally relevant skill objectives that are stated in the uniform CBS format (conditions, behaviors, and standards of performance). The 339 skills were extracted from 21 previously developed vocational assessment instruments and organized into seven content areas: Prevocational Skills, Job-Seeking Skills, Interview Skills, Job-Related Skills, Work Performance Skills, On-the-Job Social Skills, and Union and Financial Security Skills. Client skill mastery is recorded on a skill summary chart and may be quantified in a skill objective profile, which translates vocational achievement levels into a percentage of the critical behaviors mastered in each of the seven areas.

Work Adjustment Rating Form The Work Adjustment Rating Form (WARF; Bitter & Bolanovich, 1970) was constructed to measure the work readiness of rehabilitation clients. The instrument was designed primarily for use by counselors and workshop foremen working with mentally retarded clients to assess potential for training and workshop adjustment progress. The WARF contains eight subscales, each having five items, for a total of 40 items. The five items for each subscale describe five different levels of performance from low to high and require a simple yes/no judgment by the rater. The subscales are: Amount of Supervision Required, Realism of Job Goals, Teamwork, Acceptance of Rules/Authority, Work Tolerance, Perseverance in Work, Extent Client Seeks Assistance, and Importance Attached to Job Training.

Workshop Scale of Employability The Workshop Scale of Employability (WSE; Gellman, Stern, & Soloff, 1963) was designed to serve two primary functions: assessment of client status as a diagnostic basis for program planning, and assessment of change during the rehabilitation program via repeated measurements. The WSE consists of 52 items that are usually completed by a workshop supervisor. The 52 items, each containing four-choice anchored scales, are grouped into five subscales: Ability to Mobilize and Direct Energy in the Work Situation; Capacity to Tolerate and Cope with Work Pressures, Tensions, and Demands; Interpersonal Relations with Co-Workers and Foremen; Functioning Level of Ability in the Work Situation; and Overall Evaluation—Agency Criteria. The specificity of the WSE items suggests that its greatest value is probably as a diagnostic instrument in the rehabilitation workshop.

Social and Prevocational Information Battery The Social and Prevocational Information Battery (SPIB; Halpern, Raffeld, Irvin, & Link, 1975a,b) was designed to assess the skills and competencies regarded as critical for the successful community and vocational adjustment of mentally retarded adolescents and young adults. The SPIB consists of 227 true/false or picture selection items that are orally administered to small groups of examinees and are scored on nine subtests: Purchasing, Budgeting, Banking, Job-related Behavior, Job Search Skills, Home Management, Health Care, Hygiene and Grooming, and Functional Signs. Form T of the SPIB (SPIB-T; Irwin, Halpern, & Reynolds, 1977; 1979) is a downward extension of the SPIB for use with trainable retarded persons, and the Tests for Everyday Living (TEL; Halpern,

Irwin, & Landman, 1980; Landman, Irwin, & Halpern, 1980) is an upward extension for use with nonretarded subjects.

Minnesota Importance Questionnaire The Minnesota Importance Questionnaire (MIQ; Gay, Weiss, Hendel, Dawis, & Lofquist, 1971) measures the respondent's salient vocational needs by means of a 210-item pair comparison format. The needs, which are learned through previous reinforcing experiences, are defined as classes of preference for reinforcers. Twenty dimensions of vocational need were formulated: Ability Utilization, Achievement, Activity, Advancement, Authority, Company Policies, Compensation, Co-workers, Creativity, Independence, Moral Values, Recognition, Responsibility, Security, Social Service, Social Status, Supervision-Human Relations, Supervision-Technical, Variety, and Working Conditions. An MIQ profile may be interpreted in terms of the relative importance to the individual of the 20 work reinforcers or in terms of the degree of correspondence with the need reinforcer patterns for 148 diverse occupations which represent 12 occupational groups (Borgen et al., 1968; Rosen et al., 1972).

Psychosocial Adjustment Instruments with Vocational Subscales

This section contains descriptions of two observer rating instruments (Rehabilitation Indicators and Service Outcome Measurement Form) and two self-report inventories (Handicap Problems Inventory and Human Service Scale). Each of these multiscale instruments includes one or more vocational subscales and several other subscales that measure psychosocial aspects of client functioning that have direct relevance to vocational adjustment.

Rehabilitation Indicators Rehabilitation Indicators (RI; Brown, Diller, Fordyce, Jacobs, & Gordon, 1980) constitute a comprehensive assessment system for describing all areas of rehabilitation client functioning. The specific RI focus on observable behaviors that are potentially modifiable within rehabilitation settings. RI are organized into four packages (Diller, Fordyce, Jacobs, & Brown, 1979): Status Indicators summarize the client's functioning in seven categories, for example, employment, self-care, and transportation; Activity Pattern Indicators describe the client's typical activities in day-to-day living; Skill Indicators describe the behavioral skills the client needs to maintain his or her functioning and carry out daily activities; and Environmental Indicators quantify physical, social, and cultural aspects of the client's living situation. Most of the RI are completed through interviews with the client or a relative and/or through direct observation of the client.

Service Outcome Measurement Form The Service Outcome Measurement Form (SOMF; Westerheide & Lenhart, 1973; Westerheide, Lenhart, & Miller, 1974; 1975) is a counselor rating instrument that was developed to reflect the employment orientation of the vocational rehabilitation counseling process. The SOMF consists of 23 items, each with five anchored alternatives, that are scored on six subscales: Difficulty, Education, Economic/Vocational Status, Physical Functioning, Adjustment to Disability, and Social Competency. Clients are rated at acceptance for services and again at case closure, with the acceptance ratings indicating difficulty, the closure ratings indicating outcome, and the difference scores indicating gain due to rehabilitation services.

Handicap Problems Inventory The Handicap Problems Inventory (HPI; Wright & Remmers, 1960) was developed to quantify the impact of disability as perceived by the disabled individual. The HPI is a checklist of 280 problems attributable to physical disability. By marking those problems that are perceived to be caused or aggravated by the handicapping condition, the disabled person reveals the significance he or she attaches to the impairment. The HPI items are categorized into four life areas or subscales: personal, family, social, and vocational. The HPI can be used clinically as an inventory of disability-related problems that require attention and as a research instrument in the study of adjustment to disability.

Human Service Scale The Human Service Scale (HSS; Kravetz, 1973) was designed to assess clients' rehabilitation needs, in order that appropriate services can be rendered, and to measure (via retest) the extent to which the services were successful in satisfying the needs. Thus, it is both a diagnostic tool and a program evaluation instrument. Eighty items that require either biographical information or self-ratings are scored on seven factor-analytically derived subscales that are closely related to Maslow's basic need categories: Physiological, Emotional Security, Economic Security, Family, Social, Economic Self-Esteem, and Vocational Self-Actualization.

Uses of Vocational Measuring Instruments

Of the four observer rating instruments that focus on aspects of client vocational adjustment, the FAI and the VBC provide assessments of a broad range of work-relevant factors, for example, medical conditions, economic disincentives, job-seeking skills, and union-financial-security skills. In contrast, the other two work adjustment scales that are completed by raters, the WARF and the WSE, are restricted to vocational behaviors that are directly observable in work settings, for example, amount of supervision required, acceptance of rules and authority, capacity to cope with work pressure, and interpersonal relations with co-workers and foremen. It is readily apparent from their breadth of coverage that the FAI and the VBC are preferred instruments for assessing the range of clients' job-relevant skills and capacities as a basis for rehabilitation program planning, especially in completing the Individualized Written Rehabilitation Program (IWRP) and similar requirements (for examples, see Walls, Zane, & Werner, 1978, Chapter 9). The WARF and the WSE have their primary application in work evaluation and work adjustment settings. They can be used to assess readiness for work or vocational training, to diagnose deficits in work abilities and attitudes, and to plan work adjustment programs.

The two psychosocial adjustment instruments that require observer ratings, the RI and the SOMF, represent vastly different levels of complexity and depth in client assessment. The RI emphasize those functional skills and daily living competencies that are essential in achieving independence, including mobility, communication, and transportation. Although the SOMF covers many of the same areas of functioning, its items require global judgments rather than detailed observation and recording of client skills.

The two self-report vocational adjustment scales, the SPIB and the MIQ, measure entirely different aspects of client vocational functioning. The SPIB assesses functional skills in such areas as purchasing, banking, job-related behavior, job search skills, and health care. In their *User's Guide*, Halpern, Raffeld, Irwin, and Link (1975c) outlined and illustrated a systematic approach to rehabilitation program planning called task analysis planning. The MIQ, which measures a client's needs or preferences for reinforcement in the work environment, was designed to be used within the conceptual framework of the Minnesota Theory of Work Adjustment (MTWA; Dawis, 1976). The client's MIQ profile can be used in conjunction with information about the need reinforcer patterns of occupations (Borgen et al., 1968; Rosen et al., 1972) to identify those work environments that are more likely to satisfy the client's salient vocational needs.

The two self-report psychosocial adjustment inventories, the HPI and the HSS, both measure various aspects of adjustment to disability from the perspective of the client. The HPI is a checklist of problems associated with one's disability, and the HSS covers many of the same areas within a framework of rehabilitation needs.

In their excellent article on the use of the HSS in rehabilitation service provision, Reagles and Butler (1976) made several suggestions that are applicable to all self-report inventories. Some of their recommended uses of inventories are: a) as an entree to the counseling relationship by establishing a point of departure of importance to the client, b) as a simple problem checklist of the client's primary concerns,

c) as an aid in identifying severely handicapped clients in terms of self-expressed service needs, d) as an inexpensive screening device that is applicable on a routine basis, and e) as a standardized format for recording the client's input to the development of the IWRP.

Readers desiring more detailed information on the uses of measuring instruments in client assessment are referred to the *Handbook of Measurement and Evaluation in Rehabilitation* (Bolton, 1976) and to the recently published *Rehabilitation Client Assessment* (Bolton & Cook, 1980).

COMPREHENSIVE CLIENT ASSESSMENT

In the mid-1970s the Arkansas Rehabilitation Service implemented an experimental Rehabilitation Initial Diagnosis and Assessment of Clients (RIDAC) unit in the Little Rock district office. The essence of the RIDAC concept is an initial, concentrated, minievaluation of rehabilitation potential and vocational capacity for new clients, as well as for "difficult" cases that are not progressing satisfactorily (Usdane, 1972). The rationale for the RIDAC concept was the realization that successful movement of cases during the referral period is often dependent to a great extent upon the expeditious provision of relevant diagnostic services. Delays in the provision of diagnostic services may result in clients' loss of confidence in the rehabilitation process, and could result in closure from referral status or difficulty in establishing rapport for planning purposes. Generally, counseling is the only direct service provided in local offices. For diagnostic services, clients are often sent to several different places in the community—a process that is often frustrating. Furthermore, with the emphasis on services to the severely disabled, the implementation of the RIDAC concept in local field offices could serve as an important resource for rehabilitation counselors in planning with those clients who present special problems.

Objectives and Anticipated Results

The specific objectives of the experimental RIDAC unit were as follows:

1. To reduce the time lag between referral of clients for services and their movement into active status
2. To reduce the number of applicants who are closed in 08 status, that is, closed from referral
3. To increase the relevance of client diagnostic information for counselors' uses in planning with their clients, or in justifying closures in 08 status

4. To increase the number of severely disabled clients accepted for services.

In addition to the results that are implied in the four primary objectives stated above, a number of more general benefits were anticipated. Clients should be better satisfied with their early exposure to the rehabilitation process when immediate arrangements for diagnostic services are made for them. Receiving these services within just a few days after their initial contact with the agency should be encouraging. Futthermore, it was anticipated that, in some cases, extended periods of evaluation might be circumvented. Information ascertained during the initial RIDAC evaluation of some clients could help determine the feasibility of programs other than lengthy evaluations.

Perhaps most important among the potential benefits of the RIDAC unit was the increase in relevance and availability of diagnostic information, facilitating the effectiveness of counselor/client planning toward the ultimate goal of successful rehabilitation. This was viewed as especially important in the process of determining a vocational objective for each client. For the more severely disabled clients, it was anticipated that the initial RIDAC evaluation would assist in planning subsequent, more intensive assessments in other facilities.

Components of the RIDAC Unit

The Arkansas RIDAC unit staff consisted of the following positions: coordinator, physician (part-time), psychiatric consultant (part-time), nurse (part-time), psychologist, two vocational evaluators, project counselor, secretary, and clerk stenographer. Complete job descriptions for each of these positions are included in Bolton and Cook (1980, pp. 301–310). The overview of the RIDAC service procedures which follows includes the general duties, responsibilities, and functions of the staff members.

The RIDAC evaluation process is initiated by the rehabilitation counselor, who completes a brief referral form requesting RIDAC services. Next, the coordinator completes a schedule card for appointments with the physician, psychologist, and psychiatrist, and for vocational evaluation. At this point the referring counselor meets with the RIDAC staff at a prescriptive staffing to determine what services are needed and to make recommendations to the psychologist regarding specific tests that seem desirable. The prescriptive staffing is crucial in that it forms the basis for all other activities the client may be involved in while undergoing the RIDAC evaluation.

An orientation interview is then conducted with the client by the coordinator; this interview helps to allay the anxiety and fears of the client. It also involves a visit by the client to each area and with each staff member. Following this orientation, the RIDAC counselor compiles basic social information about the client. This entails a study of the referring counselor's records, and at times involves securing additional information from the client, the client's family, and others. The project counselor also formulates plans for transportation of the client.

The actual RIDAC evaluation process begins with either a general medical examination or a psychological evaluation, depending upon the availability of the physician or the psychologist. General medical examinations are provided in all new cases. The examination rooms are equipped with an EEG machine, vitalor to test lung capacity, x-ray viewer, otoscope, eye charts, and other standard examination equipment. The provision of medical evaluation services in the district office enables the RIDAC team to know quickly the extent of the medical aspects of the client's disability and the residual functional capacities in relation to any proposed potential training or working plan for the client. If the need is established for a medical specialist's examination, arrangements are made at this time. Also, the physician may request assessments of supplementary physical capacities, endurance, mobility, and so forth.

The project psychologist administers a battery of clinical tests for the purpose of assessing intellectual potential, general personality functioning, and possible perceptual/motor dysfunction. Three instruments comprise the core of the psychological evaluation: the Wechsler Adult Intelligence Scale, the Bender-Gestalt, and the Draw-A-Person. Additional tests and inventories that are administered on a selective basis include the Minnesota Multiphasic Personality Inventory, the Sixteen Personality Factor Questionnaire, and the Wide Range Achievement Test. The psychologist provides a summary of the client's personal adjustment, makes a preliminary review of indications of emotional disorders, and assesses motivational factors and other potential influences on the development and implementation of the client's rehabilitation plan. Each psychological evaluation is summarized in a written report that becomes part of the case record.

Those clients who are believed to have emotional problems that might interfere with the successful completion of a rehabilitation program are referred to the psychiatric consultant for an in-depth evaluation. The psychiatrist diagnoses the specific problem, recommends services that are needed to ameliorate the problem, and identifies any limitations produced by the diagnosed condition that will affect further evaluation, training, or work. The psychiatrist usually discusses the

Table 1. The RIDAC evaluation sequence

1. The client is located in the community, and referral is made to the rehabilitation service.
2. The referring counselor makes a determination as to whether or not the case needs the services of the RIDAC unit and makes the referral to RIDAC.
3. After the RIDAC coordinator is advised that a referral is to be made, appointments are established.
4. The entire staff meets briefly at a prescriptive staffing session to determine which RIDAC services are to be provided to the client and to make recommendations to the psychologist regarding the specific tests that seem desirable. The prescriptive staffing is a crucial point in that it forms the basis for all other activities the client may be involved in while undergoing RIDAC evaluation.
5. The client is oriented to the RIDAC program by the coordinating counselor or another staff member and is advised of what to expect while receiving RIDAC services.
6. A basic social history is taken.
7. The client begins the evaluation process with either a psychological evaluation or a general medical examination, depending upon the availability of the psychologist or physician. If the need is established for a medical specialist's examination, the RIDAC staff informs the referring counselor, who arranges for the examination.
8. After completion of the psychological evaluation and the general medical examination, the client is referred for vocational evaluation, the most crucial of all the evaluation processes, and for a comprehensive social report if requested by the referring counselor.
9. The case is discussed at a staffing attended by the referring counselor and appropriate RIDAC personnel. At this staffing, all information gathered about the client during any part of the RIDAC process is presented. As a result of staffing, the need may be apparent for further evaluation, and the client rerouted, as appropriate, through previous steps.
10. The client, with findings and recommendations of the RIDAC staff, is returned to the referring counselor.
11. The referring counselor makes a determination about the feasibility of rehabilitation services for the client. If such services are found nonfeasible, the case is closed as not eligible for services. If rehabilitation services are found feasible for the client, the case is carried through the appropriate service program.

case with the referring counselor and summarizes the findings in a written report.

Probably the most important component of the RIDAC evaluation is the vocational evaluation, which is designed to provide an initial assessment of the client's level of vocational skills and potential for future evaluation, training, and employment. However, it is not an in-depth vocational evaluation and is not meant to be a substitute for a comprehensive vocational evaluation. The RIDAC vocational assessment is selected from the following: work samples, work motivation inventories, specialized aptitude tests, and the General Aptitude Test Battery. The work samples were selected from the commerical vocational evaluation systems described in Chapter 6. The work motivation inventories include the Work Values Inventory and either the California Occupational Preference Survey or the Kuder Vocational Preference Record. Manual dexterity and mechanical aptitude are measured with the Purdue Pegboard, the Minnesota Clerical Test, and the Bennett Mechanical Comprehension Test. Upon completion of the prescribed vocational evaluation program a summary report is written which concludes with recommendations pertaining to adjustment training, vocational skill training, employment, or further evaluation.

After all of the requisite component evaluations have been completed, a case staffing is held by the RIDAC staff, with the referring counselor in attendance for the purpose of coordinating all reports and data and making final recommendations for the disposition of the case. It should be emphasized that the final decision is made by the referring counselor; the purpose of the RIDAC evaluation and staffing is simply to provide information on which to base that decision. However, possible recommendations that result from the RIDAC assessment include the following: job placement, skill training, retraining, psychological or psychiatric evaluation, sheltered workshop placement, extended vocational evaluation, medical evaluation, return to school, and enrollment in various adjustment service programs. The RIDAC evaluation sequence is summarized in Table 1.

Evaluation of the RIDAC Unit

Statistical analyses of client service data for 1,357 RIDAC clients and 2,863 traditional clients of 10 Little Rock office general counselors supported the following conclusions:

1. A larger proportion of RIDAC clients were a) severely disabled, b) multiply disabled, c) psychiatrically disabled, d) mentally retarded, and e) accepted for rehabilitation services.
2. A smaller proportion of RIDAC clients were closed in 08 status from referral. Time-in-status and cost data were not substantially different for the RIDAC and the traditional clients.
3. Counselors' evaluations of the RIDAC unit were overwhelmingly positive and included perceived improvements in the following areas: case planning, case management, client benefits, financial benefits, time considerations, and convenience.

4. Clients' evaluations of the RIDAC services were also very favorable.

In summary, the available evidence indicates that the objectives of the RIDAC unit were generally achieved. Details concerning the evaluation of the Arkansas RIDAC unit are presented by Bolton and Davis (1979).

Illustrative Case Summaries

The four cases that are summarized in this section, although not representing the entire range of clients served, illustrate the types of problems and the service outcomes that characterize the RIDAC approach to client assessment.

Case 1: Severely Disabled—Successful Outcome

A 30-year-old, married, white female, SSDI recipient, was referred to RIDAC with a major disabling condition of epilepsy, partly controlled, and a secondary disabling condition of emotional and speech disorders. The client takes phenobarbital and phenytoin (Dilantin) for control of seizures. Her only work history had been in a sheltered workshop. She expressed to her counselor a desire to go to work "to satisfy myself." Referral was made to RIDAC to determine the client's physical limitations, intellectual capacity, and vocational interests and aptitudes. Psychological testing indicated that the client was functioning in the dull normal classification of mental abilities and seemed to be on the border of psychoneurosis with symptoms of anxiety and depression. Vocational evaluation indicated that the client's highest areas of interest were clerical and computational, but she did not show aptitude for this type of work. During upper body/whole body range of motion testing, she complained repeatedly about pain in her neck, shoulders, and back. A general medical examination, however, did not list any physical limitations. The RIDAC staff recommended that this woman be placed in either a work adjustment or an on-the-job training situation for several months before a final decision was made regarding training or placement. Other recommendations were to obtain a current neurological report and speech therapy. A neurological report was received by the counselor and did not present any contraindications to the proposed plan. The client refused speech therapy. Thus, upon full review of pertinent case material, the joint decision of the client and counselor was to place the client in a work adjustment training program in a local sheltered workshop to ensure that she would receive the necessary intensive and supportive services of a therapeutic milieu. The IWRP enabled the client to develop the necessary self-confidence and self-esteem to seek out and secure gainful competitive employment in the community. She is presently employed in the housekeeping department of a local hospital.

Case 2: Severely Disabled—Not Eligible for Services

A 28-year-old single male was referred to RIDAC with a diagnosis of brain damage. The client was originally referred to the rehabilitation counselor in an attempt to qualify him as a disabled adult child since his father was retiring. The counselor, however, felt that the client should have counseling and guidance to encourage him to obtain a vocational evaluation in a facility, with the possibility of training at a later date. It was felt that the RIDAC evaluation could be a preliminary step. The general medical examination stated that the primary disabling condition was mental deficiency, with a secondary condition of blindness in the left eye. Psychological testing indicated that the client was functioning in the mildly retarded intellectual classification. His scores seemed to be depressed by organicity, lack of innate ability, and emotional factors. Vocational evaluation did not find any outstanding specific skills or aptitudes. The client lacked self-confidence, gave up on more difficult tasks, had a short attention span, was easily distracted, and behaved in a childish, immature, and inappropriate manner. The parents of the client asked to attend the staffing and were welcomed. It was the recommendation of the staff that this young man be considered for the Children's Colony for two reasons: 1) he needed to gain some degree of independence, because his parents were of retirement age; and 2) he could function adequately in a highly structured environment with his peers. The client was placed at the Children's Colony and a letter was subsequently received by RIDAC from the parents expressing their gratitude for the support given them in effecting his traumatic separation. Information on the client was forwarded to the SSDI unit, which could qualify him as a disabled adult child. The case was closed as not eligible for services.

Case 3: General Medical Only (Cancer)

A 42-year-old, married, black male was referred to rehabilitation by the chief of social services at the Radiation Therapy Institute. The client had been a boiler fireman for a large paper products company. The client underwent a total laryngectomy and left radical neck dissection for a T3N1 lesion of the left pyriform sinus. He had no evidence of distant metastasis, and he communicated well with an artificial larynx. Statements from the radiation therapists on the case recommended that the client receive radiation therapy. The client was referred to RIDAC for general medical examination to determine his limitations and the need for adjunctive services. The RIDAC physician stated that the client was limited in physical activities that required walking, standing, stooping, kneeling, lifting, reaching, and pulling. He recommended that the client receive radiation therapy and a speech evaluation. The client's program was delayed because of his excessive drinking and smoking and his negative attitude toward treatment. He received support and encouragement from his counselor, the social worker, the speech pathologist, and his wife. He began to develop a more positive attitude. As of this writing, he is receiving radiation therapy daily, meets with the speech pathologist on a biweekly basis (he is learning esophageal speech), and is attending a sheltered workshop for a period of work adjustment. He hopes eventually to return to his former employment with the paper company.

Case No. 4: Worker's Compensation Case (Back Disorder)

A 37-year-old, married, white female was referred to RIDAC for identification of impairment, limitations, and potential for training. The counselor specifically asked for the General Aptitude Test Battery. The client is a Worker's Compensation case, having sustained an injury to her back at work. She had been treated by numerous specialists. Her treatment program included traction, physical therapy, and a series of William's exercises. A general medical examination by the RIDAC physician concluded that the disability was psychophysiological musculoskeletal disorder and that the client would be limited in any work that required prolonged standing or sitting, lifting, bending, climbing, or repetitive twisting. The GATB revealed that the client showed an aptitude for various occupations including keypunch operator, clerical, computing, printing, or classifying. The client and her counselor, during counseling sessions, decided that she would enter a local vocational school for training as a general office worker. The Worker's Compensation Commission and the insurance company were notified of the client's decision and the cost of necessary services. The client entered training in December 1977. In January 1978 the client received notification that the final report had been received from her physician and that she had a 15% permanent disability to the body as a whole. The client is presently functioning successfully in her training situation.

TWO SPECIAL INSTRUMENTS

In this section two instruments that were constructed for use in the assessment of rehabilitation clients, the Revised Scale of Employability and the Work Attitude Scale, are briefly described. The complete instruments are reproduced in Appendices A and B. (These instruments may be reproduced and used by practitioners and researchers without obtaining the authors' permission.)

Revised Scale of Employability

The Scale of Employability for Handicapped Persons was developed at the Chicago Jewish Vocational Service during the years 1957–1963 (Gellman, Stern, & Soloff, 1963). Three separate scales comprised the original Scale of Employability, namely, the Workshop, Counseling, and Psychology scales; however, the Psychology scale was seldom used. The Scale of Employability was designed for the purpose of assessing the employment potential of physically, mentally, and emotionally handicapped persons who are clients of vocational adjustment workshops. It has proven to be a useful diagnostic instrument in a variety of rehabilitation settings (Bolton & Soloff, 1973).

Use of the Workshop and Counseling scales by rehabilitation practitioners has probably been limited somewhat by the excessive length of the scales (they contain 52 and 44 items, respectively). Although the behavioral specificity of the items is essential for diagnosing client deficits in work-relevant functioning, the detailed assessment is not necessary for other purposes, such as measuring a client's general progress over time. For these reasons, the Revised Scale of Employability (RSE) was constructed by the present author, using the developmental research on the original Scale of Employability as a starting point.

One purpose of the original research was the identification of the major dimensions of client functioning in vocational adjustment workshops (Gellman et al., 1963). Replicated factor analyses of the Workshop and Counseling scales isolated 11 dimensions of rehabilitation clients' vocational functioning. A series of focused vignettes describing clients' behavior was prepared for each of the dimensions and rank-ordered to establish the anchor points for the scales (see Bolton (1970) for details about the scale construction procedures).

The RSE consists of 10 client-anchored scales, each requiring one global rating, and a brief summary of production data for the eleventh dimension. The 11 scales, reproduced in Appendix A, are named as follows:[1]

Workshop Scales
WI. Attitudinal Conformity to Work Role
WII. Maintenance of Quality
WIII. Accceptance of Work Demands
WIV. Interpersonal Security
WV. Speed of Production

Counseling Scales
CI. Adequacy of Work History
CII. Appropriateness of Job Demands
CIII. Interpersonal Competence: Vocational
CIV. Interpersonal Competence: Social
CV. Language Facility
CVI. Prominence of Handicap

The 11 scales of the RSE constitute a comprehensive evaluation framework for the assessment of rehabilitation clients' vocational functioning. Once the rehabilitation practitioner has internalized the common themes underlying the sets of vignettes that define the dimensions, a client can be rated in a very brief time. The most convenient schedule for using the RSE is one that corresponds to client staffings, that is, with completion of the scales at 4- to 6-week intervals. Information from the RSE can be used to measure clients' progress, to estimate clients' readiness for job placement, and to evaluate program effectiveness.

Work Attitude Scale

In conjunction with his research on the work problems of handicapped persons at the Chicago Jewish Vocational Service in the 1950s, Walter

---
[1] The RSE published here is an abbreviated version of the first edition of the RSE; the number of vignettes has been reduced from nine to five to make the instrument easier to use.

Neff developed an instrument to assess the meanings that work has for the individual. Neff and Helfand (1963) hypothesized that "there may exist in some persons an attitudinal structure—a set of opinions, beliefs, fears, expectancies, and self-perceptions—which constitutes a psychological barrier against adequately performing the role of a worker (p. 140)."

The Work Attitude Scale (WAS) is based on a theory of the meaning of work that has three facets: a) work perceptions vary from satisfaction to dissatisfaction, b) work is meaningful in terms of patterns of interrelated needs, and c) work is focused in part on the self and in part on significant others. The levels of the three facets of the theory are:

1. *Gratification:* Satisfaction, Dissatisfaction
2. *Needs:* Material, Activity, Self-Esteem, Esteem by Others, Creativity
3. *Focus:* On Self, On Others

For each of the 20 combinations of the three facets ($2 \times 5 \times 2 = 20$), three items were written to express the salient aspects of the theory. The WAS thus contains 60 items, which are reproduced in Appendix B. Although the original scoring format for the WAS was the Q-sort, Neff later constructed a Likert response form of the instrument.

The instructions for completion of the Likert form of the WAS are given in Appendix B, with a scoring key that indicates which of the 20 cells of the three-facet design each item represents. The scoring procedure can be adapted to the needs of the practitioner or the researcher. For example, an overall index of positiveness of work attitude would result from summing the 30 Satisfaction items and summing the 30 Dissatisfaction items and then subtracting the dissatisfaction score from the satisfaction score. A global index score for the focus of work could be derived by comparing the summed scores for the 30 Self and 30 Other items in a similar fashion.

More complicated scoring procedures would entail scoring the various aspects of work attitudes *within* the levels of other facets. For example, two satisfaction/dissatisfaction scores could be obtained, one for the 30 Self items and one for the 30 Other items. Likewise, an overall profile for the five work needs could be derived by summing the 12 Material items, the 12 Activity items, and so on, or need profiles could be scored separately for Satisfaction and Dissatisfaction items, or for Self and Other items. Clearly, the multidimensional theory of work meanings that is operationalized by the WAS provides a flexible information base for practitioners and researchers.

chapter 5
PRESCRIPTIVE VOCATIONAL EVALUATION

Michael Leland and B. Douglas Rice

> Vocational (work) evaluation is a comprehensive process that utilizes work, real or simulated, as the focal point for assessment and vocational counseling to assist individuals in vocational development. Vocational (work) evaluation incorporates medical, psychological, social, vocational, educational, cultural, and economic data to assist in the attainment of the goals of the evaluative process (Tenth Institute on Rehabilitation Services, 1972, p. 2).

Within the last decade, the emphasis on providing appropriate rehabilitation services to severely disabled individuals, on a priority basis, has substantially increased the demand for effective vocational evaluation programs. As a consequence, vocational evaluation has evolved into a comprehensive process for assessing the needs, strengths, and limitations of individuals with vocational handicaps. The ultimate purpose of vocational evaluation is the development of a vocational plan of action that will subsequently reduce or eliminate the vocational handicaps.

Traditionally, vocational (work) evaluation identified those vocational areas that seemed to be the most appropriate for disabled individuals. In most cases, the results obtained related to work either by direct placement or through vocational training. Several events in recent years, particularly the legislative mandate to serve severely disabled clients and the independent living movement, have served as an impetus for an expanded evaluation system that not only considers vocational potential, but psychological, personal, and social needs as well.

HISTORICAL BACKGROUND

The historical development of the vocational evaluation movement is relatively brief, having unfolded chiefly in this century. In its initial stages, the movement drew heavily from other disciplines, principally psychology. Psychometric testing became a significant force in the United States during the early 1900s, with primary emphasis during this early stage on devising methods for measuring intelligence. However, this emphasis provided a springboard for massive investigation into the development of testing instruments that could measure almost every conceivable human ability and skill, including those in the vocational arena.

During the same period that psychometric testing appeared in university laboratories, the job analysis approach surfaced within private industry. The major purpose of job analysis was to identify job skills and abilities required by workers to perform specific tasks.

With the advent of World Wars I and II came a new and dramatic need for selecting the "right person for the right job." Group testing procedures were introduced by the United States armed forces during World War I as a means for screening out individuals with little potential or limited intelligence (Boring, 1950). The military also began research on developing objective measures of various skills needed to operate a large military war apparatus efficiently. This venture gave early birth to the concept of simulated work as a technique of vocational assessment (Bregman, 1979). During World War II the Link Trainer was used as a simulated training tool by the military to assess the specific skills of selected personnel (Pruitt, 1977). As Neff (1966) pointed out, the simulated work approach attempted to incorporate the best points of psychometric testing and job analysis while trying to eliminate their weaker qualities.

World War II also brought to the forefront the use of another method for vocational assessment, namely, the situational assessment. Pruitt (1977) commented that perhaps the greatest single contribution of the military to work evaluation was made during World War II. As an example, he cites the situational assessment techniques developed by the Office of Strategic Services (OSS, formerly Overseas Secret Service) to select and train agents for spying and espionage.

From the mid-1930s until 1959, the Institute for the Crippled and Disabled (ICD) in New York worked progressively on developing and refining the first systematic approach for evaluating disabled individuals using a battery of work samples called the TOWER system (Testing, Orientation, and Work Evaluation in Rehabilitation). The TOWER system includes more than 100 different work tasks within 14 broad occupational areas (Rosenberg, 1969). Although the TOWER system was the first work sample system, during the past two decades more than a dozen commercial systems have been developed. The currently available work evaluation systems are reviewed in the next chapter.

Concomitant with the development of sophisticated vocational evaluation techniques and instruments came the obvious need for trained and competent evaluators. Short-term institutes and training programs began to emerge across the nation. These programs helped to fill the early professional needs of vocational evaluators. However, as the field of vocational evaluation progressed in technology and methodology, it became apparent that these short-term courses would not be sufficient to provide a qualified body of vocational evaluators. In response, colleges and universities developed undergraduate and graduate degree programs in work evaluation, beginning with the University of Wisconsin-Stout in 1968.

With this rapid professional growth, the need for a collective body of knowledge became apparent. Already established as an early expert in the field of vocational evaluation, the University of Wisconsin-Stout created the Materials Development Center as a national center for materials on work evaluation and work adjustment (Sax & Allen, 1973).

With increasing numbers of professionals in the field of vocational evaluation, the need for a professional organization was also recognized. In 1966 the American Association of Work Evaluators became the Vocational Evaluation and Work Adjustment Association (VEWAA), a division of the National Rehabilitation Association (Hoffman, 1971). The Association publishes a journal, the *Vocational Evaluation and Work Adjustment Bulletin*, to disseminate research and professional innovations to its members.

THE PRESCRIPTIVE APPROACH

The main purpose of this chapter is to present an overview of the prescriptive approach to vocational evaluation, an approach that merits consideration by the rehabilitation counselor, the vocational evaluator, and the facility administrator. With the new demands for rehabilitation services by severely disabled clients, counselors are increasingly turning to vocational evaluation for assistance. Evaluation units, therefore, must be receptive to new or innovative techniques that will make their services more efficient and, in turn, more useful to counselors and clients (Rice & Thornton, 1972).

Prescribing services is not a new concept to rehabilitation, since it encompasses the idea of developing a definite plan of services that has as its objective a successfully rehabilitated client. This is familiar to rehabilitation personnel, since planning is the nucleus of all client programming. The Individualized Written Rehabilitation Program (IWRP) is an example of the importance placed on combined counselor/ client planning. The basic concepts of this approach to programming can be applied to the vocational evaluation process, resulting in benefits and utility to both counselor and client.

Rice (1972a) wrote that in utilizing the prescriptive vocational evaluation approach the evaluation should not only identify client rehabilitation problems, but provide the counselor with a "prescription" for services and service delivery for correcting or reducing the handicapping aspects of the identified rehabilitation problems. This approach differs from the traditional approach in that all available resources and disciplines are brought together to assess each client's specific strengths and weaknesses. The client's rehabilitation needs are thus identified and objectives established with services prescribed for achieving both short- and long-range goals.

The established objectives for the prescription should be supported by facts, observations, test results, client and counselor concurrence, and other pertinent data. Short-term objectives should be developed and continuously evaluated for redirection toward the acquisition of established long-range goals. In addition, the prescriptive evaluation identifies who, how, and in what sequence the services are to be delivered.

Although the prescriptive evaluation differs little from the initial phase of most commonly used approaches, it is within the latter phase that a distinction can be made and the prescriptive evaluation assumes a clear identity. This primary difference is that the evaluation report identifies and prescribes a sequence of services designed to reduce client rehabilitation problems and facilitate client movement along the rehabilitation continuum.

THE EVALUATION TEAM

It is not the composition of the evaluation team that makes the difference in the prescriptive approach, but the manner in which the members work together as a team. Critical to the prescriptive evaluation approach is that each member not only understands his or her respective role but also the roles and responsibilities of every staff person and how the individual efforts are integrated into a single system. The emphasis, therefore, is not on a fragmented approach where each staff person performs a task in isolation, but on a process where frequent contact is maintained among the team members. The key to more effective individualized evaluation is the establishment of good working relationships within the team. Good communication skills, therefore, are essential, and this principle would warrant each member participating in some form of interpersonal skills training. Rice (1972b) stated:

The most elaborate facility and highly qualified staff does not assure the delivery of meaningful rehabilitation services to the client. In all probability, rehabilitation success is determined by how effectively professionals relate to each other while working toward a common goal of rehabilitating handicapped people. Without the ingredients of communication, cooperation, and mutual trust, the client may find himself the central figure in any conflict that could develop (pp. 24–25).

Because the composition of an evaluation team is generally known, the roles of each team member are not discussed in detail here. A large rehabilitation facility will in most cases have a psychologist, a counselor, and a vocational evaluator, with assistance from a broad range of disciplines including physical therapists, occupational therapists, recreational therapists, vocational instructors, physiatrists, other medical specialists, and potential employers. Other facilities, as a result of size and resources, may be limited to a vocational evaluator and counselor, with reliance upon referral to other professionals outside the unit for needed client services.

Evaluation staffings or conferences are essential at specific intervals during the client's evaluation program. First is the counselor's initial planning with the client regarding needed services including vocational evaluation to determine rehabilitation potential. These plans along with all other information should be forwarded to the rehabilitation facility for review by an admissions committee. This committee establishes an enrollment date and passes this information on to the evaluation unit. Prior to enrollment at the facility, the evaluation team should have information from the referring counselor that will enable them to plan a practical and individualized program for the client. This referring information will assist the team in determining the work samples, psychological tests (if needed), and behavioral approach to be used with each client referred for evaluation. It is here at the "prestaffing" that tentative short- and long-term objectives for evaluation are established, subject to agreement by the client when he or she arrives in the unit.

Upon reporting, the client becomes involved in the evaluation plan, with adjustments being made according to the client's behavior and performance on work samples. A progress conference is held after the client has had the opportunity to move through the preliminary phase. At this time, the team and the client review and revise the plan. A prescription is then written for specific work and psychosocial areas. At this point many clients may need more time for additional work samples or situational assessment, provided this meets the approval of client, counselor, and evaluator. The final staffing should be attended by all staff members that have been involved in the client's program (if possible, but at least the evaluation team), including the client. The conference should be chaired by one person (the evaluation supervisor, counselor, or evaluator), with this person having the responsibility to integrate all reports and assemble the recommendations into a prescriptive format.

The team approach follows the concept of the IWRP and, as a result, should be very beneficial to the referring counselor and to the client as services beyond vocational evaluation are planned. At the conclusion of the final staffing, needed services can be identified, as can vendors or providers, time limits, and potential costs.

COMPONENTS OF THE PRESCRIPTIVE APPROACH

The systematic program of vocational evaluation under the prescriptive approach consists of eight components that provide the basis for effective vocational development. The components include: 1) obtaining initial client information, 2) the evaluation interview, 3) preparing the vocational evaluation plan, 4) vocational exploration, 5) assessment (evaluator tools include psychometric testing, work sample testing, job analysis, situational assessment, and job tryout or job site evaluation), 6) formal staff conference, 7) the prescriptive evaluational report, and 8) follow-up. Each of these components provides for a systematic building of the evaluator's knowledge about the individual client.

Obtaining Initial Client Information

To ensure that good evaluation decisions are made in developing an evaluation plan, an extensive data-gathering and exchange process between the rehabilitation counselor, the vocational evaluator, and the client must exist. The referring counselor should provide or make provisions for ensuring that adequate information regarding the client is received by the vocational evaluator. One critical task of the referring counselor that is often neglected is that of providing the evaluator with general and specific referral questions. The reason for a referral should be stated by the referring counselor in terms of specific client needs or questions to be addressed during the evaluation.

To develop the vocational evaluation plan and to address effectively the referring counselor's questions regarding the client, it is necessary to gather as much vocationally relevant information as possible. The basic relevant data that need to be examined fall into several major categories. These are: demographic information, work history, education and training, personal/social/environmental factors, physical and mental capacities, vocational interests and goals, and job-seeking experience (Esser, 1980).

The Evaluation Interview

The evaluation interview is the initial contact or exchange between the evaluator and the client. It serves two major functions: a) to develop a relationship between evaluator and client that will facilitate the evaluation process; and b) to allow the evaluator to gather additional client information and clarify any referral information. Within the context of the evaluation interview, it is important that the evaluator focus the information exchange process; that is, the client should be involved in the process as a vital member rather than as just an information giver (Rubin & Farley, 1980; Anthony, Pierce, Cohen & Cannon, 1980).

The amount and type of information covered in the evaluation interview is contingent upon the quantity and quality of information obtained from the referral source. In many instances, the interview will serve principally to clarify or confirm information supplied by the referral source.

Preparing the Vocational Evaluation Plan

The evaluation plan attempts to set the stage for individualizing the client's assessment program. Its preparation is the product of the initial data-gathering process. It should be noted that in preparing the evaluation plan, the evaluator is aware of the numerous methods and techniques for client assessment and selects only those that are relevant for obtaining specific client information.

McCray (1978) has delineated the preparation steps or processes culminating in the evaluation plan. These are:

Step 1: Accumulation of referral information
Step 2: Examination of referral information
Step 3: Identifying the referral questions
Step 4: Identifying appropriate evaluation techniques
Step 5: Listing persons involved and clarifying their roles
Step 6: The initial interview
Step 7: Plan modification

Vocational Exploration

Vocational exploration attempts to involve the client in the development of a vocational awareness of himself or herself, leading to a decision-making role as the client gains firsthand knowledge of relevant occupations. It is also an opportunity for the vocational evaluator to assist the client through work samples, job tryouts, or situational assessment in exploring various vocations before deciding upon a career that is in keeping with the client's potential and interest.

There are several distinct tools for use by the evaluator in this exploration process, such as the *Dictionary of Occupational Titles*

(DOT) and the *Occupational Outlook Handbook* (OOH). More recently, evaluators have seen the development of commercially available occupational information and exploratory packages such as the Chronicle Guidance Occupational Library, the Science Research Associates Career Information Kit, and the Career, Inc., Exploratory Kit.

By utilizing this wealth of occupational information, the evaluator can equip clients with an awareness of the world of work that is most meaningful to them as well as to assist clients in narrowing the focus upon that area of work that is of direct interest and concern.

Assessment

Utilizing the range of assessment tools and methodologies available, the evaluator, with the aid of the evaluation plan, selects the most appropriate approach. These assessment tools and methodologies include: a) psychometric testing, b) work sample testing, c) job analysis, d) situational assessment, and e) job tryout or job site evaluation. Major aspects of each are detailed below by their respective category.

Psychometric Testing During this approach the client begins to move toward an in-depth understanding of his or her vocational assets and limitations. Testing generally includes a battery of tests or psychometric instruments selected according to the individual needs of the client. The tests most frequently used are those that measure intelligence, aptitude, achievement, interests, personality, dexterity, and level of adjustment.

Psychometric testing can be a useful tool in the evaluator's arsenal of assessment tools by providing some objective measures of the client's strengths and liabilities. Testing results may also provide a basis for modifying the evaluation plan to include additional appropriate and meaningful evaluation procedures. Psychometric testing is a relatively fast, inexpensive, and objective procedure that can be used by the evaluator in shaping the vocational development of the client.

Work Sample Testing A work sample is an attempt to simulate a given task within an industry. The underlying assessment principle is that the most realistic method to evaluate work behavior and skills is to observe and measure an individual's behavior at work. Primarily, work samples can be used to determine an individual's work aptitudes and abilities to function within a given occupational area. According to Neff (1966), "Significantly enough, it has been the rehabilitation movement that has developed the most systematic schemes to evaluate work potential through structured work samples. . . . (p. 685)."

According to the Tenth Institute on Rehabilitation Services (1972, p. 19), the major assets and limitations of work samples are the following:

Assets The practical, hands-on experience of work samples; immediate and direct feedback to the client in terms of performance and vocational exploration; allowance for personal involvement to a significant degree; the high degree of approximation to work and the concrete, meaningful nature of the tasks; and the performance aspects which lead to more effective measurement of clients with verbal limitations.

Limitations The expense of developing, maintaining, and administering work samples; the continuous need to reconstruct and standardize samples; the fact that some client groups, such as the adult offender, may perceive transparency and reject the relevance of simulated tasks.

During the past few years several well designed, practical work sample systems have been developed, including the well known TOWER, the JEVS, the Valpar, and the McCarron-Dial. The next chapter examines in detail the merits and limitations of these and other work sample systems.

Job Analysis According to Hoffman (1973), job analysis is a process of defining the significant worker traits and requirements and the technical and environmental facts of a specific job. The evaluator can use this occupational knowledge in ascertaining how well a client's abilities and limitations fit within a particular job. It should be pointed out that job analysis is a technique seldom used by the vocational evaluator primarily because it is time-consuming and individualized in nature. It is a technique more often used by placement specialists within the vocational rehabilitation process.

Situational Assessment Pruitt (1977) stated that situational assessment is perhaps the most widely used approach in vocational evaluation today. Situational assessment has been defined and redefined in several contexts, but situational assessment refers primarily to the observation of the general work personality rather than specific abilities and skills, with the critical assessment skills in this technique being the observational powers of the evaluator.

The work personality being assessed generally includes the meaning of work to the individual, the manner in which the client relates to important other persons on the job, and the client's attitudes to supervisors, peers, and subordinates (Neff, 1966).

The process of situational assessment has been outlined by Pruitt (1977) and includes:

Step 1: Planning and scheduling observations
Step 2: Observing, describing, and recording
Step 3: Organization, analysis, and interpretation
Step 4: Synthesis of data.

There are a number of strengths and weaknesses of this approach that bear mention. Generally speaking, the situational approach has a strong reality-based factor in that it closely simulates actual work demands in a controlled environment. However, it is a particularly expensive and time-consuming method requiring trained observers.

Job Tryout or Job Site Evaluation These terms apply to an evaluation that occurs in an actual job setting, usually within a specific industry or business in which the client has previously shown some aptitude or interest. In this evaluation situation, the client is observed by the employer in fulfilling the requirement of a specific job or task.

The advantage to using this method is that the individual client is placed in an actual work setting with the competitive standards and expectations required of the normal worker. However, one of the major difficulties with this approach is establishing a cooperative relationship with employers within the community.

The Formal Staff Conference

The formal staff conference provides a structured mechanism for sharing and integrating all the data collected for a specific client. The evaluator assumes a leadership role in the staffing in order to present all the pertinent findings that have been accumulated, as well as to gain additional insight into the client's strengths, weaknesses, and needs as perceived by other staff members.

Using this method, the evaluator is able to reject or confirm certain perceptions of the client's vocational potential. Further, the staffing helps the evaluator to share the expertise of fellow staff members in formulating the prescriptive evaluation report.

The Prescriptive Evaluation Report

Using the prescriptive approach, the vocational evaluator provides the referring counselor with a report that includes vocational, personal, social, and other traditional information, and a "prescription" for services that will meet the client's individual needs with reference to identified assets and deficits. The report includes a sequential plan of action, as appropriate, for improving behavior, developing work potential, reducing educational deficits, and improving personal relations, personal appearance, and so on. As discussed earlier, the prescriptive evaluation report develops both short- and long-range goals in order of priority, the programs needed, the specific services to be emphasized, and, if possible, the approach that the staff should use in working with the client. Consequently, the client's needs are identified in sequential order for the referral source's consideration and/or implementation (Rice & Thornton, 1972). The example at the end of the chapter illustrates the typical prescriptive evaluation report.

Follow-up

A crucial key toward ensuring that the evaluator continues to identify correctly the needs, strengths, and limitations of his or her clients is the process of follow-up. By making contact with their referral sources, evaluators can ascertain the accuracy of their client prescriptions and determine whether there were any difficulties in carrying out the recommendations.

CONCLUSION

The prescriptive approach to service delivery is not a new concept to rehabilitation personnel; plan development has always been a vital part of a client's program. Utilization of the prescriptive technique in vocational evaluation is a departure from the traditional method of making recommendations based on test results and observations. The prescriptive approach not only makes service recommendations as a result of the client's performance and behavior, but provides information concerning how these services should be provided. Included in the prescription, when possible, are recommendations as to who could provide these services, the approximate time period required, expected outcomes, and estimated costs. In certain cases, the prescription might call for additional information from medical specialists or for results of the client's performance in job tryouts or on-the-job training. Both short- and long-term rehabilitation goals, acceptable to the client and counselor, are specified for the counselor's use in preparing the individual program of services.

Evaluation Report

Name of Client: George Marshal   Evaluation Supervisor: Dr. Metcalf
Date of Birth: 11/26/51   Total Days of Evaluation: 4
Referred by: Sherry Hemmer   Total Days to be Charged: 4
Referral Agency: Dept. of Rehab.   Dates Attended: 7/17, 18, 19, 20
Evaluation Intern: Joe Jones   Date of Report: 7/28/80

Reason for Referral

George Marshal was referred to the Rehabilitation Center for evaluation services by his counselor. Referral information indicated Mr. Marshal's disability to be an acute lumbosacral strain (ruptured disc) requiring lumbar laminectomy, which was performed on 1/23/80. The client is restricted from heavy lifting and extensive bending. Subjective complaints are reported to be minimal, but become moderate with work activity or excessive sitting or bending. Information expected to be gained through this evaluation was an assessment of the following:

1. Tolerance for performing various work tasks
2. Aptitudes for performing various work tasks
3. Exploration of vocational choices to determine areas of interest also requested.

Socioeconomic Factors

George Marshal is a 28-year-old, married, white male who is currently residing with his wife and two children. Mr. Marshal indicated completion of the 11th grade as the extent of his formal education. He further stated that he has been employed as a mill operator at two different lumber companies, totaling 4 years of experience.

His most recent employment was at Milton's Lumber Company, where he worked until the fall of 1978, when it was necessary for him to leave as a result of a back injury.

Mr. Marshal reported his present monthly income to be $616.00. In addition, Mr. Marshal indicated that his wife, Suzanne, is currently employed as a nurse's aide.

Mr. Marshal initially indicated that he possesses few outstanding interests and he might benefit from exploring various occupational areas. Mr. Marshal did report that he enjoyed working with his citizen band radio and is currently a member of Valley REACT, an emergency volunteer citizen program using C.B. communication.

In addition, Mr. Marshal reported that he is currently prescribed Empirin and codeine for relief of pain, but dislikes taking any pain medication because of the mental "cloudiness" he reported that it induces.

Test Results

The client was administered a variety of test and work samples to explore vocational areas and aptitudes, as well as to assess specifically the client's physical tolerance and endurance for standing and sitting for extended periods of time.

Mr. Marshal had undergone testing prior to this evaluation through another agency. The reported scores are summarized below.

Wide Range Interest Opinion Test

    Mechanics: Very High

    Physical Science: High

    Machine Operation: High

Intelligence Testing

    Raven Standard Progressive Matrices 50th percentile

    Revised Beta Examination: 99 Beta IQ

Wide Range Achievement Test

    Reading: 9.1 grade level

    Math: 4.9 grade level

Manual Dexterity

    Purdue Pegboard Test

    Right Hand: 60th percentile

    Left Hand: 35th percentile

    Both Hands: 20th percentile

    Crawford Small Parts Dexterity Test

    Pin and Collar: 99th percentile

    Screw: 97th percentile

The following tests were administered during Mr. Marshal's evaluation at the Rehabilitation Center:

Vocational interest was further assessed with the use of the Gordon Occupational Check List. Additional vocational exploration was accomplished with the use of the Viewscripts, Occupational Outlook Handbook, the Dictionary of Occupational Titles, and the California Occupational Guides.

Results of the Gordon Occupational Check List indicated interest in the following job-related activities:

1. Perform a variety of duties on a small farm
2. Operate a tractor or other machinery on a farm
3. Fuse metal parts together by welding
4. Be a member of a ship's crew
5. Repair radio and television sets
6. Repair and overhaul automobile engines
7. Perform routine tests in a laboratory
8. Take, develop, and interpret X-ray pictures.

Through vocational exploration, Mr. Marshal was able to focus on several specific vocational areas, which were as follows:

1. Television and radio serviceman
2. Dental laboratory technician

3. Locksmith

4. Radiological technologist

Mr. Marshal was administered several aptitude tests for the purpose of assessing his basic mechanical abilities.

The Bennett Mechanical Comprehension Test is a nonverbal, pencil-and-paper test designed to measure the ability to perceive and understand the relationship of physical forces and mechanical elements in practical situations. Mr. Marshal's score fell at the 47th percentile using the norm group of male applicants for mechanical jobs, indicating average ability in this regard.

The O'Rourke Mechanical Aptitude Test, a two-part, nonverbal, pencil-and-paper test, was originally designed as a screening device for the selection of applicants for mechanical training or occupations. It is considered to be a more accurate measure than other similar aptitude tests. Mr. Marshal's score fell at the 54th percentile, which is an average score.

The Bennett Hand Tool Dexterity Test assesses an individual's proficiency in using ordinary mechanic's tools. Mr. Marshal's score fell at the 80th percentile, which indicates above average to superior ability in this respect.

The JEVS Manipulating Work Sample Battery measures abilities that involve the dextrous use of hands, hand tools, or special devices to work, move, guide, or place objects and materials. In this battery there exists some latitude for judgment in selecting the appropriate tools, objects and materials, and in determining work procedures in conformance to standards.

Three work samples were selected from this battery to assess manipulating and tending skills (DOT codes .884 and .885, respectively).

Mr. Marshall received the following time and quality rating for the assigned work samples.

Work Sample	Time	Quality
Union assembly	Superior	Average
Grommet assembly	Superior	Superior
Lock assembly	Average	Average

In addition, Mr. Marshal was administered several work samples from the Valpar Component Work Sample Series, which measures an actuarial level of client performance in the tasks described below:

The Valpar Component Work Sample #2, Size Discrimination, is designed to measure a person's ability to perform work tasks requiring visual size discrimination. The client received an assembly score falling at the 72nd percentile and a disassembly score at the 30th percentile. No errors were recorded for this work sample.

The Valpar Component Work Sample #4, Upper Extremity Range of Motion, is designed to measure the mobility of the shoulders, upper arms, forearm, elbow, wrist, and hand. In addition, the work sample is designed to provide insight into related factors such as neck and back fatigue, dexterity, and finger tactile sense. The client's scores fell at the 22nd percentile for assembly and below the 5th percentile for disassembly. During this work sample, the client expressed physical discomfort as a result of sitting for a prolonged period of time, but indicated no physical discomfort occurring in the upper body or upper extremities.

The Valpar Component Work Sample #6, Independent Problem Solving, is designed to measure a person's ability to perform work tasks requiring the visual comparison and proper selection of a series of abstract designs. The client received an average score falling at the 58th percentile. No errors were recorded.

The Valpar Component Work Sample #8, Simulated Assembly, was assigned to assess the client's physical tolerance for standing (20 minutes). The work sample was originally designed to measure an individual's ability to work at an assembly-type repetitive task and the effective utilization of both upper arms. The client received a score falling at the 70th percentile for this work sample, indicating above average ability in this regard.

The Valpar Component Work Sample #9, Whole Body Range of Motion, measures the agility of a person's gross body movements of the trunk, arms, hands, legs, and fingers as they relate to the functional ability to perform job tasks. It was necessary to modify the required physical positions due to the client's inability to assume a bending position. The client received a score falling below the 10th percentile on this task and reported pain and fatigue in the back area. It should be noted that throughout the administration the client was questioned concerning discomfort. Although he reported that he was experiencing pain, he indicated that he wished to continue. This would seem to indicate a high level of motivation on the client's part.

In addition, the Valpar Component Work Sample #14, Integrated Peer Performance, was administered. This work sample is designed to facilitate worker interaction during completion of assemby tasks. Behavioral observations are a critical factor in this work sample. It was observed that Mr. Marshal initially interacted well with the other participants and accepted negative as well as positive criticism appropriately. Although the work sample may induce frustration in the participants, it was observed that the client remained calm and exhibited little frustration. Due to the required 1½ hours of assumption of a sitting position, Mr. Marshal did indicate that he was experiencing physical discomfort.

Because of the client's interest in TV and radio repair, the Adult Basic Learning Examination, Level II, was administered. The test is designed to measure the level of educational achievement among adults. Scores are recorded as percentile rankings derived from a norm group of individuals with 10th grade educational levels. Mr. Marshal's scores on the arithmetic subtests were as follows:

Arithmetic Computation - 8th percentile

Arithmetic Problem Solving - 26th percentile

Behavioral Observations

During the initial orientation by the Vocational Support Staff, it was reported that Mr. Marshal appeared angry about being "made to come here by his counselor." Upon discussion it was found that Mr. Marshal had previously undergone testing with another agency. Arrangements were subsequently made with the client's counselor which eliminated the need to repeat various tests, and Mr. Marshal then demonstrated a willingness to participate in the evaluation.

It may be noted that with the exception of the initial morning, Mr. Marshal willingly cooperated in the evaluation.

Throughout the evaluation, Mr. Marshal arrived promptly each morning and was punctual when returning from scheduled lunch and breaks. His personal appearance and attire were appropriate. With regard to physical tolerance and stamina, it was observed that Mr. Marshal expressed physical discomfort subsequent to sitting for time periods in excess of 50 minutes. Minimal discomfort was reported from prolonged standing (1-2 hours). In addition, it was observed during the Whole Body Range of Motion work sample that Mr. Marshal experienced great difficulty in bending at the waist as well as assuming a squatting position.

Mr. Marshal was referred to the Vocational Adjustment Unit for one day for the purpose of situational assessment. He reported excessive fatigue and low back pain upon the completion of 2 hours of work at the collating assignment. He attempted to complete a task utilizing a rivet machine; however, it was necessary for Mr. Marshal to discontinue working and return home. Mr. Marshal reported that prior to the situational assessment he was "not feeling very well," but wanted to try it. In addition, he stated that he had taken his medication earlier that morning for relief of pain and physical discomfort.

It was noted that on occasion the client would appear to overexert himself physically to complete certain tasks. This would seem to indicate a high level of motivation.

Conclusions and Recommendations

The results of this evaluation indicate that it would not be wise for Mr. Marshal to return to his former occupation or to similar physically demanding occupations. It is felt by this evaluator that Mr. Marshal may have a prognosis for success in an occupation of a semisedentary nature. Results of the testing indicate that the client possesses a basic mechanical aptitude, as well as the required manual dexterity, to succeed in occupations of a mechanical nature. In light of this, the following recommendations and plan of action are offered for consideration.

Vocational Goal: Locksmith   **DOT** 789.281

Intermediate Steps   **Resources**

Within the next 4 weeks the client will consult his physician regarding the feasibility of an exercise program to assist him in improving his stamina and decreasing the possibility of further back injury.

Client's physician:

    Dr. Charles Metcalf
    800 West Grand
    Westminister, Ohio

Intermediate Steps

Contingent upon the recommendations of the physician, the client will engage in an appropriate physical therapy program.

On the basis of client self-report of visual difficulties, the client will consult with his optometrist within the next 2 weeks for the purpose of improving his vision to the maximum extent.

After attending 4 weeks of remedial academic training, the client will demonstrate successful understanding of basic high school subjects by receiving a passing grade on the GED test.

At the completion of a 4 month training course on locksmith skills, client will demonstrate competency by receiving a passing grade ("C" or better).

Resources

May wish to consult:

    Phil Esterhouse, P.T.
    Director, P.T. Dept.
    Grant County Rehab Ctr.

Client's optometrist:

    Dr. William Graybow
    Southgate Plaza
    Suite 40
    Westminister, Ohio

Remedial academic training is available at Lakeside High School during the evenings at no charge to city residents. Contact:

    Elizabeth McCord
    Evening Class Coordinator
    223-4567

GED testing is available every second Tuesday of the month at Grant County Community College.

Contact: Larry Bracken, V.P.
         789-1234

Only available locksmith training within 50-mile radius is at:
    Ohio Vo-Tech School
    145 Commercial Drive
    Lexington, Ohio
    Administrator:
    Jeffrey Lindrell

Intermediate Steps

Following the completion of locksmith training, the client will cooperate with a job placement center by making a minimum of five employer contacts per week for the next 3 months in order to obtain employment.

Resources

Two employment agencies that offer professional services for individuals with handicaps are:

    Merton Placement Services
    Westminister, Ohio

    Columbus Rehabilitation Center
    Columbus, Ohio

chapter 6
COMMERCIAL VOCATIONAL EVALUATION SYSTEMS

Karl F. Botterbusch

In the past 10 years, one of the major factors influencing vocational evaluation has been the development and active marketing of commercial vocational evaluation systems. Today there are at least 14 commercial vocational evaluation systems being marketed. If all of the purely occupational information systems were included, this number would be almost doubled.

There are two reasons for this explosion in technology. First, changes in educational and rehabilitation legislation, initially at the federal level, have wisely mandated that all persons in our society must be served and that all must be served as individuals. State vocational rehabilitation agencies, school systems, and others have created a market for vocational evaluation services. Rehabilitation facilities, educational institutions, and private sources have provided the services to fill this need for client evaluation. In filling this need, they demanded instruments that, although not tests, would still permit assessment to occur under fairly controlled conditions within a limited time period. Hence, the spread of commercial work sample systems.

Second, the field of vocational evaluation has grown at a rate far exceeding the number of qualified persons available for positions. When persons who were not trained in evaluation techniques were hired by facilities and schools as evaluators, it became easy to install hardware, read a manual, and start to determine the future of disabled persons. Lacking specific skills and perhaps a degree of confidence, many evaluators came to rely on commercial systems.

There are two problems that vocational evaluators must face with regard to commercial evaluation systems. The first is that to some people, both in and out of the profession, the term "vocational evaluation" has come to mean "work samples" in general and "commercial work samples" in particular. Although this is a problem that can only be solved by evaluators themselves, it must be stressed that there are other methods of assessing persons besides commercial work samples.

The second problem is one of technical standards. Although some development of norms, reliability, and validity has occurred in the last 10 years, most work sample systems are technically inadequate. The evaluator who would carefully read the administration and technical manuals before selecting a new test would often be the same person who would select a work sample system on the basis of face validity and on "norms" developed on limited or nonexistent populations. Although the developers of these systems are at fault, it is the evaluator who is ultimately responsible to his or her clients for the selection of adequate assessment tools.

SELECTING A COMMERCIAL VOCATIONAL EVALUATION SYSTEM

The first area of consideration in selecting a commercial evaluation system is the relationship between the community and the vocational evaluation unit. The evaluator must carefully investigate the range and type of jobs that are available in the local labor market. Thus, a small rural facility or a facility in a one-industry community will have a narrower range of job evaluation stations than a facility in an urban area. Labor market information can be obtained through vocational surveys, local employment offices and agencies, and client placement records. Once potential employment opportunities have been determined, intelligent decisions can be made on what type of evaluation tools can best assess these demands.

The second consideration is the client population. Some evaluation units must be capable of serving clients with all types of mental, physical, psychological, and cultural disabilities. Other facilities restrict themselves to serving either a single disability or a small number of disabilities. A facility dealing with many types of handicaps would generally need to have techniques covering the entire range of occupational areas and skill levels within these areas. A facility providing services to a single disability group could safely limit its evaluation areas. At the present time, all commercial vocational evaluation systems are designed for persons who can see and hear; these systems contain no special instructions or modifications for the blind or deaf. The evaluator should be aware that he or she frequently will have to make modifications in commercial work samples so that they meet the special needs of his or her clients (Botterbusch, 1976; Dickson, 1976).

The third area to be considered is the purpose of evaluation. Although all vocational evaluation techniques should provide career information, a particular technique may either emphasize occupational information by providing a hands-on experience or it may emphasize the assessment of present skills and aptitudes without relating it to career information. Some systems attempt to provide a thorough evaluation of the client's aptitudes and work behaviors; others provide occupational information and experience, often at the expense of a thorough ability assessment. The evaluator should check the final report format to determine exactly what information it contains; this goes a long way in determining the purpose of a particular system.

These three considerations should only be used as general guidelines, because each facility is unique. A critical factor in purchasing a system should be knowledge of what is needed and not the cost or attractiveness of the hardware. Usually, no one system will meet all the needs of a facility, and the purchased system should be integrated with facility-constructed devices, other evaluation systems, on-the-job evaluation, and psychological tests.

COMMERCIAL VOCATIONAL EVALUATION SYSTEMS

The remainder of this chapter contains summary descriptions of 14 commercial vocational evaluation systems. Each description follows a standard format with six sections: basis of the system, organization, work evaluation process, method of instruction giving, utility, and reviewer's summary and comments. More detailed information about the evaluation systems is available in the comprehensive report by Botterbusch (1980).

Comprehensive Occupational Assessment and Training (COATS)

Basis of the System The COATS is based on several sources; studies done by Prep, Inc., and research reports taken mainly from federally funded projects were used to establish the need for and the content of each of the four components listed below.

Organization The COATS system consists of four components that are intended to give the evaluator a complete picture of the client. (Each component may be used independently.) Each component contains three different program levels: a) assessment and analysis, b) prescription and instruction, and c) evaluation and placement. The four components are as follows:

1. *Job Matching System* This component is an assessment program designed to match a person's preferences, experiences, and abilities to employment and/or training opportunities. The COATS Job Matching System is essentially an audiovisual version of the Cleff Job Matching System. The basic method is to match the client to

24 occupational clusters, each of which includes a number of job titles. The matching process uses 16 skill categories, which are grouped into three major areas: Concrete, Social, and Information. These are obviously taken from the Data-People-Things hierarchy of the *Dictionary of Occupational Titles* (DOT). The clusters can also be used to refer persons to the appropriate COATS Work Samples. Fifteen audiovisual cartridges present photographs and drawings from each of the skill categories. Five cartridges deal with worker preferences, five with experience, and five with capabilities.

2. *Employability Attitudes System* In this component the client determines what his or her attitudes and behaviors are and compares them with the attitudes that employers see as being important for the hiring, promoting, or firing of an employee. Thirteen job-seeking categories (e.g., integrity, time management, and concern for details) and 23 job-keeping and job-advancing categories (e.g., concern with details, persistence, and social judgment) are used. Student results can be compared with employer norms for several groups, including type of industry, geographical regions, size of company, and union. Six audiovisual cartridges containing what the developer calls 25 "real life" adventures are used. Some of these adventures seem to be contrived and are not too realistic.

3. *Work Sample System* This component contains 26 work samples that were developed on the basis of content analysis of tasks common to job families (e.g., electrical work). These job families are based on U.S. Office of Education Career Clusters rather than the DOT. The 26 work samples are: Drafting, Clerical Office, Metal Construction, Sales, Wood Construction, Food Preparation, Medical Services, Travel Services, Barbering/Cosmetology, Small Engines, Police Science, Masonry, Electrical, Electronics, Automotive, Commercial Art, Nutrition, Bookkeeping, Fire Science, Real Estate, Extraction Technology, Clothing and Textiles, Communication Services, Refrigeration, Solar Technology, and Computer Technology. Each of the 26 work samples can be used independently. Instructions are contained on audiovisual cartridges. Each work sample contains occupational information that is used to elicit the degree of client interest in the work sample. The instructions are given in a step-by-step manner, and the cartridge stops when a task is to be performed.

4. *Living Skills System* This component deals with what skills are needed to be functionally literate in contemporary society. The program classifies literacy into skills (reading, writing, computation, problem solving, and speaking-listening) and knowledge areas

(consumer economics, occupational knowledge, community resources, health, and government-law). Six cartridges containing 18 "adventures" are used to evaluate literacy skills and knowledge areas. As with the employability attitudes component, many of these adventures are contrived.

Work Evaluation Process
1. *Preliminary Screening*   No preliminary screening is required.
2. *Sequence of Work Sample Administration*   The four components may be given in any order. The 26 work samples need not all be administered or administered in any particular order. Because each component is more or less independent, components may be purchased and used independently of each other.
3. *Client Involvement*   There is extensive client involvement following the assessment part of the Employability Attitudes and Living Skills. Employability Attitudes instructions involves a Learning Activity Package with 337 Job Seeking and Job Keeping lessons; Living Skills instructions involves a series of 24 audiovisual lesson packages addressed to basic skill development. The evaluator monitors client progress, helps when necessary, and coordinates the activities of several clients.
4. *Evaluation Setting*   Although the manuals do not specify a particular setting, the use of audiovisual materials, answer sheets, handbooks, as well as the emphasis on activities give the COATS a classroom atmosphere.
5. *Time to Complete the Entire System*   The developer states that a total of from 52 to 93 hours are required to complete the evaluation with all 26 work samples. However, in actual use, only from four to ten work samples are usually given. All components except work samples can be administered to small groups.

Method of Instruction Giving   Instructions for all four components are presented on a cartridge containing an 8-track audiotape synchronized with a 16-mm filmstrip. In work samples, the client responds to performing work activities as directed by the cartridge. The client also completes a form on which he or she rates self-interest and self-performance. In the other three COATS components, the client responds by completing a machine-scorable answer booklet. The work samples do not require the client to complete tasks on a time basis.

Utility
1. *Vocational Exploration*   The Job Matching, Employability Attitudes, and Work Sample Systems provide the client with a wealth of occupational information.

2. *Vocational Recommendations* The COATS provides vocational recommendations for both individual jobs and groups of related jobs.
3. *Counselor Utilization* At present the COATS is basically designed for client (or student) self-interpretation followed by activities designed to change client behavior. The evaluator must be able to provide the counselor with a usable report using the wealth of data generated by the COATS.

Summary and Comments The COATS is the most comprehensive evaluation system presently available for use in educational and rehabilitation settings. The system is logically consistent, well designed, and based on a wide range of research studies. Two unique aspects are: a) the emphasis upon the client using the results of the assessment to plan and, it is hoped, change his or her own behavior and b) the fact that each component can be used independently. This means that a facility could use, for example, the Work Samples and Job Matching Systems in an evaluation unit, the Employability Attitudes System in a work adjustment program, and the Living Skills System in a literacy training program. The COATS was basically designed for school populations, and this results in several potential problems for rehabilitation facilities: a) the client must be able to read at about the eighth grade level to use the written materials effectively; b) the use of audiovisual format and separate answer sheets may present some problems for persons with hearing, visual, and/or learning handicaps; and c) except for the hand-scored work sample option, the turnaround time of 1 week is a problem for facilities that typically have a period of evaluation of 2–3 weeks. From a technical point of view, the weakest component is the Work Samples, which do not presently contain adequate norms.

Motivational Occupational Vocational Evaluation (MOVE)

Basis of System The MOVE, formerly called the Hester Evaluation System, is based almost exclusively on the third edition of the DOT; recent revisions in the fourth edition of the DOT have resulted in a change in the scoring system. The system stresses the Data-People-Things hierarchy, physical conditions, environmental conditions, general vocational preparation, and specific vocational preparation. It must be stressed that the MOVE is not a work sample system but a battery of psychological tests and ratings designed to relate client scores to the DOT.

Organization Twenty-six separate performance and paper-and-pencil tests are used to measure 27 ability scores. These scores evaluate the client's abilities on the Data and Things hierarchies. (The system requires the evaluator to determine People hierarchy levels based on interviews, case histories, and behavior observations.) These ability scores are grouped into seven areas below; the equipment or test used to obtain each score is given in parentheses:

1. *Finger Dexterity* (Purdue Pegboard); *Wrist-Finger Speed* (Tapping Board); *Arm-Hand Steadiness* (Lafayette Motor Steadiness Kit).
2. *Manual Dexterity* (Minnesota Rate of Manipulation; *Two-Arm Coordination* (Two-Arm Tracing Apparatus); *Two-Hand Coordination* (Etch-A-Sketch with Maze Overlay); *Hand-Tool Dexterity* (Hand-Tool Dexterity Test); *Multiple Limb Coordination* (foot-operated stapler); *Machine Feeding* (folding machine)
3. *Perceptual Accuracy* (projector with slides); *Perceptual Speed* (Tachistoscope); *Spatial Perception* (Revised Minnesota Paper Form Board Test)
4. *Motor Coordination-Aiming* (Lafayette Motor Steadiness Kit); *Reaction Time* (Multi-Stimulus Reaction Timer); *Fine Perceptual Motor Coordination* (Polar Pursuit Tracker); *Visual Motor Reversal* (Mirror Tracing Apparatus)
5. *Abstract Reasoning* (Raven Progressive Matrices); *Verbal Ability* (SRA Verbal Ability, SRA Verbal Test—L Scale); *Numerical Ability* (SRA Verbal Test—Q Scale); *Decision Speed* (same equipment as Perceptual Accuracy); *Response Orientation* (same equipment as Reaction Time); *Oral Directions* (Personnel Tests for Industry—Oral Directions Test)
6. *Reading* (Gates-McGinitie Comprehension Test); *Arithmetic* (Level 1 of the Wide Range Achievement Test)
7. *Hand Strength* (grip dynamometer); Lifting Ability (standing platform).

Work Evaluation Process

1. *Preliminary Screening* No preliminary screening is required. In the 3-week Vegas Evaluation Program designed by and used at Chicago Goodwill, the MOVE is administered at the beginning of the program to determine basic abilities.
2. *Sequence of Work Sample Administration* The tests do not have to be given in any specific order.
3. *Client Involvement* Because of the formal nature of the testing process and the emphasis upon accurate measurement, there is little client involvement during actual testing. However, the evaluator is urged to explain the entire system to clients prior to test administration.
4. *Evaluation Setting* The psychometric basis of the MOVE creates a formal testing atmosphere. The emphasis on accurate measure-

ment using psychophysical devices to determine reaction time, dexterity, and so on, could easily create a laboratory-like environment.
5. *Time to Complete the Entire System*   The developer estimates that the entire battery can be administered in about 5 hours. The individually administered tests take a total of about 1 hour to administer. The remaining 4 hours are devoted to tests that can be administered to small groups.

Method of Instruction Giving   All instructions are read aloud to clients, and many are accompanied by short demonstrations. The manner of communication of the instructions may be varied to accommodate any special client problems (e.g., hearing problems, low intelligence).

Utility

1. *Vocational Exploration*   The formal testing atmosphere and the lack of introductory explanations relating the tests to jobs offers the client almost no chance for vocational exploration. However, the jobs listed on the computer printout are intended to provide the client with information that can be used as a basis for vocational exploration.
2. *Vocational Recommendations*   The major purpose of the MOVE is to make specific vocational recommendations. As stated above, the printout lists specific job titles that are consisered as being feasible.
3. *Counselor Utilization*   The system is designed to report jobs that are within the client's abilities. This information, if communicated to the referring counselor effectively, could be very useful.

Summary and Comments   The MOVE uses the trait-and-factor approach that has been used as a test development model for over 40 years. This approach has proven successful for many psychological tests. The system attempts to present a picture of the client's abilities and to match these abilities with the structure of the DOT. The logical structure has a definite appeal to persons who stress ability testing as part of the vocational evaluation process. It must be emphasized that the lack of detailed information on the development and the validity of the system is a major source of concern. Descriptions of the development process and the scoring procedures are critical for all work sample systems, but are even more critical in a system that handles a large mass of data in ways that are not really available for the user's inspection. The lack of details on the process, coupled with the almost total lack of technical data, force the potential user to accept the results on faith. The system does not claim to be a complete vocational evaluation system—the developer realizes the need for occupational information, interest determination, accurate behavioral observations, and evaluator interaction with the client. The system could be best described as a very logical series of tests designed to relate client abilities to the Data-People-Things hierarchy of the DOT. The system is probably best used for initial screening at the beginning of the vocational evaluation process.

McCarron-Dial Work Evaluation System (MDWES)

Basis of the System This system is based on five factors: verbal-cognitive, sensory, motor, emotional, and integration-coping. These five factors were derived from an assessment of three dimensions: verbal and synthetic-spatial skills, sensory-motor skills, and emotional-coping skills.

Organization The MDWES consists of eight separate instruments grouped into five factors:

1. *Verbal-Cognitive* Wechsler Adult Intelligence Scale (or the Stanford-Binet Intelligence Scale) and the Peabody Picture Vocabulary Test. In many instances, an achievement test such as the Wide Range Achievement Test (WRAT) or the Peabody Individual Achievement Test (PIAT) is also given.
2. *Sensory* The Bender Visual Motor Gestalt Test (BVMGT) and the Haptic Visual Discrimination Test (HVDT). For visually disabled clients, the Haptic Memory Matching Test (HMMT) is used in place of the HVDT and the BVMGT.
3. *Motor* McCarron Assessment of Neuromuscular Development (MAND). The following 10 tasks assess fine and gross motor abilities:
   a. Fine Motor Skills Assessment: Beads-in-Box; Beads-on-Rod; Finger Tapping; Nut-and-Bolt Task; Rod Slide
   b. Gross Motor Skills Assessment: Hand Strength; Finger-Nose-Finger Movement; Jumping; Heel-Toe Tandem Walk; Standing on One Foot.
   There are 39 possible scoring options for these 10 measures.
4. *Emotional* Observational Emotional Inventory (OEI). In some instances, the Minnesota Multiphasic Personality Index (MMPI) and the House-Tree-Person are also used.
5. *Integration-Coping* The Dial Behavior Rating Scale (BRS) and the Street Survival Skills Questionnaire (SSSQ) are used.

Work Evaluation Process

1. *Preliminary Screening* An interview with the client and the referral source is urged to obtain background data on the client.

2. *Sequence of Work Sample Administration*   Administration begins with factor one and continues through factor five.
3. *Client Involvement*   Client involvement is encouraged during the assessment period. Upon completion, the manual recommends individual counseling to provide help for the client to move toward realistic work-training goals and expectations.
4. *Evaluation Setting*   A formal testing setting is used for factors one through three and for the SSSQ in factor five. The other two factors require a period of placement in a work setting, most commonly a sheltered workshop. When used in clinical or educational settings, office or classroom situations are used for making behavioral observation.
5. *Time to Complete the Entire System*   The first three factors and the SSSQ (factor five) can be completed in a day or less. A minimum of 1 week (2 weeks are recommended) for systematic observation in a work setting, most commonly a sheltered workshop, is required for the emotional and integration-coping factors when used in work evaluation.

Method of Instruction Giving   All instructions for factor three (MAND) and parts of factor two (HVDT) and five (SSSQ) are given orally through demonstration accompanied by kinesthetic cues or total communication systems as needed. Factor one and the BVMGT (factor two) are given according to their manuals.

Utility

1. *Vocational Exploration*   The formalized assessment procedures required for the first three factors offer almost no chance for client vocational exploration. The observation period either in a sheltered workshop or on a job site provides chances for exploration, but this depends on the program of each facility.
2. *Vocational Recommendations*   The system assesses the client's ability to function in one of the five following vocational program areas: day-care work activities, extended sheltered employment, transitional training, and community employment. The system also provides guidelines for assessing the client's potential functioning in one of five living programs: institutional, intermediate care, group home, halfway house, and community independent living. Examples of final reports for work, educational, and clinical uses are provided in the various manuals. Emphasis is on training, placement, educational and vocational development.
3. *Counselor Utilization*   The system is designed for disability determination, which includes a description of assets, functional limitations, and adaptive capacities. The system is aimed at providing counselor information and counselor involvement is recommended.

Summary and Comments The McCarron-Dial was designed for the purpose of assessing the mentally disabled person's ability to function. It uses a combination of widely accepted, individually administered psychological tests, assessments of fine and gross motor ability, and an extended period of observation. Rather than discard those tests that have proven useful, or rely solely on performance and behavior observation, the McCarron-Dial attempts to combine them into a single prediction tool. It is encouraging to note that some detailed, well designed studies have been conducted with the MDWES. In a vocational evaluation setting, the system may achieve its best use as a preliminary assessment device for assessing general levels of functioning prior to a systematic exploration of interests and specific skills.

Micro-TOWER

Basis of the System The system is basically a group aptitude test that uses work sample methodology to measure seven aptitudes as defined by the third edition of the DOT and the General Aptitude Test Battery (GATB). The statistical basis consists of studies on the factor analysis of several work samples and concurrent validity studies.

Organization The system contains 13 work samples, which measure seven specific aptitudes, plus general learning ability, or G. The work samples are, however, organized into five major groups of what can be thought of as second-order factors. The primary aptitude(s) of the DOT/GATB abbreviation for each work sample are given in parentheses:

1. *Motor* Electronic Connector Assembly (F—finger dexterity); Bottle Capping and Packing (M—manual dexterity); Lamp Assembly (K—motor coordination)
2. *Spatial* Blueprint Reading (S—spatial reasoning); Graphics Illustration (S—spatial reasoning; K—motor coordination)
3. *Clerical Perception* Filing (Q—clerical perception; K—motor coordination); Mail Sorting (Q—clerical perception); (M—manual dexterity); Zip Coding (Q—clerical perception); Record Checking (Q—clerical perception)
4. *Numerical* Making Change (N—numerical reasoning); Payroll Computation (N—numerical reasoning)
5. *Verbal* Want Ads Comprehension (V—verbal comprehension); Message Taking (V—verbal comprehension).

Work Evaluation Process

1. *Preliminary Screening* No preliminary screening is required prior to the administration of Micro-TOWER. The manual states, however, that a period of general orientation to the system should be given prior to work sample administration.

2. *Sequence of Work Sample Administration* The manual contains several suggested schedules for administration of the work samples and for group discussion. These schedules are only suggestions and the work samples do not have to be given in any set sequence. However, because the Want Ads Comprehensive Work Sample tests the ability to read and understand English, it is usually first. Within each work sample a carefully defined sequence is followed. All instructions to the clients are recorded on a cassette tape. The first step is the presentation of a series of occupational photos that illustrate jobs requiring the skills assessed by the work sample. Each work sample provides an untimed learning/practice period which includes taped instructions, visual illustrations, evaluator demonstration, and an opportunity for clients to practice. During this period, the cassette tape automatically stops at preselected places so that the evaluator can give additional instructions. The evaluator is also free to stop the tape at any time if additional help in needed. After this learning/practice period comes the evaluation period. Here clients work entirely on their own without any help. After completion of the task, the clients fill out a self-report form rating their interest and perceived ability.
3. *Client Involvement* Micro-TOWER emphasizes client involvement. This is accomplished in several ways. Prior to administration of the work sample, occupational information is provided; during the instruction period, the evaluator stops at several points to answer questions and provide additional instructions. The practice period also permits feedback. The greatest client involvement is during the group discussion program. Here, client values, interests, needs, and so forth are discussed. Suggested activities (e.g., job values, lifelines, choose your supervisor) are provided in a separate manual. Clients also receive formal feedback of their performances on the work samples.
4. *Evaluation Setting* The evaluation setting could best be described as a combination of a formal testing situation and a group counseling environment. The Micro-TOWER is best administered in a room that is separate from the rest of the evaluation unit; a U-shaped table arrangement is suggested. These factors add to the formal testing atmosphere.
5. *Time to Complete the Entire System* Total testing time is about 15 hours; if group discussions are included, the total evaluation takes 19–20 hours. Depending on what schedule is used, the battery can be administered in between 3 and 5 days. The manual contains several suggested schedules which vary in the number of hours per day that the work samples are administered and in the presence and duration of the group discussion periods.

Method of Instruction Giving Instructions are given by several methods. Each work sample begins with a series of large photographs showing jobs requiring skills related to the work sample. The major instructional method, however, is a separate audio cassette tape for each work sample which is coordinated with the evaluator's demonstration. This tape is programmed to stop at certain critical points so that the evaluator can provide help, give additional explanations, or check the results of the practice exercises. The system emphasizes standardized instructions and timing; it uses the audiotape as the major means of ensuring standardization. No written instructional materials are used. However, to complete some of the verbal and clerical tasks a third to fourth grade reading level is required. In summary, there are five steps in each work sample: a) occupational orientation, b) basic instructions, c) practice period, d) timed evaluation, and e) completion of self-evaluation.

Utility

1. *Vocational Exploration* The information given at the beginning of each work sample is designed to make clients aware of what jobs are related to the aptitude(s) being measured by the work sample. Many of the topics covered in the group discussions center on relating personal needs to job demands and occupational interests.
2. *Vocational Recommendations* The system relates aptitudes to worker trait groups (WTG) that require aptitude patterns similar to those of the client. Thus, in making recommendations, the evaluator would match the client's aptitudes with those required by the WTG. This process would be further broken down according to interests, interpretations from behavior observations, and the results of group discussions. These recommendations would be written in narrative form in the narrative summary report.
3. *Counselor Utilization* The Micro-TOWER has two major uses. The first is to present a relatively accurate assessment of job-related aptitudes in a brief period of time. The second is to be a first or screening step in an extended period of evaluation.

Summary and Comments Micro-TOWER may best be described as a group aptitude battery that uses work sampling techniques as the assessment method. The system claims to measure seven of the nine aptitudes that are used in the WTG arrangement of the DOT/GATB. The system has the advantage of being group-administered in a fairly short period of time, thus making maximum use of evaluator time. The system attempts to go beyond the mere assessment of aptitudes by providing occupational information and group discussion. Adequate norms are available, except for employed workers. The system generally takes a standardized, psychological test approach with emphasis on carefully controlled administration conditions, the separation of learning from performance, and the reporting of results in terms of percentiles. One of the most encouraging aspects of the Micro-TOWER is the apparent concern with continued development and refinement, as evidenced by the numerous technical articles. One major problem with the system is the lack of thorough behavioral observational materials. Another possible problem is the converse of the advantages of a group-administered test, namely, the evaluator may not be able to provide the client with the one-to-one relationship that is needed for some severely disabled persons.

Philadelphia Jewish Employment and Vocational Service Work Sample System (JEVS)

Basis of the System The worker trait groups arrangement of the third edition of the DOT is the basis for this system. The philosophical basis is a trait-and-factor approach between the common aptitude and behavioral demands of the represented WTG and related work samples. It is also related to the *Guide for Occupational Exploration*.

Organization The system contains 28 work samples arranged in 10 WTG as follows:

1. *Handling* Nut, Bolt, and Washer Assembly; Rubber Stamping; Washer Threading; Budgette Assembly; Sign Making
2. *Sorting, Inspecting, Measuring, and Related Work* Tile Sorting; Nut Packing; Collating Leather Samples
3. *Tending* Grommet Assembly
4. *Manipulating* Union Assembly; Belt Assembly; Ladder Assembly; Metal Square Fabrication; Hardware Assembly; Telephone Assembly; Lock Assembly
5. *Routine Checking and Recording* Filing by Number; Proofreading
6. *Classifying, Filing, and Related Work* Filing by Three Letters; Nail and Screw Sorting; Adding Machine; Payroll Computation; Computing Postage
7. *Inspecting and Stock Checking* Resistor Reading
8. *Craftsmanship and Related Work* Pipe Assembly
9. *Costuming, Tailoring, and Dressmaking* Blouse Making; Vest Making
10. *Drafting and Related Work* Condensing Principle Drawing.

Work Evaluation Process

1. *Preliminary Screening* No preliminary screening is required.
2. *Sequence of Work Sample Administration* The 28 work samples

are administered in order of difficulty beginning with Nuts, Bolts, and Washer Assembly and ending with Condensing Principle Drawing. If a client is obviously not able to complete the work samples at any one level, more complex work samples are usually not administered.
3. *Client Involvement* Because work sample administration resembles a formal testing situation, client contact with the evaluator is minimized; feedback on performance and behavior occurs at the end of the evaluation process. However, a client orientation is given at the start of the work samples and a motivational group interview is held at the end of the first day.
4. *Evaluation Setting* A realistic work atmosphere and setting are stressed in the manual.
5. *Time to Complete the Entire System* The average client takes 6 or 7 days for the 28 work samples.

Method of Instruction Giving Most instructions are oral and include demonstration. Reading is required of the client only when it is a requirement in the job area being sampled.

Utility

1. *Vocational Exploration* Client vocational exploration is seriously limited by two factors: a) many of the work samples tend to be abstract, and b) there is no orientation relating the work samples to jobs.
2. *Vocational Recommendations* The final report has a space for two worker trait group arrangements that are suggested for additional planning. The recommendations are closely related to the third edition of the DOT and are geared for both training and job placement.
3. *Counselor Utilization* The system and the final report are oriented toward the counselor; however, counselor familiarity with the DOT is necessary for optimal counselor use.

Summary and Comments The JEVS system is a highly standardized and well integrated procedure for client evaluation based on 10 of the DOT worker trait groups. The strongest points of the system are its stress upon careful observation and accurate recording of work behaviors and performance factors. The use of a trait-and-factor approach ties in well with the assessment of specific abilities. The major problems with the system seem to be the abstract nature of many of the work samples, which hinders vocational exploration, limited evaluation feedback of the client, and the lack of job information presented to the client. The system is best used when a thorough evaluation of the client's potential is desired.

Pre-Vocational Readiness Battery (Valpar 17)

Basis of the System The manual contains no discussion of the basis of the system.

Organization The system contains five areas, each of which has several separate subtests:

1. *Development Assessment* This area contains four parts, which are "simple, functional, non-medical measures of physical and mental abilities": a) Patterning/Color Discrimination Manipulation; b) Manual Coordination; c) Work Range/Dynamic Strength/Walking; and d) Matching/Vocational Knowledge/Measurement.
2. *Workshop Evaluation* This area consists of a simulated assembly process during which three clients use a three-step assembly process. A fourth person (either client or evaluator) acts as an inspector.
3. *Vocational Interest Screening* A sound and slide interest assessment is conducted in which the client compares two jobs. There are six area scores: social service, sales, machine operation, office work/clerical, physical sciences, and outdoor.
4. *Social/Interpersonal Skills* This consists of a two-page form containing descriptions of commonly found barriers to employment. Four major areas are covered: a) personal skills; b) socialization; c) aggravating behaviors; d) work-related skills.
5. *Independent Living Skills* This consists of an assessment of: a) transportation; b) money handling; c) grooming; and d) living enviornments. The transportation and money handling areas contain three levels. Simulation and gaming techniques are used heavily in this area.

Work Evaluation Process

1. *Preliminary Screening* The manuals do not mention a need for preliminary screening. It is assumed that no advance screening is necessary.
2. *Sequence of Work Sample Administration* Information presented by the developer states that the five sections can be given in any order. However, because the method of instruction given for the rest of Valpar #17 is at least partially determined during the Development Assessment section, this part should be given first.
3. *Client Involvement* Although the degree of client involvement with the evaluator varies with the section, in general there is a considerable degree of client-evaluator contact. Most of the tasks are administered individually. The manuals do not contain any discussion on procedures for feedback or for sharing the results with the client either during or after completion of the five areas.

4. *Evaluation Setting* The setting is not specified. However, the use of the various sections would imply that a formal testing situation would be created.
5. *Time to Complete the Entire System* Although the time varies with the population tested, the general manual estimates 5½ hours for the entire battery.

Method of Instruction Giving Instructions are given using a variety of methods. During the administration of the Development Assessment section, the evaluator first determines at which of three possible levels the client functions: a) verbal, b) verbal plus demonstration, or c) verbal plus demonstration with a sample to follow. The appropriate level is used throughout the remainder of the Valpar #17. The Vocational Interest Screening uses a slide/cassette instruction method. Independent Living Skills uses a combination of gaming and comparing pictures with accompanying verbal instructions.

Utility

1. *Vocational Exploration* Two parts of the Valpar #17 offer some direct vocational exploration: Vocational Interest Screening and Workshop Evaluation. The Vocational Interest part allows for some exploration and provides some occupational information. The Workshop Evaluation, as a simulated assembly task, could give the client some concept of production line work.
2. *Vocational Recommendations* Each of the sections provides data that can be used to provide vocational recommendations. The specific recommendations would be based upon the final reporting format used.
3. *Counselor Utilization* The battery is designed specifically to facilitate counseling and/or training after assessment. The scoring format specifies goals and potentials by providing counselor insight into relative strengths and weaknesses. It also provides score sheets with pictorial representations of the work performed in that task to remind both the counselor and the evaluee of the activity and performance in each area. Each subject also provides both a possible means of remediation or training and a format for reassessment to gauge improvements over time.

Summary and Comments Valpar #17 is apparently intended to be an assessment of the variables that must be considered when assessing a mentally retarded person's interests, vocational skills, and social maturity. The system is designed to be used by a person who is not trained in psychology, medicine, or occupational therapy. The system is well designed, attractive, and novel in many ways. The use of audiovisual and gaming materials will make it attractive to clients as well as evaluators. Data collection forms are unusually well designed. The major problems are in the technical areas. The manuals contain no background as to why certain components were selected, and no relationship to previous work done in this field. No data are given on reliability and validity; there is not even a statement on these two factors. The norms data are impossible to interpret without additional information. In summary, this is a very attractive assessment device, but much more needs to be known about it.

Talent Assessment Programs (TAP)

Basis of the System The results are organized according to specific jobs within occupation clusters (e.g., construction, food services, assembly).

Organization Ten tests are included in the system:

1. Structural and Mechanical Visualization
2. Discrimination by Size and Shape
3. Discrimination by Color
4. Tactile Discrimination
5. Fine Dexterity without Tools
6. Gross Dexterity without Tools
7. Fine Dexterity with Tools
8. Gross Dexterity with Tools
9. Flowpath Visualization
10. Retention of Structural and Mechanical Detail

Work Evaluation Process

1. *Preliminary Screening* There is no mention of preliminary screening.
2. *Sequence of Work Sample Administration* Work sample 1 must be given first and work sample 10 last; the rest may be given in any order. The reason for this is that the last work sample requires the client to construct the same structure as does the first work sample, except that it is done without a model. Thus, the separation is needed as a measure of retention.
3. *Client Involvement* The type and degree of client involvement during administration are not specific. Because of the shortness and formal nature of the tests, there is probably little client involvement. The client is given a copy of his or her scoring profile upon completion, and this is discussed as desired by the client.
4. *Evaluation Setting* Although the evaluation setting is not specified, the TAP lends itself to a formal testing atmosphere.
5. *Time to Complete the Entire Battery* The tests can be administered in from 2 to 2½ hours.

Method of Instruction Giving Although the basic method of instruction giving is oral with accompanying demonstrations, the evaluator is to "make certain that clients have complete understanding of directions" by using other techniques, if necessary, for example by "having clients demonstrate, having clients repeat directions, [and] permitting clients to practice." No reading is required for any test.

Utility
1. *Vocational Exploration* Because the system really consists of standardized perceptual and dexterity tests, they are too abstract to provide much direct vocational information to the client, without interpretation by the evaluator.
2. *Vocational Recommendations* Using occupational clusters, the manual lists specific job titles with DOT codes within each cluster together with the tests that relate to specific job requirements. This listing is not intended to be comprehensive.
3. *Counselor Utilization* The profile sheet with its occupational recommendations is designed for the counselor, teacher, or employer.

Summary and Comments As opposed to other work evaluation systems which attempt to present a complete picture of the client, the TAP can be characterized as a battery of perceptual and dexterity tests designed to measure gross and fine finger and manual dexterity, visual and tactile discrimination, and retention of details. Thus, it is limited to the assessment of these fairly specific factors. The developer does not claim that this system will assess all vocationally significant capacities and behaviors; in fact the manual states that other assessment devices should be used in addition to the TAP to obtain a complete evaluation of the client.

The TOWER System

Basis of the System The source of this system was job analysis of positions that were considered open to handicapped persons in the New York City area.

Organization The system contains 93 work samples arranged into 14 job training areas:

1. *Clerical* Business Arithmetic; Filing, Typing, and One-Hand Typing; Payroll Computation; Use of Sales Book; Record Keeping; Correct Use of English
2. *Drafting* T-Square and Triangle; Compass; Working Drawing; Drawing to Scale; Geometric Shapes
3. *Drawing* Perspective; Forms, Shapes, and Objects; Shading; Tone and Texture; Color; Freehand Sketching
4. *Electronics Assembly* Color Perception and Sorting; Running a

10-Wire Cable; Inspecting a 10-Wire Cable; Lacing a Cable; Soldering Wires
5. *Jewelry Manufacturing*   Use of Saw; Use of Needle Files; Electric Drill Press; Piercing and Filing Metals; Use of Pliers; Use of Torch in Soldering; Making Earring and Brooch Pin
6. *Leather Goods*   Use of Ruler; Use of Knife; Use of Dividers; Use of Paste and Brush; Use of Scissors and Bond Folder in Pasting; Constructing Picture Frame; Production Task
7. *Machine Shop*   Reading and Transcribing Measurements; Blueprint Reading; Measuring with a Rule; Drawing to Measurement; Metal Layout and Use of Basic Tools; Drill Press Operation; Fractions and Decimals; Measuring with the Micrometer Caliper; Mechanical Understanding
8. *Lettering*   Lettering Aptitude; Alphabet and Use of T-Square; Use of Pen and Ink; Use of Lettering Brush; Brush Lettering
9. *Mail Clerk*   Opening Mail; Date-Stamping Mail; Sorting Mail; Delivering Mail; Collecting Mail; Folding and Inserting; Sealing Mail; Mail Classification; Use of Scale; Postage Calculation
10. *Optical Mechanics*   Use of Metric Ruler: Use of Calipers; Lens Recognition; Lens Centering and Marking; Use of Lens Protractor; Hand Beveling and Edging
11. *Pantograph Engraving*   Introduction to the Engravograph; Setting-up, Centering Copy, and Determining Specific Ratios; Use of Workholder and Adjustment of Cutter; Setting Up and Running Off a Simple Job
12. *Sewing Machine Operating*   Sewing Machine Control; Use of Knee Lift and Needle Pivoting; Tacking and Sewing Curved Lines; Upper Threading; Winding and Inserting Bobbin; Sewing and Cutting; Top Stitching
13. *Welding*   Measuring; Making a Working Drawing; Identifying Welding Rods; Use of Acetylene Torch; Use of Rods and Electrodes; Use of Torch and Rod; Measuring and Cutting Metal; Soldering
14. *Workshop Assembly*   Counting; Number and Color Collation; Folding and Banding; Weighing and Sorting; Counting and Packing; Washer Assembly; Inserting, Lacing, and Typing; Art Paper Binding.

Work Evaluation Process

1. *Preliminary Screening*   This is emphasized for planning purposes, but the specific information needed prior to administration of the system is not specific.
2. *Sequence of Work Sample Administration*   Administration is pro-

gressive within the major areas; the choice of areas depends upon client interest and/or the evaluation plan.
3. *Client Involvement*   No client involvement procedures are specified in the manual.
4. *Evaluation Setting*   A realistic work atmosphere and setting are stressed.
5. *Time to Complete the Entire System*   The average client completes the entire system in 3 weeks; however, clients seldom take all work samples in the system.

Method of Instruction Giving   The system uses mainly written instructions that are supplemented by evaluator explanation and demonstration when needed.

Utility
1. *Vocational Exploration*   The client is exposed to many different training areas which are representative of a variety of jobs. The manual contains some specific occupational information that is given during the administration of the work samples.
2. *Vocational Recommendations*   Vocational recommendations are limited to jobs that are directly related to the work samples. The recommendations are not closely related to the DOT and are primarily training oriented.
3. *Counselor Utilization*   Counselor involvement in the evaluation process is recommended; the final report is aimed at the counselor.

Summary and Comments   The TOWER system is the oldest complete work evaluation system and over the years has served as a model for the development of many work samples. The TOWER uses a realistic job setting to evaluate clients thoroughly for a rather narrow group of jobs. The facts that the TOWER is based on job analysis and that the system has been used for many years to place and train handicapped people are indications that the system is very useful in evaluating clients for a small group of jobs. The lack of precise definitions for work performance factors and client behaviors and the lack of adequate norms are the major weaknesses of the system. The high use of written instructions and the high level of the areas evaluated restricts its use with low literate and mentally retarded clients.

Valpar Component Work Sample Series

Basis of the System   According to the developers, the work samples are based on a trait-and-factor approach taken from job analysis. The manual for each work sample relates that work sample to several WTG arrangements as well as specific occupations.

Organization At present there are 16 work samples contained in the series:

1. *Small Tools* (Mechanical)
2. *Size Discrimination*
3. *Numerical Sorting*
4. *Upper Extremity Range of Motion*
5. *Clerical Comprehension and Aptitude*
6. *Independent Problem Solving*
7. *Multi-Level Sorting*
8. *Simulated Assembly*
9. *Whole Body Range of Motion*
10. *Tri-Level Measurement*
11. *Eye-Hand-Foot Coordination*
12. *Soldering and Inspection* (Electronics)
13. *Money Handling*
14. *Integrated Peer Performance*
15. *Electrical Circuitry and Print Reading*
16. *Drafting*

Work Evaluation Process
1. *Preliminary Screening* The work samples do not require preliminary screening.
2. *Sequence of Work Sample Administration* The order and the number of work samples to be given are left to the discretion of the evaluator. It must be remembered that the Valpar is a group of independent work samples and not a system.
3. *Client Involvement* Because work sample administration resembles a formal testing situation, client involvement is minimal; feedback on performance is left up to the discretion of the facility and individual evaluator.
4. *Evaluation Setting* Although the setting is not specified, the content of most of the work samples as well as the instructions result in the creation of a formal testing situation.
5. *Time to Complete the Entire System* It is estimated by the reviewer that most work samples can be completed in 1 hour or less. The Drafting, Integrated Peer Performance, and Clerical Comprehension and Aptitude samples would take well over 1 hour to administer.

Method of Instruction Giving A combination of oral instructions with accompanying demonstrations is used by the evaluator to administer most work samples. Instructions are read verbatim from the manuals. In the Clerical Comprehension and Aptitude and the Money Handling work samples, the client is required to read instructional and testing materials.

Utility
1. *Vocational Exploration* There is limited opportunity for vocational exploration due to the abstract nature of some of the work samples.
2. *Vocational Recommendations* Because these are individual components and not a system evaluation, vocational recommendations cannot be made on the basis of one work sample. The use of the Valpar work samples for making vocational recommendations largely depends upon their use by the individual evaluation unit.
3. *Counselor Utilization* Because the system uses the purchasing facility's report format, counselor utilization cannot be specified.

Summary and Comments The Valpar Component Work Sample Series currently consists of 16 individual work samples that are physically well designed and constructed. They are appealing to clients and lend themselves to easy administration and scoring. Individual work samples can be easily incorporated into an existing evaluation program. Because these individual work samples can be purchased as needed by facilities, there are no unified final report forms, and other aspects of an integration system are lacking. The major problem with the Valpar is in the area of relationship to jobs. According to the manuals, each component is keyed to a number of specific occupations as well as worker trait groups. However, the manuals offer no convincing evidence that, for example, one work sample could be related to 10 WTG.

Vocational Evaluation System (Singer)

Basis of the System The work samples within the system are based on a group of tasks contained in closely related jobs. The basis is a combination of job analysis procedures and the job descriptions contained in the third edition of the DOT.

Organization Presently the following 25 work stations are available:
1. *Sample Making*
2. *Bench Assembly*
3. *Drafting*
4. *Electrical Wiring*
5. *Plumbing and Pipe Fitting*
6. *Woodworking*
7. *Air Conditioning and Refrigeration*
8. *Sales Processing*
9. *Needle Trades*

10. *Masonry*
11. *Sheet Metal Working*
12. *Cooking and Baking*
13. *Small Engine Service*
14. *Medical Service*
15. *Cosmetology*
16. *Data Calculation and Recording*
17. *Soil Testing*
18. *Photo Lab Technician*
19. *Production Machine Operating*
20. *Household and Industrial Wiring*
21. *Filing, Shipping, and Receiving*
22. *Packaging and Materials Handling*
23. *Electronics Assembly*
24. *Welding and Brazing*
25. *Office Services*

Work Evaluation Process
1. *Preliminary Screening* No preliminary screening is required.
2. *Sequence of Work Sample Administration* The order and the number of work stations given is left to the discretion of the evaluator.
3. *Client Involvement* The client is involved in the evaluation process through a series of self-ratings on interest and performance. Due to the frequent evaluator checkpoints in each work sample, the possibility for client contact with the evaluator is high. The manual does not specify whether formal feedback is to be given to the client at the end of the evaluation process.
4. *Evaluation Setting* The use of the carrels and audiovisual instructions could not help but to create a school-like atmosphere.
5. *Time to Complete the Entire System* The manual states that "a general Rule of Thumb is to allow two to two and one-half hours per job sample." Because any number of stations may be administered, no realistic estimates on the length of time to complete the total system can be given.

Method of Instruction Giving All instructions are given using an audio cassette tape and filmstrip format with the client controlling the rate of advancement. Typically, the client hears several frames of instruction, turns off the equipment, performs a specific task, and then calls the evaluator to check that task. The linear programmed material is occasionally supplemented with written material. Additional evaluator instructions are discouraged because they would interfere with the standardization; evaluators are to record any type of reinstruction.

Utility
1. *Vocational Exploration* An extensive amount of occupational information is provided to the client; each work sample contains an introduction to some jobs related to the work sample. Many schools and facilities use the Singer primarily as an interest and career exploration device.
2. *Vocational Recommendations* Because the system contains no final report format, it is difficult to judge the type and quality of vocational recommendations. These would depend upon the user.
3. *Counselor Utilization* For the reason given above, this aspect cannot be accurately judged.

Summary and Comments The Singer manual provides all the data that the evaluator would need. The process of developing MTM and employer worker norms is one of the strong points of the Singer. Also encouraging is the publication of some basic studies on the system. Presently the system provides a measure of interest measurement and skill assessment for jobs mostly in the skilled trades and technical areas. The occupational information remains the strong point of the system. The major problems are the lack of work atmosphere, the use of expendable supplies, and the possible need for a superstructure to integrate the units into a functional whole.

Vocational Information and Evaluation Work Samples (VIEWS)

Basis of the System The VIEWS is based on four areas of work and six worker trait groups in the third edition of the DOT. These areas of work were chosen because they represent the most common areas of training and employment for mentally retarded persons.

Organization The 16 work samples are organized according to the DOT as follows:

1. *Elemental Area of Work*
   a. Handling WTG: Tile Sorting; Nuts, Bolts, and Washers Sorting; Paper Count and Paper Cutting; Collating and Stapling; Stamping; Nuts, Bolts, and Washers Assembly; and Screen Assembly
   b. Feeding-Offbearing WTG: Machine Feeding
2. *Clerical Area of Work*
   a. Routine Checking and Recording WTG: Mail Sort and Mail Count
   b. Sorting, Inspecting, Measuring, and Related WTG: Nut Weighing; Valve Disassembly
3. *Machine Area of Work* Tending WTG: Drill Press

4. *Crafts Area of Work* Manipulating WTG: Budgette Assembly; Valve Assembly; Circuit Board Assembly

Work Evaluation Process
1. *Preliminary Screening* No preliminary screening is required.
2. *Sequence of Work Sample Administration* The work samples are given from least complex to most complex. Each work sample has three phases: a) demonstration—the evaluator follows the manual to provide an oral description and a physical demonstration for the client; b) training—the client is trained to a predetermined criterion of mastery on each work sample (during this phase the evaluator is free to use a wide variety of techniques to make certain that the client learns the task); and c) production—after the criterion has been achieved, the client is assigned a set number of cycles of the work sample to perform independently. The purpose in separating the training and production phases is to make sure that the client has learned each task before performing it.
3. *Client Involvement* There is extensive client involvement. In the training phase for each work sample, the evaluator and the client have a significant amount of interaction during the learning process. The *Evaluator's Handbook* accompanying the VIEWS calls for an informal client feedback session after the first day as well as on subsequent days when needed. There is little client involvement during the production phase.
4. *Evaluation Setting* A realistic work atmosphere and setting are stressed in the *Handbook* and during evaluator training.
5. *Time to Complete the Entire System* The developer estimates that the VIEWS can be administered in from four to seven 5-hour days (i.e., 20–35 hours).

Method of Instruction Giving No reading is required of the client for any work sample. The demonstration phase uses oral instructions plus modeling. During the training phase the evaluator is free to use a variety of verbal and nonverbal techniques; flexibility is stressed here. Because each work sample is individually administered, the client can receive instructions using the methods that best meet his needs.

Utility
1. *Vocational Exploration* Because some of the tasks are not actual jobs because almost no occupational information is provided, the VIEWS is of little use in occupational exploration.
2. *Vocational Recommendations* Specific recommendations are made; these are related to the six WTG covered by the VIEWS.
3. *Counselor Utilization* The system and the final report are oriented toward the counselor.

Summary and Comments The VIEWS attempts to evaluate the vocational potential of mentally retarded adults for jobs in six WTG. The system relates to job areas that are very common in the national economy and more important to job areas where many retarded persons have found successful employment. The most unique feature of the system is the attempt to separate learning from performance. The developers believe that the client should be thoroughly taught the task prior to performing it under timed conditions. The VIEWS also uses standardized behavior observations that are combined with time and quality scores to produce a well organized final report. The major problem with using the VIEWS by itself is the lack of occupational information.

Vocational Interest Temperament and Aptitude Systems (VITAS)

Basis of the System The VITAS is based on 15 worker trait groups in the third edition of the DOT. Apparently, these were selected because of employment and/or training opportunities. Since the original development, the system has been related to 16 work groups in the *Guide for Occupational Exploration.*

Organization The 15 WTG are assessed by 21 work samples as listed below (note that several of the work samples assess for more than one WTG):

1. *Handling WTG* Nuts, Bolts, and Washers Assembly; Packing Matchbooks
2. *Tending WTG* Pressing Linens
3. *Manipulating WTG* Budget Book Assembly; Pipe Assembly
4. *Switchboard Service* Message Taking
5. *Routine Checking and Recording* Verifying Numbers; Proofreading
6. *Sorting, Inspecting, Measuring, and Related Work* Packing Matchbooks; Tile Sorting and Weighing; Nail and Screw Sort, Part I
7. *Computing and Related Recording* Calculating; Bank Teller; Payroll Computation
8. *Inspecting and Stock Checking* Tile Sorting and Weighing; Collating Material Samples; Nail and Screw Sort, Part II; Circuit Board Inspection
9. *Cashiering* Calculation; Bank Teller
10. *Classifying, Filing, and Related Work* Filing by Letters; Calculating
11. *Information Gathering, Dispensing, and Verifying* Message Taking; Census Interviewing

12. *Paying and Receiving* Calculating; Bank Teller; Payroll Computation
13. *Technical Work, Science and Related* Laboratory Assistant
14. *Craftmanship and Related* Lock Assembly; Spot Welding
15. *Drafting and Related* Drafting

Work Evaluation Process
1. *Preliminary Screening* The manual does not mention that any preliminary screening is needed.
2. *Sequence of Work Sample Administration* The client usually begins with the easiest work sample (i.e., Nuts, Bolts and Washers Assembly) and progresses to the most difficult (i.e., Drafting). However, the work samples can be given in any order.
3. *Client Involvement* The client is involved in the vocational process at several different times: a) new clients are given an orientation session when first coming into the evaluation unit; b) a group motivational session at the end of the first day of evaluation; and c) a feedback and interest interview after the work samples are administered.
4. *Evaluation Setting* The VITAS manual stresses a realistic work setting.
5. *Time to Complete the Entire System* According to the manual, "most clients can complete the work sample within three five-hour days."

Method of Instruction Giving All client instructions are given orally and by demonstration. Although the client is not required to read any administration instructions, reading and the use of mathematical skills are needed to complete many of the work samples successfully.

Utility
1. *Vocational Exploration* The VITAS is of little use for providing the client with occupational information. The nature of many of the tasks is abstract, and no job information is provided during the instruction period for each work sample.
2. *Vocational Recommendations* Recommendations are made in two specific areas: a) the most feasible WTG for employment or training, and b) specific supportive services needed to obtain the employment goal. Apparently, recommendations within each WTG are kept general. No specific jobs are suggested.
3. *Counselor Utilization* The final report is aimed at the counselor who needs to make fairly specific vocational decisions.

Summary and Comments The VITAS system is the third work sample system developed by the Philadelphia JEVS. Like the JEVS and VIEWS systems, it stresses the importance of careful and accurate behavior observations. The system also uses the work sample-to-WTG approach that has served JVS and VIEWS so well in the past. It must also be pointed out that many of the VITAS work samples are refinements and modifications of the original JEVS system. Although the system could provide accurate assessment of CETA populations in a relatively short period of time, it has two problems: a) a lack of client occupational information, and b) the failure to make any real distinction between learning and performance. The emphasis upon close client contact, careful observations, and the practical reporting format are the three major advantages of the system.

Vocational Skills Assessment and Development Program (Brodhead-Garrett)

Basis of the System   The three manuals do not contain a discussion of the basis of the system. Apparently, the system is based upon the selection of vocational training programs and the providing of occupational information. No job classification using either the DOT or the U.S. Office of Education classifications is contained in the manuals.

Organization   The system contains three phases; only the first phase uses work samples. The second and third phases consist of specific tasks within a general vocational area.

1. *Phase I*   During this phase, the client is engaged in three types of activities.
    a. Sorting: six activities involving objects of different sizes and shapes as well as letters
    b. Assembly: six activities in putting together pipes, collating, using a doorbell, nuts and bolts, and hand packaging
    c. Salvage: six activities involving the disassembly of the items put together in the Assembly component.
2. *Phase II*   The following seven separate vocational components are intended to provide occupational information and to develop entry level skills: a) basic tools, b) sheltered employment, c) building maintenance, d) health, e) agribusiness, f) clerical/sales, and g) construction trades. Each of these seven component programs is also composed of units. For example, the sheltered employment section includes the following: a) collating, b) engraving, c) injection/rotation molding, d) salvage/sorting, e) packaging, and f) contracts/production.
3. *Phase III*   The seven separate program areas are designed to provide "basic job entry level skills for specific occupations": a) health, b) agribusiness, c) building maintenance, d) clerical/sales,

e) automotive, f) small engine, and g) construction. As with Phase II, each Phase III program is composed of numerous subunits. For example, the small engine program includes the following: a) use of tools, b) service and operation, c) disassembly of major parts, d) assembly of major parts, and e) diagnosing problems.

Work Evaluation Process
1. *Preliminary Screening* Apparently no preliminary screening is required. However, prior medical and psychological recommendations are encouraged for use.
2. *Sequence of Work Sample Administration* According to the developer, the sequence is dependent upon the implementation of the system, i.e., the number of participants and scheduling. Although each phase is interrelated, any phase can be utilized without the other phases. Any appropriate assessment method can be used prior to the Phase II vocational exploration.
3. *Client Involvement* The manuals contain no information about giving client feedback. However, because the work samples must be administered on an individual basis without formal instructions, it is expected that there would be a high degree of client-evaluator contact. A Learner Comment Sheet is completed by the client; this general form includes likes and dislikes, duties performed, and problems encountered. Phases II and III would assume a teacher-student relationship, and here the amount of client involvement would depend upon the individual teacher.
4. *Evaluation Setting* Phase I implies either a classroom or an evaluation setting. Phases II and III are mostly educational in nature, although, depending on the type of instruction, they could also be industrial.
5. *Time to Complete the Entire System* According to the manual, Phase I is "not to exceed six weeks." However, this reviewer estimates that the work samples could be given to most clients within the course of a full week. Phases II and III are training stages and each will last "at least six months" and until placement. Some of the training curriculum in Phase III could take over a year.

Method of Instruction Giving Instructions are given using a combination of oral and demonstration techniques.

Utility
1. *Vocational Exploration* The system's Phases II and III offer the opportunity for specific occupational exploration in selected areas. In particular, Phase II is intended specifically for vocational exploration. Because of the nature of the tasks and the lack of detailed

instructions, Phase I appears to offer little in the way of career exploration.

2. *Vocational Recommendations* Each of the separate job areas for Phases II and III contain checklists of the major tasks covered in the areas. The overall level of proficiency is also rated. The usefulness of this data would depend on how it is used by client and teacher.

3. *Counselor Utilization* The Brodhead-Garrett manuals contain no mention of the rehabilitation counselor or a referral source. The system is designed to be used as an assessment and training device with the "end product" being a person ready for work.

Summary and Comments The Brodhead-Garrett is a system that is intended to provide continuous service from initial assessment through training and eventually job placement. In this aspect it is unique. Phase I is the only part of the system that can be considered as a work evaluation system as this term is usually used in vocational evaluation. Phase I lacks detailed evaluation and client instructions, norms, proper setup procedures, and scoring methods. In short, the manual for Phase I does not give the evaluator enough information to use the system accurately. In using Phase I, the evaluator must also ask how the content of assessment tasks is related to the specific training given in the other two phases. The success of Phases II and III depends in large part upon the quality of instruction and the physical facilities. These two phases have the potential for being very useful for training clients in both basic skills and for some entry level positions.

Wide Range Employability Sample Test (WREST)

Basis of the System The WREST is based on a group of work samples originally developed at a sheltered workshop in Wilmington, Delaware, for "referral of handicapped individuals who may be trained in basic work production skills." The work samples were used in conjunction with other techniques to train and select persons for various areas of the workshop.

Organization There are 10 work samples, the first two of which each have two parts:

1. *Folding* includes a) single folding and b) double folding, gluing, labeling, and envelope stuffing
2. *Stapling* includes a) stapling accuracy and b) collation and stapling
3. *Packaging*
4. *Measuring*
5. *Stringing*

6. *Gluing*
7. *Collating*
8. *Color Matching*
9. *Pattern Matching*
10. *Assembling*

Work Evaluation Process
1. *Preliminary Screening* No preliminary screening is required.
2. *Sequence of Work Sample Administration* The 10 work samples may be administered in any order. However, most evaluators "will find it more convenient to follow the designated order."
3. *Client Involvement* The manual stresses that the client(s) should be told what the work samples involve and how the results will be used. The need for individualized attention is also mentioned. There is, however, no statement in the manual on providing feedback after specific work samples.
4. *Evaluation Setting* The evaluation setting would most likely be that of a formal testing situation.
5. *Time to Complete the Entire System* Administration time for individual clients is about 1½ hours; small groups of three to five persons take about 2 hours.

Method of Instruction Giving All instructions are oral with demonstration; no reading is required. The manual warns that instructions must be closely followed: "any change from the manual may cause confusion, thus invalidating the norms of that test."

Utility
1. *Vocational Exploration* The very simple nature of most of the work samples makes the WREST of little use in job exploration for a normal population.
2. *Vocational Recommendations* The manual contains no information on the making of vocational recommendations from the work sample results.
3. *Counselor Utilization* The manual contains no information on use of WREST results for the counselor.

Summary and Comments The WREST consists of 10, short, low level tasks apparently designed to assess mainly the manipulation and dexterity abilities of the client. Although it is not stated in the manual, the WREST seems most useful in assessing new clients for assignment to suitable work projects within a sheltered workshop. The emphasis upon repeating the work samples many times should provide an evaluation of the client's ability to improve his or her performance under repeated practice conditions. The major problems of the system center around the lack of systematic behavior observations, failure to relate results to the competitive job market, and the apparent lack of a usable final report for the referring counselor or agency. Finally, the WREST has an adequate norm base, good estimates of test-retest validity, and an attempt at establishing concurrent validity. In a field that is all too often characterized by poor technical development, the WREST can serve as a good example.

PUBLISHERS

For further information about the 14 vocational evaluation systems the reader may consult Botterbusch (1980) or write to the publisher of the system.

1. *COATS* Prep, Inc., 1575 Parkway Avenue, Trenton, NJ 08628
2. *MOVE* Evaluation Systems, Inc., 640 N. La Salle St., Suite 698, Chicago, IL 60610
3. *MDWES* McCarron-Dial Systems, P.O. Box 45628, Dallas, TX 75245
4. *Micro-Tower* ICD Rehabilitation and Research Center, 340 East 24th Street, New York, NY 10010
5. *JEVS* Vocational Research Institute, Jewish Employment and Vocational Service, 1700 Sanson Street, Philadelphia, PA 19103
6. *Valpar 17* Valpar Corporation, 3801 E. 34th Street, Suite 105, Tucson, AZ 85713
7. *TAP* Talent Assessment, Inc., P.O. Box 5087, Jacksonville, FL 32207
8. *TOWER* ICD Rehabilitation and Research Center, 340 East 24th Street, New York, NY 10010
9. *VALPAR* Valpar Corporation, 3801 E. 34th Street, Suite 105, Tucson, AZ 85713
10. *Singer* Singer Educational Division, Career Systems, 80 Commerce Drive, Rochester, NY 14623
11. *VIEWS* Vocational Research Institute, Jewish Employment and Vocational Service, 1700 Sanson Street, Philadelphia, PA 19103
12. *VITAS* Vocational Research Institute, Jewish Employment and Vocational Service, 1700 Sanson Street, Philadelphia, PA 19103
13. *Brodhead-Garrett* Brodhead-Garrett Company, 4560 East 71st Street, Cleveland, OH 44105
14. *WREST* Jastak Associates, Inc., 1526 Gilpin Avenue, Wilmington, DE 19806

chapter 7
BEHAVIORAL ANALYSIS OF WORK PROBLEMS

John N. Marr

Behavior modification and behavior therapy have been applied in a wide range of rehabilitation settings and have yielded significant gains for a variety of behavior problems that interfere with the rehabilitation of handicapped persons. Settings have included university laboratories, schools, homes, institutes for special handicapped conditions, sheltered workshops, comprehensive rehabilitation centers, and outpatient clinics. Targeted populations have ranged across almost all handicapping conditions. Behavior problems for which successful interventions have been developed have included blindisms, speech deficits, self-abusive behaviors, withdrawal and depression, dependency behaviors, bladder control, disruptive behaviors, and work-related behaviors. Although this chapter focuses on deficit and surplus behaviors that are related to obtaining work and to working, other applications of behavior modification in rehabilitation are presented in Fordyce (1971), Ince (1976), Walls (1969), and Marr and Means (1980).

Applied behavioral analysis is based on the extensions of methodological behaviorism, a philosophy for studying behavior first described by John B. Watson (1919) and later developed by B. F. Skinner (1953) and his students. Methodological behaviorism calls for the use of the scientific method in the study of behavior. Thus, the optimal use of behavioral procedures requires five elements:

1. Specific definitions of problems and objectives in terms of observable behaviors or the products of these behaviors
2. Measurement of behaviors prior to intervention
3. Selection of intervention procedures on the basis of research evidence of success
4. Continuous measurement of the behavior during intervention to assess success

5. Attribution of failure of intervention to the method employed and not to the person.

FUNCTIONAL ANALYSIS OF WORK-RELATED BEHAVIORS

One behavioral assessment approach applied to the analysis of work-related behaviors is the ABC model. The relevant behaviors (B) of the individual are specified, the antecedent (A) events of stimuli that control and precede the behaviors are identified, and the consequences (C) of the behavior for the individual are noted. This approach to vocational rehabilitation focuses on the person interacting with the environment. It emphasizes the control of behavior (B) by environmental events (A and C) and suggests that behavior can be modified by changes in those events. In rehabilitation, changes can be made by the service delivery provider or by the rehabilitation client. For a more complete discussion of the rationale for the approach in comparison to the more traditional approaches to assessment, the reader is referred to Craighead, Kazdin, and Mahoney (1981), Fordyce (1971), and Skinner (1974). This chapter describes the assessment process, measurement, and development of interventions as applied to work behaviors. The behavior assessment procedure and instruments for behavior modification and behavior therapy are more completely described in Lutzker and Martin (1981) and Craighead et al. (1981).

Work Behaviors

The analysis of a particular client's work behaviors requires that three categories of behaviors be identified. These are behavior assets, behavior deficits, and behavior surpluses. The information about these classes of behaviors can be obtained from records, other persons who are familiar with the client, the client, and direct observation. Relevant records include rehabilitation case files, school records, and employment histories. Persons who know the client include relatives, friends, previous employers, dormitory counselors or houseparents, previous teachers, and rehabilitation counselors and instructors who are familiar with the person. Clients can furnish information by interview, self-report instruments, or by self-monitoring of their own behavior.

Behavioral Assets Any behaviors or sets of behaviors that the client already has and that would enhance employability, persistence at work, or the learning of new work skills should be described in specific terms. These skills can be used in planning the vocational rehabilitation program. The value of behavioral assessment of assets is revealed by the following case:

> Recently, I was asked to consult with the instructor, foreman, and counselor of a deaf-blind man. The man had a history of being discharged

from a number of different vocational rehabilitation settings across the nation because of his violent displays of aggressive behavior. At this institution, they had tried him at a number of tasks but he worked too slow, made many errors in the products being manufactured, and displayed anger when given correction. There was nothing in his records about behavioral assets. Observation of his work behavior showed that he worked very steadily except for pauses to tactually explore materials, nearby objects, or persons (as we do with our eyes and ears). The interview with the staff started with behavioral assets. In addition to attending to initial instruction through manual placement of his hands, attending to manual sign, arriving at work on time, returning from breaks on time, and wearing clean clothes, he kept his room, clothes, and person immaculate. Everything was dusted, swept, and put away; his bed was made every morning, and activities of daily living were carried out quickly with no displays of anger. Further questioning revealed that he had learned this set of skills from his mother. She then became a source of information about successful methods of teaching him to work without error at a fast rate. This approach to intervention would not have been apparent without the focus on behavior assets.

Behavioral assets serve a number of functions. They serve as strengths on which new skills can be built and to which similar skills can be related. When written into the client records, they can be used by other rehabilitation staff in evaluation, counseling, vocational instruction, or placement. Finally, they are very important to the client because they present a more complete picture than a list of rehabilitation needs and behavioral problems.

Behavior Deficits and Surpluses Behavioral problems are classified as deficits or surpluses. Deficits in work behaviors are those that are necessary to prepare for, obtain, or maintain work and that the client does too infrequently. Classes of behavior identified by Walker, Anderson, and Hutchins (1968) that are necessary for reemployment of multiply handicapped clients are job objective problems, job-seeking skill deficiencies, and job retention problems. Examples of each are listed in Table 1.

Behavior deficits must be described so specifically that two different persons can agree on the occurrence of the behavior when it does appear. Such a description produces agreement among staff who might be observing the client at different time periods or in different situations. An excellent manual for teaching staff to identify problems in specific terms is available from the Stout Vocational Rehabilitation Institute (Materials Development Center, 1974).

Work-related problems also include behavioral surpluses or excesses. These are behaviors that should occur only infrequently or not at all. Examples of behavioral surpluses in work environments are: talking to other workers who are distracted from work by the talk, violating safety rules, throwing or breaking tools, and annoying other

Table 1. Classes of behavior deficits

Problem	Deficit
Job objective	1. Does not seek information about work that he or she can do or could learn to do
	2. Does not complete work samples to allow assessment of abilities
	3. Does not attend job information meetings
Job-seeking skills	1. Does not read want ads or, if unable to read, does not ask others to read ads to him or her
	2. Does not describe skills to interviewer
	3. Does not complete application form
Job-retention skills	1. Does not arrive for work on time
	2. Does not stay on-task
	3. Does not put tools away at end of workday

workers. Each behavioral surplus also must be specified in exact terms, for example, annoying other workers by grabbing and poking.

MEASUREMENT OF WORK-RELATED BEHAVIORS

Defining the client's problem in behavioral terms allows for precise measurement of targeted behavior problems. Consider the ambiguity of each of the terms in the lefthand column of Table 2. It would be

Table 2. A comparison of traditional and behavioral descriptions of work-related problems[a]

Traditional description	Behavioral specification
Work Break (Surplus)	
"Goofs off," "Easily distracted," or "Poor work endurance"	Too many minutes away from the work station in activities not related to production
Care of Materials (Surplus)	
"Careless," "Irresponsible," or "Lazy"	Too many tools left in work area and too many tools and machines broken
Work Quantity (Deficit)	
"Lazy," or "Unmotivated"	Too few finished products produced in a day (or hour)
Personal Appearance (Deficit)	
"Inappropriate dress" or "Poor grooming"	Hair not combed
	Slacks or skirt not closed
	Shoes not tied
	No socks

[a] These examples are taken from the chapter on Work Problems in the *Behavior Management Manual* (Marr & Means, 1980).

very difficult to measure or treat the problems if they were used to describe the client.

When the problems are behaviorally specified, it is possible to measure the severity of the problem, to select a specific intervention to treat the lack of motivation or carelessness or irresponsibility, and to determine whether or not the intervention is having an effect on the problem. Thus, specific definitions allow accurate measurement of problems and permit one to hold the interventions accountable for success or failure.

Methods of Measurement

The procedure selected for measurement of the severity of the problem should be sensitive to change in the behavior, should be easy to obtain, and should not interfere with ongoing activities of the workshop or facility. The four types of measurement that are commonly used in applied behavior analysis are behavior products, frequency counts of ongoing behavior, fixed interval counts, and time-sample counts.

Behavior Products This is the easiest measure to obtain because it can be done at any time after the client has had an occasion to perform the behavior. Properly combed hair is a product of hair combing. Inches of whetstone not polished is the result of a client attempting to polish and buff whetstones in a workshop. Number of tools left on a workbench is a product of the behavioral deficit of not putting tools away. Number of skills listed in a job application letter is a measure of adequacy of self-presentation when seeking a job.

Frequency Count The most commonly used method of recording client behaviors is the frequency count. It consists of counting the number of times the behavior occurs during a period of the day. If the behavior occurs frequently and is a surplus, 1 hour of observation a day should suffice. If the behavior is infrequent, the period might be from 8 a.m. to 12 a.m., 1 p.m. to 4 p.m., or all day. Whatever time period is chosen, the behavior should be measured during the same period every day. The time periods selected should also depend upon the staff knowledge about when the client is most likely to show the problem behaviors.

The following are examples of frequency counts:

1. Count the number of times the client argues with other students in the training area from 8 a.m. to 4:30 p.m.
2. Count the number of minutes the client is late per day, based upon morning arrival and returns from break and lunch.
3. Count the number of occasions that the client leaves the work station.

Table 3. Examples of frequency and fixed interval counts

	8 a.m.	9 a.m.	10 a.m.	11 a.m.	12 noon	Total
Frequency						
First morning	2 0 5 1	0 3 0 0	1 1 2 1	0 4 0 1		20
Second morning	1 1 3 4	0 0 0 0	0 0 0 0	0 0 0 0		9
Fixed Interval						
First morning	× ○ × ×	○ × ○ ○	× × × ×	○ × ○ ×		11
Second morning	× × × ×	○ ○ ○ ○	○ ○ ○ ○	○ ○ ○ ○		4

Fixed Interval Counts If the intervals of time in which the problem behavior occurred are counted, the procedure is called a fixed interval count. The method consists of breaking a unit of time such as the morning work period into equal intervals of time, for example, 15-minute intervals. One is concerned only with whether or not the behavior occurs during that interval, and the number of times that the behavior occurs during the interval may be ignored. If during the period from 8 a.m. to 8:15 a.m. the client leaves the work station twice, only one X is marked in the period from 8 to 8:15 a.m. If from 8:15 to 8:30 a.m. the client does not leave the work station, an O is put in that interval. If from 8:30 to 8:45 a.m. the client leaves the station five times, one X is placed in the interval, indicating the client had left the station at least once. At the end of the 4 hours the number of 15-minute intervals with an X in them would be counted. Thus the total possible score would be 16. Examples of frequency and fixed interval counting are presented in Table 3.

Notice that the interval count gives a different score, in the example above, than would a frequency count. The frequency count would have given the exact number of occasions that the client was away from the work station, but the interval count does not require that the staff person watch the client all the time. If the client leaves his work station at 9:02 a.m. and does not return until 11:55 a.m., the frequency count would show only one occasion of the client leaving his work station, but the interval count would show each of the 15-minute intervals during which the client was not at his work station, a total of 12. To avoid watching a clock to mark off intervals, a kitchen timer that rings every 15 minutes or a cassette tape with recorded beeps at 15-minute intervals can be used to mark off intervals.

Time Sampling In this method the observation period is also divided into equal intervals, but the client is observed only at the end of each interval to determine whether the behavior is occurring at that moment in time. An X is recorded if the behavior is occurring at the end of that interval, and an O if the behavior is not occurring at that moment in time. This method is especially useful for recording behaviors that occur for different durations, and it has the advantage of not requiring the observer to watch the client during other times. This method of measurement allows the evaluator, instructor, or foreman of the shop to continue giving instruction and only to glance at the client at the end of the interval to determine whether or not the behavior is occurring. Time sampling is especially appropriate when durations of the problem behavior are long or when the behavior occurs frequently.

Portable timers designed for behavioral programs are described by Foxx and Martin (1971), and a more complete description of behavioral measurement techniques is given by Marr and Means (1980). Methods of measuring quality of work are presented by Martin and Pear (1978). Methods of graphing the results of measurement to show the changes in behavior before and after intervention are given in Koorland and Martin (1975), and examples of graphing are given by Marr and Means (1980).

Baseline

Measurement of the problem behavior prior to the implementation of the behavior change program is referred to as the baseline data. Collection of data during that period permits an estimation of the severity of the problem. Consultation in schools has shown that teachers will often report that a child is never on-task, never does his or her school work, or is always bothering the other children. When the baseline data are collected, however, it is determined that the child is on-task as much as 60% of the time; the problem is that when off-task, the child's behavior toward others seriously disrupts the classroom. If the child's behavior were not measured until after the intervention was put into effect, one might judge the 60% of the time that the child is on task as indicative of the success of intervention.

The baseline data should be collected for a long enough period for the staff to estimate the range of severity of the problem. On some days the behavior may not appear at all, but on other days the behavior occurs eight or nine times during the work period. In such a case baseline data should probably be collected for at least 10 days or 2 weeks prior to intervention. On the other hand, if a behavioral deficit is so severe that the individual never exhibits the necessary correct behavior, it would be possible to start the intervention with only a 1-week baseline period to confirm that the behavior does not occur when the observer is specifically watching for it.

Intervention Data

Measurement must continue after intervention so that the effect of the intervention can be assessed. Many persons who work in service settings believe that they do not need precise measurement because their experience with the service population gives them special knowledge about client change. A fast change of large magnitude in client behavior is readily apparent to staff who are familiar with the client, but staff often do not notice large magnitude changes in behavior that occur slowly. It is analogous to the common observation that parents do not notice their children's physical growth as readily as relatives and visitors who only see them once every few months.

Our conclusions about the effect of treatment are based on the comparison of the measurement of behavior during intervention with that taken during baseline. Thus, it is desirable to measure the behavior during treatment as often as it was done during baseline.

BEHAVIORAL INTERVENTIONS

Techniques of behavior modification and behavior therapy have been developed from classical conditioning, operant conditioning, social learning theory, and cognitive psychology. All have been tested and found to have success in modifying behavior of persons in education, health, prison, industry, and rehabilitation settings. Illustrations of actual applications in work settings have been selected to represent the variety of successes in work settings. There are other behavior problems that occur during rehabilitation, and the reader can find measurement and treatment strategies for those types of problems in the *Behavior Management Manual* (Marr & Means, 1980).

Positive Reinforcement

Reinforcement refers to any event that occurs immediately after the behavior and that increases the probability of that behavior occurring in the future. Rewards differ from reinforcement in that the former are given for service or attainment and are not defined by their effect on the behavior. Reinforcements may be positive or negative, but they are both defined by their effect of increasing behavior. Verbal statements of "good," "great," and "bad" are all positive reinforcements if they increase the behavior they followed. Things such as candy, ice cream, toys, money, surprise bags, and tokens are all positive reinforcements if they increase the behavior they follow.

Negative reinforcements are defined by their withdrawal immediately following the behavior and their effect of increasing behavior. Leaving work after cleaning up the work station, and returning to work to escape the foreman's long, sober stare are both examples of negative reinforcement if they serve to increase the behaviors of cleaning up and going back to work, respectively. Notice that negative reinforcement is an aversive stimulus that is removed when the target behavior occurs, whereas punishment is the application of the aversive stimulus immediately following a behavior for the purpose of suppressing the behavior. Greene and Hoots (1969) used television distortion to increase the work rate of a mildly retarded man by wiring the television signal to the work response levers. If the desired rate of work was not maintained, the television picture and sound became distorted. Although the authors of that study described the procedure as negative reinforcement, it could also be called positive reinforcement because fast work not only escaped the distortion, it also gained interesting visual and auditory stimulation.

Too often clients are given attention only when they are doing the wrong thing. Sometimes that attention, even when it is scolding, acts as a positive reinforcement. A successful intervention strategy calls for frequent positive reinforcement for appropriate behaviors. Positive reinforcement is usually one component of every behavioral program, as the reader will see in the remaining sections of this chapter.

There are four sources of information that assist in identification of a client's positive reinforcement. First, knowledge may be obtained about preferred activities and objects of other clients who are similar in age, sex, intelligence, and background. Second, the client may be observed in the settings where an intervention is to be initiated. What a client does most frequently can be used to reinforce target behaviors (Premack's Principle). For example, if a client is observed associating with a particular person, a work station next to that person can be used as reinforcement for on-task behavior. The third source of information is that from records, friends, relatives, and other service delivery providers who are familiar with the client. In the case of the deaf-blind client, described in the section on behavioral assets, further questioning of the staff revealed that riding in the car could be used as a positive reinforcement. The fourth information source is that supplied by the client. Ask the client or use one of the reinforcement checklists; for adults, see Cautela and Kastenbaum (1967), and for children, see Phillips, Fisher, and Singh (1977).

Shaping Positive reinforcement is a powerful tool not only for increasing the frequency of a behavior that is infrequent but also for initiating a deficit behavior that is not in the client's repertoire, for example, never on time or never speaks to co-workers. In the method of shaping, the supervisor gives positive reinforcement for small approximations of the correct response. If one waited to reinforce until the client reaches 100% of the targeted production rate, one might have to wait forever. If, however, the client is reinforced for a 5% improvement, then only if he or she gets another 5% improvement, and so on, the client's behavior can be shaped to the desired form or level.

Illustrations of Positive Reinforcement

Sometimes positive verbal reinforcement is used to increase a behavior, in combination with other techniques. In the following case, the client was reinforced for behavior he was already performing, and subsequently only for longer durations of that behavior.

> **Problem** Mentally retarded client with bilateral cateracts stops work, acts "silly," and mumbles about 8–10 times a day.
> **Treatment** Frequency count continued during intervention and 5-minute time sampling recommended for on-task behavior. Decision was made to give positive verbal reinforcement for on-task behavior before client stopped working. Intervals of reinforcement were 10 minutes at first and then lengthened. Periodic public reinforcement of other on-task clients was also initiated. If that procedure has not been successful, a point economy (point for every 10 minutes of on-task) was recommended. Points would earn group reinforcements (extra work breaks). (Hinman & Marr, 1982).

In the next case, positive reinforcement was used to treat quality of work. Measurement allowed estimation of the success of the verbal reinforcement so that a token economy could be used if the verbal approval did not improve the quality of work.

> **Problem** A 17-year-old cerebral palsy client made many mistakes at his work station in a sheltered workshop because he worked too fast. He also wandered away from his work station frequently.
> **Treatment** Measurement of on-task behavior was by 15-minute time samples during daily 2½-hour periods, and measurement of errors was taken by frequency count. Increased positive verbal reinforcement was first given for working carefully and slowly. In addition, other clients were loudly reinforced for being on-task when client was away from station. A second intervention was recommended if the first did not produce significant gains. Tokens were to be given every half-hour for work products completed without errors. Tokens were also to be given at random periods for on-task and slow work. Tokens were to be exchanged for group events listed on a reinforcement menu (Hinman and Marr, 1982).

Reinforcement in one location for behavioral improvement in another location is illustrated by this next case.

> **Problem** Client was classified as borderline retardate by staff of group home. In one year, he had been fired from eight jobs. He was fired for not completing designated tasks or for too many work breaks. The longest he had worked was 3 months. He could read and write. Part of

the difficulty in this case is that the person applying the intervention was not at the location where the client had started a new job.

Treatment A brief work report form was designed for ratings of poor, satisfactory, or good to each job category, i.e., promptness, work rate, work quality, and cooperation. This form was completed daily by his boss. The client was informed that if he received 4 "satisfactories" the first day he would have access to reinforcers such as one hour of TV, swimming pool, etc. Each "good" would receive additional hours of TV. Additional reinforcers, i.e., pass to movie, were tied to "good" performance across 4 days of the week and for number of weeks worked. All behaviors and reinforcers were specified in writing so that the client could refer to them at any time (Hinman & Marr, 1982).

Positive Reinforcement to Decrease Surplus Behaviors

Often the selection of an intervention becomes easier when the surplus problem behavior is redefined as a deficit problem behavior. This redefinition uses the principle of incompatible behaviors. Two behaviors are incompatible if they both cannot occur at the same time. Like the ends of a teeter-totter, they both can not be up at the same time. A person cannot be sitting in his chair and standing at the same instance. If the client's problem is that he is standing too much, the problem is redefined as sitting too little. If sitting is reinforced, sitting increases in frequency and duration and the surplus problem of standing has to decrease.

Similarly, the deficit behavior problem of staying on-task is incompatible with a host of surplus problems identified by work supervisors and vocational instructors. These include bothering other workers, talking to others, taking too many work breaks, and the class of behaviors that are often referred to as "horsing around," "goofing off," "dawdling," and "short attention span." If on-task behavior is increased from a baseline of 50% to 90%, the surplus behaviors would automatically decrease because they are incompatible with those behaviors classed as on-task.

Fading a Prompt

The first choice of methods to change deficit behaviors is prompts, that is, telling the client that he or she should perform the behavior in a situation where the client has not been performing it. The client may not have been doing it or may have been working faster because he or she did not know that the behaviors should occur in that situation. The client has the behavior in his or her repertoire, but it is not habitually emitted in the presence of the appropriate stimuli. Sometimes, however, the client must be told again and again. An effective procedure for teaching the client to initiate the appropriate behavior without being told is the method of presenting a prompt and then fading it, that is, gradually eliminating it.

Marr and Means (1980) have described two procedures for first prompting a client to get to work and then fading the prompt. One procedure consists of presenting complex instructions or rules on a sign or card such as the following

> When you report to work, go immediately to task area. This is the same area in which you worked yesterday morning, unless your instructor has told you to change areas. Get your tools and equipment, start working. When you finish one project, start another project. Keep working until the instructor tells you to stop. If you run out of material, go get some more or ask the instructor where you can find some more material. Before leaving your area for breaks, lunch, or at the end of the day, put your tools, equipment, and materials away and then clean and sweep your area (Marr & Means, 1980, p. 36).

After the client is consistently following the directions on the card, it is removed or a less detailed sign is substituted for it,

> Go to your assigned area, and start working. When you finish, start another project. Keep busy and keep your area clean.

Finally, the instructions are faded out completely. In using fading procedures, staff give reinforcement for slight improvements in behaviors. When the appropriate behaviors are occurring at an acceptable rate, the reinforcement is thinned until it is given only as often as would occur in the natural work environment.

Aversive Consequences to Decrease Surplus Behaviors

Fifty years of research has shown that very intense physical punishment will permanently suppress behavior but that moderate and light punishment will not. Although there are very important ethical reasons why strong punishment should not be used, there also are important practical reasons for using other procedures. Punishment not only suppresses the target behavior but also suppresses other behaviors that are desirable. In addition, punishment may produce undesirable side effects, such as aggression, hostility, and fear.

Other methods that have been successful in decreasing surplus behaviors are extinction, time out, overcorrection restitution, overcorrection positive practice, negative practice, and response cost (used within a token economy).

Extinction This procedure refers to the removal of reinforcement following the behavior. If a client no longer receives attention for making "silly" faces or gestures, the client will stop making them.

Time Out This procedure refers to the removal of the client from a preferred activity or place for 5–10 minutes as a consequence of inappropriate behavior. If a client likes working at a certain job but violates a safety regulation (such as wearing safety goggles), he would be immediately given 5 minutes of sitting at the work station without operating the equipment or talking to others. Another variation of time out is given in the following case.

> ***Problem*** Client in a sheltered workshop comes to work with very bad body odor. Other clients refuse to work near him.
>
> ***Treatment*** Baseline measurement was taken by counting the number of mornings that he carried an unpleasant oder detectable by staff person standing two feet from him. Intervention recommended was to be initiated by a counseling session where causes of body odor and the relationship between obtaining work and holding a job to cleanliness was discussed. Discussion of his behavioral assets was also recommended. Joint planning of bathing and clothing behaviors followed and additional training was scheduled. Finally, he was to be informed that if he had an unpleasant odor in the morning, he would have to work in a corner alone, (time-out) and if he had no odor, he could work alongside others. Heavy praise was also to be initiated by all staff for slight improvements in hair and clothing appearances and decreases in odor (Hinman & Marr, 1982).

Negative Practice In this procedure the person must repeat the inappropriate remark or activity a number of times as a consequence of performing it (limit this procedure to 3–4 minutes). If a client cursed the supervisor, he might be made to curse for 4 minutes "to get it out of his system." Other variations in the use of negative practice are given in the following case.

> ***Problem*** Client complains frequently during the day about changing work stations, medications, doctors, her mother, and so on. She walks with a limp and has limited use of one hand.
>
> ***Treatment*** Complaining behavior was measured by frequency count. Intervention had three parts. a) During counseling and training session, client was given practice on talking about positive memories (dance, movies, television, parties, etc.) and positive attributes of self and others. She was taught to distinguish between interesting topics of conversation and those that are uninteresting (complaints). She was encouraged to try out the interesting talk and report back on the effects. b) Workshop staff were alerted and instructed to positively reinforce her positive comments. c) Staff were carefully instructed to ignore complaints, and if she persisted the following modified negative practice procedure was to be used.
>
> The staff member would immediately tell her in a neutral manner, "You are complaining. Let's put your complaints on tape." The staff member was then to have her complain 3 minutes into a tape recorder and then tell her she would be able to tape some more every time she complained in the workshop. The client would then get to listen to her own complaints whenever she complained after filling up a 15-minute cassette. Staff were reminded to warmly praise client for other kinds of talk after taping sessions.

Overcorrection Restitution The procedure involves cleaning, repairing, or making restitution for that part of the environment that was damaged by the behavior of the client. The overcorrective activity should usually be limited to 5–10 minutes and must be related to the problem. For example, if the client throws his cigarette butt on the floor in the break room, he must empty and wash all the ashtrays "so there will be room for his cigarette butt in the future," or he must pick up the butt, sweep that part of the floor, wash it, and dry it.

Overcorrection Positive Practice In this procedure the client must practice the correct behavior for 3–5 minutes as a consequence of inappropriate behavior. For example, if a client cuts across a danger area that is marked by red safety lines on the floor of the workshop, he must practice walking around the area for 3–5 minutes.

Response Cost The procedure involves a penalty in tokens for an inappropriate behavior. It is discussed in the section below on "Token Economies."

Guidelines for Successful Use of Time Out, Negative Practice, and Overcorrection

Research and observation of the effects of these procedures have revealed a number of guidelines for successful utilization.

1. The consequences must be applied immediately after the inappropriate act.
2. The client must be told specifically what behavior was inappropriate.
3. The client must be informed of the consequences.
4. The consequence should be limited to 5–10 minutes, less if the client is very young or retarded. Lengthening the limit to 15 minutes for repeated violations has not been found to be effective except for overcorrection. Time measurement begins and continues only when the client has ceased "hollering, screaming, fighting, kicking, complaining, etc."
5. After the time is up, again tell the client exactly what he did to earn the consequence and that the consequence will again occur if the behavior occurs.
6. Make sure that all staff are trained to properly carry out the procedure on the same client in the same manner every time it occurs.
7. Be prepared for a temporary increase in high-frequency behaviors before the decrease begins. It is believed that this characteristic increase is due to the consistent attention given to the inappropriate behavior. The decrease will occur faster if all staff remain neutral when carrying out the consequence (no affect: no display of anger, hostility, joy, or grief). Later is the time to be open about the feelings created by the behavior.
8. Look for opportunities to give positive reinforcement for appropriate behaviors of the client.

Token Economies

Much has been written about token economies; the reader is referred to Ayllon and Azrin (1968) and Kazdin (1977) for more complete descriptions. Only the basic principles are presented here with some examples of their application to teaching and managing work-related behaviors. The simplest token economy system has three components: the target behaviors, the token, the back-up reinforcers.

Target Behaviors These are the behaviors that the rehabilitation professional wants to change. They must be specified in sufficient detail that all staff in contact with the client know what to reinforce and when to reinforce. The general rule is to limit the target behaviors to five in any one setting and in any one period of the day. For example, at the start of the day, the client might be given tokens for arriving on time, for starting work immediately, for wearing clean clothes, for wearing appropriate work clothes, and for being clean (hair combed, shaven, face and hands clean, and no body odor). During the work period, tokens might be given for being on-task, for following directions, for quality of work (must be specified, i.e., all of whetstone polished and no corners chipped), for production rate (i.e., one token for each piece of 10 complete per hour), and for returning from work break on time.

The Token The token bridges the gap between the occurrence of the target behavior and the delivery of the reinforcement. It might be something that is very concrete such as a poker chip, or more abstract such as a point on a card. The lower the level of intelligence of the client, the more concrete the token must be and the more immediately it must be delivered. The client accumulates the tokens and then purchases the back-up reinforcements.

Tokens may be individualized by giving those of a particular shape and color to one client and those of a different shape or color to another client. Individualization prevents stealing of tokens, allows more accurate measurement of individual progress, and facilitates record keeping by staff (they only need to count the individual tokens that have been dispensed to record progress). Different colors or shapes can also be given for different types of behavior, be used to represent different dominations, or be dispensed by different staff (if there is need to monitor reinforcement activities of staff).

Back-up Reinforcements The tokens have value for the clients because they can be used to purchase objects, events, or activities that are reinforcing to the clients. Objects that might be purchased are such things as candy, soft drinks, pictures, clothing, badges, certificates of achievement, cigarettes, or money. Events might include parties, picnics, or field trips. Examples of activities are choice of work station, extra work breaks, renting a cassette recorder with music and earphone for 15 minutes, using the office telephone, or leaving the job early.

The list of back-up reinforcements with the cost of each is called the reinforcement menu. It should be posted so that clients can see them at the time they are earning the tokens. For mentally retarded clients who cannot read, they are represented by pictures with the cost shown in actual tokens. For visually impaired clients, the menu is placed on a cassette tape that they can listen to occasionally.

The cost in tokens of the back-up reinforcers is determined by the same principles as in any economy, i.e., supply, demand, and staff effort. The more time and difficulty required by staff to offer the item, the higher the purchase price. Activities that the staff are trying to decrease in clients (behavior surpluses) might be listed at the bottom of the menu with token prices of each. Such activities are called response costs and might include spitting on the floor, throwing tools, or putting cigarettes out on the floor. The price of these items should be just high enough to decrease the response.

Back-up reinforcers might be purchased on demand, only at certain periods of the day, once or twice a week, and sometimes all of the above. For example, extra work breaks might be purchased at any time, money at the end of the day, a party on Fridays, and a field trip once a month.

Graduated Levels of Token   One of the most common reasons given by rehabilitation professionals for not using a token economy to teach and maintain behaviors that facilitate work is that clients differ in their needs for reinforcement of work-related behaviors. A token economy system overcomes this objection by allowing assignment or advancement of clients to a level within the token economy where they no longer receive tokens on a "piece rate" but do receive tokens on salary.

Generally, the system has three levels. In the first level, clients receive tokens immediately after demonstrating the appropriate response. In the second level, clients receive a salary in tokens at the end of the week and then use the salary to purchase items from a different reinforcement menu. Their menu contains everything that is listed on the first level menu plus additional incentive items or activities, such as use of office phone, preferred work stations, recommendations for promotions or passes.

A committee composed of at least two staff and an appointed or elected client representative from the third level make assignment to the different levels. They might determine when a client from the first level has demonstrated habitual work behaviors that would warrant promotion, whether a new client already has the basic behavior warranting second level assignment, whether a second level client should be given probationary status for inappropriate behaviors, a first warning, or even demotion to first level, and whether a client is ready for promotion to third level.

The third or most advanced level signifies that the client is characteristically demonstrating all behaviors necessary for successful work and not exhibiting any behaviors that would interfere with obtaining a job or persevering at work. Although no tokens are given at this level, the client would still receive verbal reinforcement, certificates of achievement, and all activities on the reinforcement menus plus access to additional activities or items (high pay, special name tags, supervisory position, etc.).

Token economies have been used extensively to modify work behaviors in homes, schools, sheltered workshops, comprehensive rehabilitation facilities, hospitals, and prisons. For more detailed descriptions of procedures, the reader is referred to the following: a) on individualized token economies see Marr and Means (1980) and Schaefer and Martin (1969); b) on types of work and work descriptions see Ayllon and Azrin (1968); c) on rules for earning and spending tokens see Ayllon and Azrin (1968) and Petrak (1971); d) on back-up reinforcers see Sulzer-Azaroff and Mayer (1977).

Modeling Pro-Work Behavior

Modeling refers to the learning process in which an individual changes behavior as a result of seeing, hearing, or reading about the behavior and its consequences for another person. Modeling can be used to teach a person new job-obtaining behaviors, to practice habitually those behaviors that have been previously learned, or to decrease inappropriate work-related behaviors. Bandura and Walters (1963) initiated the research that demonstrated the impact on behavior of observing others, and Bandura (1977a) has described and summarized much of the more recent research.

Television and movies have greatly influenced the behaviors of all ages through modeling of inappropriate behaviors and positive consequences for both appropriate and inappropriate behaviors. The "drugstore cowboy" wears the symbols of boots, jeans, shirt, and hat that have been modeled in film as clothes of the working cowboy. Adolescents and adults model the cowboy in their clothes and also model the clothes and mannerisms of the successful rock star and professional athlete in commercials. But television does not model the hours of work that produced or earned the high-priced clothes and automobiles that are displayed.

Four determinants of successful modeling programs have been outlined by Bandura (1977a) and are described here in terms of learning work behaviors.

1. *Attention* The client must attend to and understand the information that is relevant to obtaining work or working that is being modeled.
2. *Retention* After attending to and understanding the relevant information, the client must attach the information to codes and classification schemes that are used to remember new material. Clients can be taught how to code and classify their observations. In some ways this is similar to how a film is presented for teaching new material: a) tell the audience what they are going to see, what is important, why it is important, and try to relate it to what they already know; b) show the material; c) tell them afterward what they saw, what was important, and why it was important; d) answer their questions.
3. *Motoric Reproduction* The skill demanded in performing motor behaviors requires not only attention and retention but also overt practice. Watching another person assemble a product and remembering the sequence of steps does not produce success until the client has practiced the assembly sequence a number of times (see Bandura, 1977b, for a discussion of self-efficacy).
4. *Motivation* After all of the above, the person may not perform the act unless there is some expectation of success and positive reinforcement. Even when the person has practiced sufficiently to allow an expectation of success, he or she must see that the model receives positive consequences, i.e., reinforcement, for effort.

In the *Behavior Management Manual*, Marr and Means (1980) described different methods of using modeling to modify work behaviors. Modeling should be planned because new workers may model themselves after the worst workers when starting new assignments. Planning should include the decision about who should be assigned to give the new worker on-the-job instruction. Some effective workers are not good models because they do all the work themselves while allowing the trainee to stand around. The experienced worker who is selected should be instructed to demonstrate tool care, clean-up, rates of working, and work-break termination, as well as technical execution of the job.

The supervisor must monitor the training, reinforce the experienced worker in the presence of the trainee, and be prepared to reinforce the trainee for attending, remembering, and practicing.

Examples of Modeling of Job-Seeking Behaviors

One approach to increasing and improving job-seeking skills is the job club method developed by Jones and Azrin (1973). This approach includes a variety of behavioral methods to facilitate obtaining a job. A more complete description of these methods is presented in Chapter 10. Among the methods is modeling to enhance motivation of the client. Because job seekers often become discouraged, the job club includes frequent presentation of taped commentaries by former job seekers who have been successful in obtaining jobs. Thus, the job club method is primarily serving the fourth determinant of modeling success, motivation; those in the job club who have practiced the skills learned receive observable positive reinforcement—a job.

Another use of modeling to facilitate the learning of job-seeking skills is contained in a program developed by the Minneapolis Rehabilitation Center (Prazak, 1969). In this program, the specific skills needed to obtain a job are identified and then taught. Modeling a desirable job interview is demonstrated by 10-minute videotape recording of a staff member applying for a job. Clients ask questions and react immediately after viewing the tape, and then the staff member draws their attention to the important interview behaviors of the model.

Following the discussion, clients try 5-minute mock interviews which are recorded on videotape. These are critiqued by the clients, and a staff member reinforces the clients for the good portions of their interviews. Thus the group witnesses others being reinforced for a variety of behaviors that comprise a good interview.

Chaining

A complex task is composed of many behaviors that must be performed in sequence. The performance of the first response is the stimulus that controls the next response. The performance of the second response is the stimulus for the third response, and so on, as presented below:

$$\text{walk in the door} \rightarrow \text{walk to work station} \rightarrow \text{obtain tools or materials} \rightarrow \text{start work}$$

Forward chaining refers to teaching a client the first response, then the next, then the third, and so forth. Backward chaining refers to the procedure of teaching the client the last response first, then the one before the last, and so on. Generally, for a mentally retarded client or for a client who has considerable difficulty carrying out the steps in the correct order, backward chaining is advisable. For a more complete description of chaining, see Martin and Pear (1978, pp. 146–148).

Usually modeling accompanies the chaining procedure. For example, the supervisor or experienced worker models the first four steps of a five-step job and then teaches the client to carry out the fifth step. Next the model demonstrates the first three steps, teaches the fourth step, asks what is the next step, reinforces the client for describing the fifth step, and reinforces the client for performance of the fifth step. Each step is mastered and reinforced before proceeding to teach the client the previous step. The following case represents the use of backward chaining.

Problem A client in a sheltered workshop was required to correctly use a wood lathe to prepare a wooden bowl, then use another machine to polish the bowl, then use a stamping machine to cut a piece of leather, and finally use a hand stapler to staple the leather to the bowl. The client correctly carried out the first three steps but did not perform the stapling task properly. Clients received pay on the basis of the number of their products that passed inspection. The supervision of the sheltered workshop reported increasing frustration and aggression on the part of the client because he was only getting about 10–20% of the pay of other clients.

Treatment The client's past production rate served as the baseline and a backward chaining procedure for stapling was initiated. The supervisor modeled placing the leather in the correct position on the bowl, modeled placement of the staple gun and stapling the first three staples, modeled the placing for the fourth staple, and then held the gun in position allowing the client to trigger the gun. The client was verbally reinforced and then told he would receive payment for that completed product. Next the procedure was repeated but the client had to hold the staple gun in position and trigger the gun by himself for the last staple. Reinforcement was again given. Again the procedure was repeated except for placement in the last two positions; the client being reinforced for correct execution. In one week the supervisor reported that the client was already at 90% of the production rate of other clients.

CONCLUDING CONSIDERATIONS

This chapter has described a number of procedures for analyzing and modifying work behavior problems. Guidelines and cases have been presented but success of the interventions is still dependent upon the proper selection of treatment, monitoring outcome, and preparation of staff.

Choice of Treatment

The choice of behavioral treatments applied to work-related behaviors often leads to a consideration of intrusiveness and effectiveness. The least intrusive and most effective method is always the treatment of choice. The methods of changing surplus behaviors can be ordered from least obtrusive to most intrusive: extinction (ignoring the behavior so that it does not receive staff attention), prompting (telling the individual to stop it), positive verbal reinforcement of incompatible behaviors, time out, response costs, and overcorrection restitution.

The difficulty in selecting an intervention comes when the most effective method is also a highly intrusive method. Extinction might be the treatment of choice for suppressing the client's behavior of telling the supervisor about television shows she sees every night. The same treatment would not be effective for spitting on the floor, whereas negative practice and overcorrection restitution might. A committee that includes community representatives can make the decision that the treatment is in the best interests of the client and is preferred over alternative treatments that have been considered.

Accountability

The use of applied behavioral analysis assumes a commitment to continuous measurement as described in the earlier portion of this chapter. Comparisons of the records obtained after treatment with those obtained at baseline allows one to hold the treatment accountable. As indicated in every chapter of the *Behavior Management Manual* (Marr & Means, 1980), the last step of behavioral intervention calls for revising the treatment, monitoring staff for proper application, or choosing another behavioral procedure if the treatment is not showing success.

Staff Training

Ideally, a specialist in applied behavioral analyses would be the person responsible for proper utilization of behavioral procedures. However, when such a specialist is not present, a behavioral psychologist can usually be obtained as a consultant. Staff should be thoroughly trained in every procedure used in the facility, and supervisors should monitor behavioral applications routinely. Staff need positive reinforcement in carrying out their responsibilities, and research has shown that staff service delivery behaviors also can be significantly influenced by positive reinforcements (Iwata, Bailey, Brown, Foshee, & Alpern, 1976).

chapter 8
PSYCHOSOCIAL ADJUSTMENT SKILLS TRAINING

Robert L. Akridge and Bob L. Means

This chapter introduces a model of interventions described as psychosocial adjustment skills training. Two major assumptions underlying the model are: a) that behavior is a function of both the person and the situation, and b) that the most effective and economical therapeutic intervention for adjustment problems is that of systematically teaching the person more functional ways of behaving in his or her situation. This approach is variously referred to in the professional literature as psychoeducational training, life skills training, systematic training, structured learning, and training-as-treatment.

A skill is simply the ability to behave in some prescribed manner at a given level of competence. Most persons demonstrate some competence in all the basic adjustment skills. The skill level may be adequate for successful adaptation within the person's situation, or the skill may be insufficiently developed and adjustment problems may arise.

A large portion of human behavior can be conceptualized into constellations of skills. We commonly group some behaviors (e.g., occupational, mobility, and artistic) into general skill areas. Viewing the behaviors associated with psychosocial adjustment as skills allows a more operational description of how the major domains of life activity are structured. Thinking of psychosocial adjustment in terms of skills may seem strange at first because of other concepts and theories that have been learned. For example, most readers can easily relate anxiety to such concepts as ego defense mechanisms, but are less likely to view anxiety in terms of relaxation or stress management skill deficits. The psychosocial skills training approach is based on translating common psychological adjustment problems into skill deficits and providing systematic educational experiences to develop needed adjustment skills. The approach is straightforward: it identifies what the person needs to do to adapt to a particular situation and teaches him or her how to do it.

The aim of psychosocial adjustment skills training in vocational rehabilitation is to develop whatever additional skills the client needs to adapt effectively at work and in work-related situations. This chapter presents a set of concepts and operations relating to psychosocial adjustment skills training that the rehabilitation professional may apply at each stage of the rehabilitation process to help clients adjust successfully. The process and content of psychosocial skills training are described briefly in relation to rehabilitation settings at both theoretical and practical levels. Considerations and guidelines for initiating psychosocial skills training in rehabilitation are discussed.

DESCRIPTIONS OF PSYCHOSOCIAL ADJUSTMENT SKILLS

Within the constant flux of each person's situation, spontaneously selecting and employing the most adaptive concepts and operations is termed psychosocial adjustment. A psychosocial adjustment skill is a demonstrated potential for making an adaptive response or organized series of responses to some specific aspect of a particular domain of life activity. Psychosocial skills are learned response patterns usually described in terms of large, observable units of behavior. Successfully relating to co-workers is an example of a psychosocial adjustment skill (at a fairly high level of abstraction) in the vocational adjustment or career development domain.

Psychosocial skills are structured hierarchically within domains of activity so that more complex, difficult-to-master competencies are combinations or transformations of simpler, concrete, specific skills. Many specific skills at lower levels of abstraction are critical in more than one broad, major domain of life activity such as vocational adjustment. Consider the skill of communicating attentiveness in interpersonal situations. This skill is critical in both the vocational adjustment and social adjustment domains. Any behavior sufficiently discrete to be recognized as a skill will likely be a part of a larger skill. Complex skills require a task analysis to determine the number and arrangement of subskills that comprise them.

Additional salient characteristics of psychosocial adjustment skills are: a) the individual can reliably emit the behavior upon request; b) the behavior may be initiated through self-monitoring and self-instruction, and may be maintained through self-reinforcement; and c) given a minimum level of trainer skills, the individual can teach the competency to others.

ORIGINS OF PSYCHOSOCIAL ADJUSTMENT SKILLS TRAINING

Among the developing human service professions, vocational rehabilitation has contributed considerably to a skills training approach to helping handicapped persons. During its early years, vocational rehabilitation emphasized physical restoration and the provision of vocational training. Subsequently, legislative mandates, more effective consumer advocacy, and the growth of the rehabilitation profession broadened the vocational rehabilitation focus to include persons with intellectual and emotional disabilities. Additionally, a large proportion of clients served by the state/federal vocational rehabilitation program and private facilities are from the lower socioeconomic levels of society and are frequently characterized as culturally disadvantaged and lacking adequate adaptive skills.

Professional experience and research support the proposition that, even with persons whose disabilities are primarily physical, successful rehabilitation programs usually include attention to psychosocial and general vocational preparation in addition to the more strictly medical and occupational concerns. As vocational rehabilitation has approached these new opportunities to serve, a continued strong emphasis on training has characterized rehabilitation practice.

This trend is exemplified by developments in the vocational evaluation and work adjustment specialty. Most of the early leaders of this movement insisted that work adjustment training be conducted in actual work settings such as the sheltered workshop. As technology was refined and the concepts and skills that clients needed for successful employment were more clearly specified, it became obvious that much of this training could be accomplished in simulated work environments, classrooms, and other structured situations that provide purposefully mediated learning experiences. This systematic training approach utilizes a workshop format that combines teaching, modeling, coached practice, trainer and peer feedback and support, and focused feedback from paper-and-pencil assessment instruments or videotaped performance. The training group or laboratory learning methodology has been widely used in educational and mental health settings and is rapidly becoming a major treatment modality within rehabilitation settings. From a methodological standpoint, the Personal Achievement Skills Training Package (Means & Roessler, 1976) illustrates this approach.

The development by rehabilitation professionals of a skills training approach to adjustment problems was paralleled in clinical psychology by the development of behavioral group therapy (Upper & Ross, 1980), and in counseling psychology by the development of deliberate psychological education, mental health education, and life skills training

(Authier, Gustafson, Guerney, & Kasdorf, 1975; Skouholt, 1977). These trends were paralleled in education by such movements as progressive education, affective education, and confluent education, all of which advocate that personal and interpersonal learning objectives be given equal priority with cognitive and occupational objectives. The fields of special education and special vocational education have been particularly active in developing skills training programs to improve personal, interpersonal, educational, and career competencies of handicapped persons (Goldstein, Sprafkin, Gershaw, & Klein, 1979).

Much of the methodology used in psychosocial adjustment skills training with clients was developed within the context of competency-based training for human service professionals and management personnel. To the extent that common skills such as goal setting have been identified across many professions and professional support groups, competency training has also contributed substantially to the content of psychosocial skills training (Carkhuff, 1971; Ivey & Authier, 1978).

Social psychology, because of its focus on person-environment interaction, has contributed to the development of psychosocial adjustment skills training. Consider, for example, the study of "meaning attribution" (Kelly, 1967), or how people assign different meanings to events and how these differences affect their behavior. Skills training programs to prevent or correct the kind of problems people have as a consequence of misconstruing events are based on this line of inquiry. The therapeutic approach known as cognitive behavior therapy (Lazarus, 1973; Mahoney, 1979; Meichenbaum, 1977) is also consistent with this information base and tends to use a skills training approach. The basic thrust is to train clients to conceptualize their experience in more personally satisfying and socially acceptable ways.

The concept of "explicit personality theory" provides another example. The response of a human service professional to clients is heavily influenced by how the professional conceptualizes human behavior in general, rehabilitation clients as a group, and the specific client. The responses of clients are also heavily influenced by how they conceptualize themselves in their situations. Many of these images of how people operate, or self-in-situation conceptualizations, are below the threshold of the person's awareness. Psychosocial skills training programs help participants make their "personal constructs" (Kelly, 1955) more explicit and therefore more available to self-examination and corrective feedback from the trainer and peer group members.

The existential theme of meaning is inherent in the skill areas of value clarification and goal setting. Attention to experiential states (e.g., feelings) is both existential and phenomenological. The emphasis on modeling and practice with reinforcements comes from social learning theory.

Not only has psychosocial adjustment skills training developed from numerous theoretical perspectives, it also bridges many of them. The psychosocial adjustment skills training approach has been described by its developers mainly as a *method* of intervention. Methodologically, the approach is behavioral in that the primary emphasis is on preparing clients to behave in desired ways. Goals have generally been selected on a pragmatic basis. Different approaches to therapy have tended to produce demonstrable change in different areas of functioning. Behavioral change goals that have been described more explicitly, prescribed more frequently, and demonstrated more reliably have tended to become the curriculum of psychosocial adjustment skills training.

THE CONTENT OF PSYCHOSOCIAL ADJUSTMENT SKILLS TRAINING

Conceptual Model

The term *human behavior* refers to consistent patterns of change in the relationship between a person and the environment. Any intervention designed to influence human behavior may focus on person variables, situational variables, or both. Although it is recognized that a comprehensive rehabilitation process will attend to both, the emphasis of this chapter is on person variables.

Hershenson's (1977) three-dimensional model of evaluation in rehabilitation was modified as shown in Figure 1 to depict the hypothesized components of psychosocial adjustment and their relationships to each other and to the general field of rehabilitation. The model is essentially eclectic in that it incorporates elements from all the major theories of human behavior and behavior change. General systems theory (sometimes referred to as information theory) provides a unifying perspective for integrating these diverse elements. The most consistent metaphor used to portray the person-environment adaptation process is that of information processing. This metaphor organizes the five basic behavioral processes shown in Figure 1 and directs attention to the aspects of the client's internal and external environment that are attended to (input), how the client processes these perceptions (conceptualizing, feeling, and intending), and what the person does (output). This is not a singular, linear process, however, because the person/environment transaction is continuously modified by feedback and feed-forward. When the response has an effect on the environment and this effect is perceived by the person, this is called feedback. Feed-forward occurs when the person engages in selective perception that

Figure 1

Spheres of Functioning
- I. Physical
- II. Intrapersonal
- III. Interpersonal
- IV. Ideological
- V. Financial
- VI. Technical

Basic Behavioral Process
- A. Perceiving
- B. Conceptualizing
- C. Feeling
- D. Intending
- E. Acting

Levels of Action
1. Physiological
2. Self-Management
3. Interpersonal
4. Task Performance
5. Life Planning

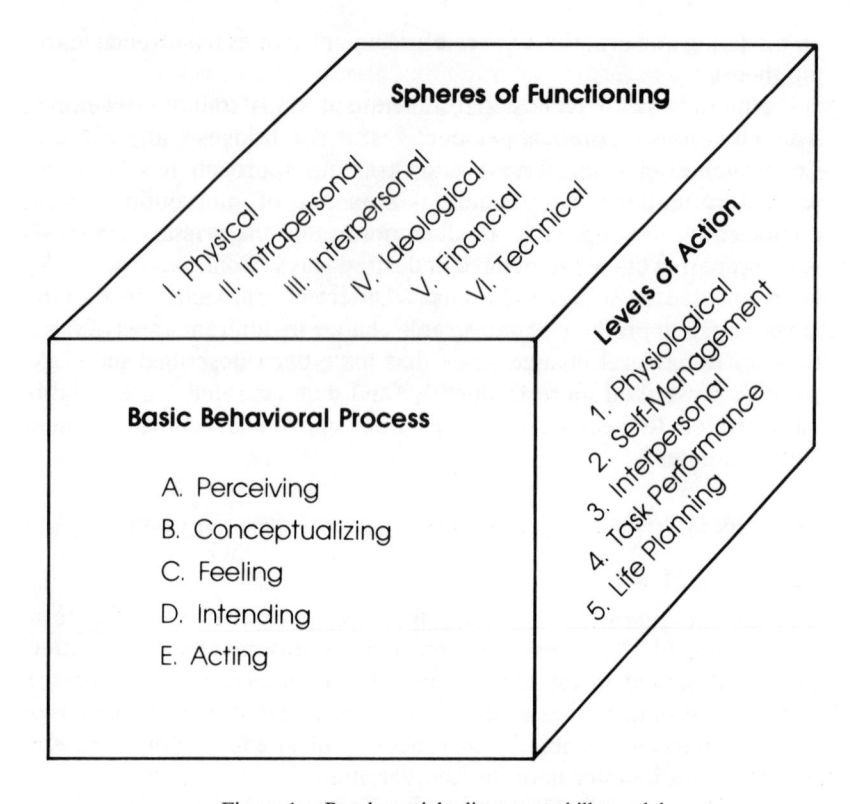

Figure 1. Psychosocial adjustment skills model.

is influenced by previously learned response patterns (traits) or temporary feeling states (emotions, sexual arousal).

Another major concept of the model is that of integration. All psychosocial adjustment interventions may be understood in terms of increasing integration or decreasing disintegration. The person or self-system is viewed as five integrated, basic behavioral processes, all of which are mutually influencing in terms of the total adjustment process.

The model defines the content parameters of psychosocial adjustment skills in terms of healthy, adaptive living within particular spheres of functioning. The phrase "psychosocial adjustment skills" refers to the process of employing, in an integrated fashion, the basic behavioral processes (perceiving, conceptualizing, feeling, intending, and acting) within particular spheres of functioning (physical, intrapersonal, interpersonal, ideological, financial, and technical) as shown schematically in Figure 1. The level of action dimension, encompassing the content of psychosocial adjustment skills, results from the interaction of basic behavioral processes and spheres of functioning. The action dimension orders interventions from the most person-centered to the most environment-centered. These levels of action (physiological, self-management, interpersonal relations, task performance, and life planning) shown in Figure 1 represent the whole of the rehabilitation process. It was hypothesized that psychosocial adjustment skills would cluster at three of Hershenson's levels of action. A factor analysis of the Psychosocial Development Matrix Questionnaire items representing the five basic behavioral processes within the six spheres of functioning confirmed the presence of three factors that were defined by item content as Self-Management, Interpersonal Relations, and Life Planning (Akridge, 1981).

In the next section, the content of psychosocial adjustment skills training is organized around these three competency areas (Table 1). It should be remembered that each of these competency areas includes employing and integrating all the basic behavioral processes in different kinds of situations. The situation may be subdivided in various ways. The six spheres of functioning (physical, intrapersonal, interpersonal, ideological, financial, and technical) represent an ecological perspective.

The level of action dimension of the model is most relevant for discussing rehabilitation interventions. Physiological functioning is the major focus of the medical and allied health professions. Some psychosocial interventions at the self-management level, such as relaxation and stress management, may be applied from a medical or psychosocial perspective. Self-management, interpersonal relations, and life planning cover the major concerns of psychosocial adjustment.

Task performance is the domain of basic education, vocational training, recreation, activities of daily living training, rehabilitation engineering, and similar interventions. A primary characteristic of task performance behaviors is that they are power responses. For assessment purposes, we need only be able to say whether the person can perform the responses in a standard situation. In contrast to this emphasis on performance capability, the assessment of psychosocial skills (levels 2, 3, and 5) is primarily concerned with typical responses.

Traditional work adjustment programs in rehabilitation have emphasized task performance behaviors, such as performing a particular work behavior or a particular activity of daily living. Many work adjustment programs, however, are much more sophisticated and provide an array of services which, for a given individual, may impact on any one or a combination of physiological, self-management, interpersonal relations, task performance, or life planning levels of action. Such programs will usually include some attempt to influence clients' typical response patterns within certain domains of life activity.

A Taxonomy of Psychosocial Adjustment Skills

Any attempt to construct a comprehensive, although tentative, listing of psychosocial adjustment skills is complicated by the ambiguity of the language. Different terms are frequently used to refer to similar processes. Behavioral processes may be described at various levels of abstraction.

The listing of personal adjustment skills in Table 1 is representative of a comprehensive program of psychosocial interventions needed by rehabilitation clients. Although the list suggests a substantial investment of time and resources, the personal adjustment skill deficits of many rehabilitation clients are such that a large investment is required for them to achieve successful rehabilitation and stable employment. Rehabilitation clients not only must learn to cope with specific disabilities, but as a group they have less well developed psychosocial adjustment skills with which to live independently in our culture (Akridge, 1981).

Representative examples of skills which make up the three major psychosocial adjustment skill areas are listed and defined in Table 1. The skills in the self-management area are sometimes referred to as

Table 1. Representative psychosocial adjustment skills by competency areas

Self-Management Area
1. *Fitness Skills*—The ability to implement and maintain an exercise, nutrition, and sleep program supporting health, growth, and extended life
2. *Relaxation Skills*—The ability to monitor and control one's level of arousal
3. *Stress Management Skills*—The ability to control anxiety and react positively to tense situations
4. *Pain Management Skills*—The ability to monitor and control physical discomfort
5. *Affective Self-Monitoring*—The ability to identify emotional responses
6. *Rational Thinking Skills*—The ability to use logic to interpret data and events
7. *Behavior Change Skills*—The ability to apply learning principles to change one's own typical behavior

Interpersonal Relations Area
1. *Conversing Skills*—The ability to listen and speak appropriately to others
2. *Self-Revealing Skills*—The ability to reveal thoughts, feelings, and actions appropriately in interpersonal contexts
3. *Befriending Skills*—The ability to locate potential friends and develop friendships
4. *Assertiveness Skills*—The ability to reasonably represent one's desires and defend one's rights
5. *Teaming Skills*—The ability to work and contribute in a group
6. *Interpersonal Support Skills (Helping)*—The ability to help others understand and cope with their experiences

(Continued)

Table 1. *(Continued)*

Life Planning Area
1. *Value Clarification Skills*—The ability to conceptualize categories of behaviors that are personally desired and self-satisfying
2. *Goal-Setting Skills*—The ability to convert problems or opportunities into observable and measurable objectives
3. *Program Development Skills*—The ability to schedule activities that lead to goals
4. *Program Implementation and Monitoring Skills*—The ability to initiate, evaluate, and modify personal behavior change programs
5. *Time Management Skills*—The ability to view time as a limited resource and accomplish goals on time
6. *Understanding Human Behavior Skills*—The ability to apply some theory which leads to adequate prediction of human behavior
7. *Lifestyle Analysis Skills*—The ability to conceptualize the relationship between individual choices and behaviors and the general patterns or behavioral trends one develops over time. A method of viewing life as a whole in relation to other lives and to one's vision of what is possible.

intrapersonal or personal adjustment skills. Relaxation, pain control, and rational thinking are examples. The interpersonal area may be referred to as social skills. Empathy and assertiveness are examples of interpersonal skills. Other possible names for the life planning area are environmental coping skills or cultural skills. Such skills facilitate adjustment to the physical environment, social institutions, and cultural mores. They allow one to participate in the prevailing communication system, economy, technology, transportation system, and cultural resources. Specific examples include such skills as value clarification, life style analysis, goal setting, and program development.

THE PROCESS OF PSYCHOSOCIAL ADJUSTMENT SKILLS TRAINING

The process of psychosocial skills training includes client assessment and the implementation of a specified intervention program. Assessment is concerned with identifying skill strengths and deficits in relation to symptoms or problems expressed by the client or diagnosed by rehabilitation professionals. (Client assessment procedures and techniques are considered in more detail in a later section.) Once the skill deficits are identified, the client is encouraged to join a training group with other clients who exhibit similar skill development needs. The actual training process is primarily composed of the following elements:

Group Cohesion The adjustment skills training class is similar to group counseling in that experiencing the freedom to discuss personal data is desirable. This is typically the first stage of the process in the skill training groups. In some content areas such as relaxation skills training, which requires less self-referenced verbalization, group process is initially less important but becomes important when helping clients integrate the relaxation response into their typical behavior.

Rationale The second step of the process is to explain why the skill is necessary for successful adaptation. Clients are taught a method of analyzing their behavior that suggests that problem behaviors result from personal skill deficits and that the remediation of problems and avoidance of further problems depend on learning what they need to do to cope successfully.

Concept Development and Modeling the Skill The third stage of the process is to teach clients functional knowledge about skill development in general, and the what, when, where, and how of this particular skill. An example of functional knowledge in the communications area is that to engage someone in friendly conversation, it is necessary to spend some time listening to what the person is saying. Listening might be broken down into communicating attention, listening to affect, listening to content, and communicating understanding. These subskills may be demonstrated by the trainer and also with various media. The participants also observe the other training group members practice the skill.

Practice, Performance Feedback, and Shaping Clients participate in structured practice which requires them to emit the desired behavior. More difficult responses are composed of combinations of simpler responses. Monitoring and feedback are provided by both the trainer and the peer group. Approximations of the response are reinforced, with the emphasis on positively reinforcing the most correct portion of the attempted response.

Generalizability Structured practice is pursued until the skill is overlearned. This overlearning along with specific activities to enhance transfer of training to other environments are two aspects of this approach which go beyond traditional behavior modification.

Clients are provided assignments for real-life practice. This behavior is critiqued in subsequent group meetings and, where possible, performance feedback is obtained from other persons in the client's environment such as instructors and family members. Every feasible effort is made to ensure that clients receive positive reinforcement for emitting the desired behavior so as to integrate the desired response into their typical behavior. Participants are also taught to provide self-reinforcement for successfully employing the skill in real-life situations.

Management of Training Groups

The training consists of one or two trainers, a training program, and the training context. In most instances it is advisable to have two trainers. When one trainer is directing the action, the other observes the group, helps individuals, serves as a model, and provides feedback to the other trainer. Co-trainers help each other sharpen their skills so as to better model and demonstrate the behavior.

How the trainer is experienced by the group members is important in determining the outcome. The authors' experience parallels the findings of experimental studies of interpersonal attraction and influence. Effective trainers are trustworthy, capable, and attractive (likeable). An effective interpersonal style is one that balances high levels of empathy and assertiveness.

In addition to being proficient in the skill being taught, specific trainer skills are also required. Some of the more important teaching skills are concept development, modeling, and shaping behavior. The trainer facilitates individual self-exploration, problem/goal identification, program development, and self-assessment. The trainer also needs to be effective in group facilitation skills. Training and experience in group counseling or other types of small-group intervention are helpful.

Example of Psychosocial Training

The following example could take place in an evaluation center, a rehabilitation center, a work adjustment facility, or other similar setting. Some professional in the setting assesses the client's personal adjustment skills. The assessor may utilize behavioral observation, paper-and-pencil instruments, interviews, or a range of other techniques and would involve the client to some degree in self-assessment, the extent being dependent on the degree of client-centeredness of the assessor's approach. Which skill dimensions the assessor measures depends on how he or she organizes or conceptualizes healthy behavior and probably to some extent on what training and intervention resources are available.

Suppose that during the assessment process Bill is found to be unable to relax. This skill deficit may be manifested in a number of adjustment difficulties (e.g., insomnia, psychomotor complaints, disturbed interpersonal relationships) and might be diagnosed in as many ways (e.g., anxiety, neurosis, impulsive personality, conversion reaction). If the problem-causing personal skill deficit is the inability to relax, regardless of how or where it is manifested, the therapeutic intervention is to teach Bill relaxation skills.

On the hypothesis that Bill's major skill deficit (i.e., the skill deficit that is or will be the greatest impediment to successful adjustment) is inability to relax, he is placed in a relaxation training group. The group consists of 15 clients, all of whom have varying degrees of relaxation skill deficits, and a trainer who has some level of expertise in relaxation. The process of the training is something like the following:

1. Clients are taught functional knowledge related to relaxation and learning to relax (e.g., why it is important, evaluating one's skill level, different approaches).
2. Clients are then guided through one or more methods of achieving relaxation in a setting and with resources that facilitate relaxation. The clients learn how it feels to relax and one or more ways of achieving it.
3. A good deal of time is then spent on getting *more* relaxed, sooner, with less support. At the end of this phase the clients should be able independently to achieve a deep state of relaxation in less than 2 minutes in a facilitative environment (i.e., quiet, comfortable, with few distractions).
4. The focus of the training then moves to integrating relaxation into their daily lives. First, the clients are influenced to practice regularly in a structured manner. The usual practice scheme is once or twice a day in a quiet place for 15–20 minutes. The frequence and success of individual practice is monitored in the training group, and plans to overcome implementation problems are formulated.
5. Somewhere around this point the functional knowledge related to moment-to-moment use of relaxation skills would be reiterated and expanded. Clients would then be given assignments to relax in nonfacilitative settings (e.g., at work, in the face of conflicts).
6. By this time the trainees know how to achieve deep relaxation in a supportive setting and can apply this response to some degree, or at least not become anxious, in a nonfacilitative setting and are improving. The training ends usually after 20–25 hours.

Throughout the process a number of things occur. A group of unique clients with unique symptoms learn a common thing: what it is like to relax, how to achieve relaxation, and how to respond with less stress in a range of situations.

THE CLIENT ASSESSMENT PROCESS

Client assessment from a skills training perspective emphasizes training clients to engage in self-assessment and requires answering a different question than that asked in traditional approaches to assessment. Rather than merely asking what problems, symptoms, or undesirable outcomes the client has, the following two questions are also asked: a) what concepts and operations could the person employ to optimize self-maintenance and growth? and b) in what order and combination can the person best learn and apply these adaptive skills?

Assessment from the skills training perspective requires instruments and procedures to measure healthy behavior and development, yet most available instruments emphasize problem behavior. Even those instruments based on a positive theory of personality (e.g., that of Maslow) such as the Human Service Scale (Reagles & Butler, 1976) and the Personal Orientation Inventory (Shostrom, 1963) are composed mainly of items that indicate problem behavior.

Hershenson (1977) showed how matrix analysis provides a conceptual tool which incorporates more relational thinking when analyzing human behavior. The content portion of the psychosocial development matrix in Figure 1 draws attention to the relationship between basic behavioral processes and spheres of activity. When the assessment items defining each cell of the matrix are stated in terms of adaptive skills, the identification of a skill deficit is presented as one problem area or goal area among many relatively well developed skills making up the remainder of the matrix. This approach is more likely to increase the client's motivation to engage in improvement programs.

For instance, if the client experiences a traumatic loss of eyesight, one might first examine the perceptual process across all spheres of activity. Given sufficient compensation for this sensory loss, the other basic processes of conceptualizing, feeling, and so forth, may still be intact. Uncompensated perceptual skill deficits in several spheres of activity may be manifested at all levels of action or at one particular level. Suppose that the individual's physical health, self-management, and general life planning behaviors are adequate. The client is also making rapid progress in learning new job skills and activities of daily living skills sufficient to be self-supporting. Yet the individual's interpersonal relationships are deteriorating rapidly. The use of matrix analysis and a taxonomy of essential skills would direct attention to the specific skills that the client needs to develop, or to the deficits for which compensation is required. Examples of such skills may be self-expression, body positioning, recognizing feelings, and other specific skills that would allow the client to respond more empathically when being receptive, and more assertively when being expressive.

In providing rehabilitation services, it may be essential in many instances to start the client assessment process from a problem identification perspective because the client brings this perspective to the situation. In this case, the task is to translate problem statements into skill deficits. The professional facilitates the client self-exploration process until a sufficient amount of information is gathered and organized to answer the question, "For this particular person, what might he or she be doing if he or she didn't have the problem?" This translation process is facilitated by a taxonomy of psychosocial skills or-

Table 2. Five phases of assessment

1. Screening and General Disposition
   a. Specify general type of problem and area of difficulty
   b. Decide what additional assessment information is needed
   c. Use broad band assessment methods such as interview, wide ranging checklists, and inventories
2. Definition of Problem
   a. Assess basic behavioral processes within life domains of interest
   b. Specify behavioral excesses and deficits
3. Specify Skill Deficit and Design the Intervention (Client Goal Setting and Program Development)
   a. Specify desired terminal behavior or environmental event
   b. Use narrow band, high fidelity methods of assessment (e.g., frequency counts)
   c. Establish baseline data
   d. Utilize a prescriptive teaching of systematic training methodology to develop functional concepts and skills
4. Monitoring of Progress
   a. Regularly repeat baseline measures during intervention
   b. Select measures that are relevant to the objectives of intervention
   c. Use criterion-referenced and norm-referenced assessment
5. Follow-up
   a. Are the changes in baseline measures maintained over time after the intervention?
   b. Are changes in baseline measures maintained in situations other than where the intervention occurred?
   c. To what extent did changes in one class of behavior influence changes in a related class of behaviors (generalizability)?

ganized into functional domains of life activity to determine what skill deficits are suggested by the problem enumeration.

A summary of the behavioral assessment process by Crone and Hawkins (1977) was modified and is presented in Table 2. Client assessment is an ongoing process which guides the rehabilitation intervention, provides the client and professional with feedback, and accumulates the essential data for program evaluation.

The data provided by such an assessment process are highly consistent with the mandated requirements of vocational rehabilitation. The particular combination of person variables and situational variables that make the person eligible for rehabilitation services operate to prevent the achievement of a vocational goal. These factors must be identified, a plan of services projected, and evaluation procedures implemented to provide the best chance of the person being able to secure and maintain a satisfactory and satisfying work role in the community. The comprehensive rehabilitation plan which documents and organizes these activities can be written in highly concrete and specific terms, relative to person variables, utilizing the psychosocial skills assessment/training/evaluation process. Identifying psychosocial skills that support the terminal objective (employment) and providing systematic training in these skills (intermediate objectives) along with whatever influence one can muster on situation variables, constitute the most potent intervention.

ASSESSMENT INSTRUMENTS AND PROCEDURES

Several attempts to define and measure essential skills for successful functioning in various domains of life activity have appeared in the literature recently (Akridge, 1979; Goldstein, Gershaw, & Sprafkin, 1976; MacDonald, 1978). For a review of the complex issues involved in this endeavor, the reader is referred to Crone and Hawkins (1977). Some of the assessment instruments and procedures that may be relevant to psychosocial adjustment skills training are reviewed below.

Behavior Rating Scales

Rating scales are useful for guiding and systematizing the observations of clients' behavior by rehabilitation professionals or peers. The Vocational Behavior Checklist (Walls, Zane, & Werner, 1978) and the Independent Living Checklist (Walls, Zane, & Thvedt, 1979) are representative of the more comprehensive taxonomies at the task performance level where behaviors are concrete and specific. The kinds of skills covered, such as counting to 100 or greeting a co-worker, are typical of training objectives of mentally retarded clients. The Scale of Employability produced by the Chicago Jewish Vocational Service and distributed by the Materials Development Center at Stout Vocational Rehabilitation Institute, is similar in focus but includes more complex behaviors, and the format is oriented to assessing typical behavior rather than maximum behavior. Moving to an even more general level of competencies, the Client Outcome Measure (Westerheide & Lenhart, 1973) used by the Arkansas and Oklahoma Vocational Rehabilitation Agencies and the Functional Assessment Profile (Marsh, Konar, Langton, & LaRue, 1980) developed by the Massachusetts Vocational Rehabilitation Agency, rate the client's functioning on a relatively small number of broad dimensions. The Functional Assessment Profile covers interpersonal relationships, communication, self-care, object manipulation, mobility, time management, energy reserves, self-direction, and work.

Self-Report Measures

Although there are inherent limitations to the use of self-report measures, to the extent that the scientific evaluation of rehabilitation interventions which depend solely on such measures is highly suspect, they are useful for assessing change from the client's perspective. They may also provide useful information about how the person conceptualizes self and situation. Advocates of a skills training approach generally take a behavioral perspective in interpreting self-report measures. The person's responses to the individual test items are considered behavioral events in and of themselves and are not interpreted to indicate underlying traits. When responses to items that are highly correlated are summed, such subscores are seen as summary terms to index that subset of behaviors. If the concept of personality is used at all, it is restricted to mean a summary of behavioral trends manifested by the person's response to the environment rather than a set of personal attributes which shape the person's response to the environment.

Self-report instruments that focus on skills or competencies, such as the Wolpe-Lazarus Assertion Scale or the Conflict Resolution Inventory, demonstrate considerably higher correspondence to behavioral observations than do self-report measures of pathology such as anxiety scales and fear inventories (Bellack & Hersen, 1977). The more concrete and specific the behavior referred to by the individual items and the more clearly the situation is specified, the more the measure will correspond to observable behavior. A final point regarding the use of self-report instruments in skills training is the importance of obvious face validity or content validity of the items. Empirically derived scales such as the Minnesota Multiphasic Personality Inventory may be valid and useful for some types of selection problems, but are not very helpful for engaging clients in self-assessment, identifying current skill strengths and deficits, or evaluating skills training interventions.

The Psychosocial Development Matrix Questionnaire (Akridge, 1981) is a self-report inventory of psychosocial adjustment skills based upon the three-dimensional model presented earlier. The person's response to individual items may be summed within the three major competency areas of self-management, interpersonal relations, and life planning. One may also derive subscores by spheres of activity (physical, intrapersonal, etc.) or basic behavioral processes (perceiving, conceptualizing, etc.).

The Personal Skills Self-Assessment Instrument (Means, 1980), on which the taxonomy of psychosocial adjustment skills presented earlier is based, reflects a method of self-assessment that is highly consistent with the philosophical orientation of the model. The questionnaire, which requires clients to rate their level of functioning on 25 behaviorally anchored skill dimensions, serves not only to provide an assessment of client skill strengths and deficits, but also orients the client to the psychosocial skills training model. As a result of having reviewed the behaviors associated with each of the five levels of functioning on each of the 25 skills, the client may be better prepared to set specific behavioral goals and accept specific psychosocial skills training programs which address them.

Behavioral Observation

When behavioral competencies associated with a particular domain of life activity are plotted into hierarchical arrangements to show the relationships between more general competencies and specific behaviors, it is possible to observe whether these specific behaviors occur in appropriate situations. In some instances it is feasible to make these observations in naturalistic settings, and in some instances it is necessary to construct situations such as role play, simulated work settings, and structured small group activity, to elicit the response.

Interview Setting

Clients and potential clients generally first come in contact with the rehabilitation process within an interview setting. To the degree that the rehabilitation professional is sensitive to structuring the physical and interpersonal environment of the interview, it is possible to observe the client's behavior in a rather standard situation. In addition to the professional's informal observations, he or she may carry out more systematic observations. For instance, one might simply count certain classes of behavior. Examples of such potentially useful frequency counts include information seeking, personal pronouns, impersonal pronouns, means/end or cause and effect verbalizations, and goal statements.

Training Context

Training environments provide excellent settings for assessing psychosocial competencies. In addition to observing the individual's skill in performing the prescribed training task, it is also possible to observe how the client manages himself or herself, utilizes learning resources, relates to authority figures and peers, and what meaning the individual attributes to the activity in relation to his or her overall life plan.

Many rehabilitation clients are already involved in vocational training programs or work adjustment programs that provide a context for psychosocial skills assessment. Workshops or seminars organized around basic competencies needed by everyone, such as communication skills or relaxation and stress management, also provide a context for systematic behavior observation.

Self-Observation and Recording

Teaching clients to monitor and record specific behaviors is a useful assessment procedure. It is especially appropriate when working with certain classes of responses such as thoughts, feelings, or images, which cannot be observed directly. It is also a means of modifying behavior, because self-recording of the behavior tends to increase desirable and decrease undesirable behavior. This approach to assessment offers the advantage of high client involvement in the determination of behavior and skill excesses and deficits and also provides practice in the important adjustment skill of self-monitoring. The mere act of systematically observing one's behavior facilitates self-exploration in related areas and is an essential part of self-instruction and self-reinforcement.

SUMMARY

Psychosocial adjustment skills training was presented as a method for influencing the adjustment problems of rehabilitation clients preparing for work. The content, process, and measurement of psychosocial adjustment skills training were examined in reference to their appropriateness to vocational rehabilitation systems. Considerable consistency between the benefits of the psychosocial skill training approach and the mandatory requirements of vocational rehabilitation as well as the historical and current emphasis of the vocational rehabilitation system were identified.

chapter 9
VOCATIONAL PLANNING

Richard T. Roessler

With the current state of the economy restricting the availability of jobs, and with the growing number of severely disabled individuals on their caseloads, rehabilitation counselors must have many skills if they are to guide clients through vocational planning successfully. One aspect of vocational planning emphasizes goal identification, selection of key intermediate objectives and necessary rehabilitation services, placement, and progress monitoring. However, vocational planning encompasses more than conducting vocational counseling with the individual; it also requires the counselor to intervene directly in the work setting on behalf of the client.

Whether they are helping individuals begin (assume) or return to (resume) work, counselors must have an understanding of the problems that impair client efforts to obtain work. Research indicates that success in securing work is affected by job availability, level of job-seeking skills, level of client training and work experience, and disability-related problems. To overcome these problems, the counselor must allot time in vocational planning to direct intervention at the work site through job analysis, modification, and development. Counselors must also provide job-seeking skills training or arrange for the client to receive this training.

Another necessary counselor competency for vocational planning is knowledge of the world of work. Knowledge of work roles helps the counselor develop an appropriate set of questions to guide the evaluation and feasibility determination stage of the rehabilitation process. Providing a foundation for vocational planning with the client, the results of evaluation in the medical, psychological, and vocational areas clarify client suitability for various types of work.

To increase the client's career awareness, vocational counseling relies heavily on both client and counselor discussing the routines, requisites, and rewards of work roles. Because the client must have some appreciation of the relative merits of different jobs, such knowledge is important in the process of selecting a vocational objective.

Knowledge of routines, requisites, and rewards is important information for individuals who are disabled in mid-life, because they must consider the effects of disability on each of these work dimensions.

Vocational counseling with rehabilitation clients, therefore, can be discussed in two broad categories. For example, the counselor may help the client enter the world of work or change careers. This approach to vocational counseling emphasizes a decision-making or problem-solving strategy. Other individuals seek the assistance of a rehabilitation counselor in order to return after illness or injury to a previous job. The focus of this type of vocational counseling is on the way the disability has disrupted the person/job match.

VOCATIONAL PLANNING WITH REHABILITATION CLIENTS

Among social services in the United States, vocational rehabilitation has the primary responsibility for increasing the employment potential of individuals with disabilities. By preparing people with handicaps to fill work roles in society, rehabilitation enables its clients to become taxpaying, productive citizens. Hence, on a cost-benefit basis, the program more than pays for itself. In addition, it provides services that have a direct bearing on increasing the individual's sense of self-worth in a work-oriented culture. Therefore, vocational planning, with its goal of employment of the person with a disability, is an extremely beneficial service provided by vocational rehabilitation.

Vocational planning with rehabilitation clients is a complex and difficult process both because of the type of clients typically involved in rehabilitation services and because of the current state of the economy. For example, in a recent survey of clients receiving placement services from public rehabilitation programs, Vandergoot and Swirsky (1980) found that the clientele had

> ... characteristics typical of a group that would have marginal labor market potential. A great majority of them had a high school education or less, had few skills, had low income levels, were not self-supporting, and had relatively meager work histories. This profile raises the question about the clientele of rehabilitation programs. Do only marginal work force individuals use these services? What do those with greater qualifications do? (p. 153)

Matkin (1980) underscored the difficulties rehabilitation counselors can expect in vocational planning and placement as the effects of the Rehabilitation Act of 1978 are felt. According to Matkin, the cost-benefit ratios of rehabilitation will decrease as counselors increase the number of clients on their caseloads who are less employable, that is, individuals with developmental disabilities. Matkin did not paint a very bright picture: "Rehabilitation counselors will soon be confronted with the situation of an increased caseload, less funding available for service delivery, a greater number of severely handicapped clients without potential employability, and fewer job opportunities for placement" (p. 126). Complicating this somewhat dismal perspective is the fact that the economy has remained in a state of recession for most of the past decade.

Disheartened by this scenario of more difficult clients in an era of fewer jobs and resources, one could question the value of a chapter on vocational planning—what is the point? The point, of course, is that the current challenges require the counselor to be as proficient as possible in vocational planning with rehabilitation clients. This proficiency encompasses a vast array of skills needed by counselors to conduct vocational counseling with clients and to intervene directly in the world of work on behalf of clients.

THE ROLE OF THE COUNSELOR IN VOCATIONAL PLANNING

Clients encounter a number of difficulties in securing and maintaining work. The counselor can only affect these difficulties by job analysis, job modification, and job development. At the same time, counselors are involved in the more traditional process of vocational counseling with their clients. This counseling occurs in a one-to-one relationship and focuses on planning for employment. Once a vocational objective has been selected, client and counselor must specify the vocational rehabilitation services required to prepare the person for the job. The culmination of the vocational planning process is placement and tenure on the job.

It is important to point out that vocational planning with rehabilitation clients may take two forms: helping individuals assume work (initiate a new work role) or helping them resume work (return after disability to a prior work role). Assuming work affects the vocational planning process by placing more emphasis on the procedures of vocational choice and decision making. In helping individuals make vocational choices, the counselor performs the "decision-facilitating function," which enables the client to move through the steps of problem solving (Jaques & Hershenson, 1970). Counselor and client have a mutually agreed-upon objective (to choose a feasible job) and proceed to collect the evaluation and occupational information necessary to identify job alternatives. After selecting an appropriate job goal, client and counselor participate in the development of a rehabilitation program which specifies the steps needed to prepare the individual for work.

To assist the client in resuming work, the counselor adopts less of a vocational choice-making approach and concentrates on determining how disability has disrupted or affected the previous fit between person and job. If the client had a positive work history prior to disability, the counselor can assume that the client held a job that he or she liked and could do (Lofquist & Dawis, 1969). Given the advent of disability, this match between capabilities and job demands and worker needs and job rewards may have been decreased. If the client now desires to return to work, the counselor must help him or her understand how the previous job/person equilibrium has been affected by disability and what can be done to restore the balance. The vocational rehabilitation plan contains the services needed to restore the job/person fit by preparing the person to resume a previous work role.

Integrating individuals with disabilities in the work force may require more than one-to-one vocational planning with the client. Many problems that clients encounter in becoming employed require direct counselor intervention in the work setting. This role of the counselor is a highly significant aspect of vocational planning.

EMPLOYMENT-RELATED PROBLEMS

Several studies have outlined the problems that rehabilitation clients encounter in attempting to fill a work role. Naturally, the type of problems reported depends somewhat on the perspective, that is, whether the counselor or the client is relating the problems. In a recent study (Zadny & James, 1979a), counselors ranked the problems rehabilitation clients have in getting jobs in the following order: 1) job availability (unfavorable market, high unemployment, and lack of suitable jobs), 2) deficient job-seeking skills, 3) poor employer reception of job applicants, 4) lack of client work experience, 5) lack of motivation, and 6) lack of vocational training. From the counselor's point of view, lack of client motivation could be considered almost as important as the lack of available jobs if several related concerns are grouped together (lack of motivation to work and lack of persistence in seeking work).

As Zadny and James (1979a) pointed out, counselors could respond to each of the major problems they perceived rehabilitation clients as experiencing. For example, job development would be one response to the problems of lack of job availability and negative employer attitudes toward the job applicant with a disability. Similarly, job-seeking skills training would remedy deficiencies in clients' abilities to seek and secure work. Finally, more involvement of the client in developing a valued rehabilitation program and vocational objective would improve the level of client motivation to follow the plan.

Before discussing client perspectives on work problems, it is important to reiterate that the counselor is involved in more than vocational counseling when one discusses assuming or resuming work. For example, part of the time that the counselor allots to vocational planning should be devoted to job development and to providing, directly or indirectly, job-seeking skills training for clients. Indeed, Zadny and James (1979b) reported that counselors with superior placement records had a more positive attitude toward and expended more energy in placement. These counselors were more knowledgeable about the world of work, made more employer visits and calls, and devoted more time and travel to placement and job development activities (Zadny & James, 1979b). Therefore, in allocating time to vocational planning, the counselor must consider more activities than direct contact with the client in a vocational counseling relationship.

The counselor's perspective on securing work for rehabilitation clients is, however, only one point of view. Many clients also have considerable experience in seeking work, and their perception of the issues is not entirely congruent with the perspective of rehabilitation counselors (Tichenor, Thomas, & Kravetz, 1975). For example, although counselors do not mention it as a problem, 25% of the clients in one survey said disability was a major problem in securing work (Zadny & James, 1978). They did not mention lack of motivation or lack of confidence as problems; in fact, only 3% of the clients in the survey said that they made no effort to seek a job. As did the counselors, clients in the survey emphasized certain personal characteristics as problems in returning to work; for example, 22% of the clients mentioned either lack of work experience or inadequate vocational training as problems in getting jobs.

Symptomatic possibly of a breakdown in the rehabilitation process for some clients, two-thirds of the clients in a recent survey reported that they located their own jobs (Zadny & James, 1979b). Zadny and James suggested some reasons for this; for example, counselors tended to overlook placement plans, job-seeking skills training, and help with developing job leads in their vocational planning. The finding that the majority of clients find their own jobs provides all the more reason to emphasize certain practical aspects of vocational planning such as job development and job-seeking skills training in addition to the more commonly discussed approaches to vocational choice making and midlife career planning.

VOCATIONAL PLANNING IN REHABILITATION

To assist the client in assuming or resuming work, the rehabilitation counselor must play a number of roles. Initially, the counselor must develop an adequate diagnostic understanding of the client in order to have a proper foundation for vocational planning (Rubin & Roessler, 1978; Roessler & Rubin, 1980). Developing this diagnostic understanding requires answers to questions pertinent to the individual's current and potential physical, psychosocial, educational, vocational, and economic statuses. These information needs for vocational planning can be met through systematic use of the intake interview and medical, psychological, and vocational evaluations.

The purpose of the diagnostic evaluation of the client is to answer questions of feasibility of various types of work responsibilities. To consider feasibility issues, counselor and client must understand how disability and social history factors relate to expectations and rewards of different jobs. Hence, the counselor must have a thorough knowledge of the world of work, which can only be developed by direct contact with employers and tours of their establishments. Combining information about the client with information about the world of work enables the counselor to be a competent diagnostician of client/job fit (Matkin, 1980; Myers, 1980; Roessler & Rubin, 1979).

The importance of the counselor as an occupational information specialist (an information transmitter) has been underscored in many articles (Jaques & Hershenson, 1970; Wise, Charner, & Randour, 1976). Wise, Charner, and Randour viewed knowledge of work routines, requisites, and rewards as an important part of career awareness. It is the counselor's role to convey this information to the client or to help the client secure this information. Knowledge of work routines, requisites, and rewards has a direct effect on the individual's preferences, values, and self-concept regarding different types of work.

In addition to being an occupational information specialist, the counselor must help the client manage the process of assuming or resuming work. Assuming work involves client and counselor in a careful review of evaluation data as it relates to vocational alternatives suggested by the client and counselor. The counselor's main responsibility then is to guide the client through the steps of selecting an alternative and developing a rehabilitation plan. The extent to which the client is involved in and therefore values the plan has a great deal to do with the effort the individual will invest in goal attainment. In cases where the client is contemplating resuming work, the counselor's role is one of helping the client explore the way in which disability affects his or her capability to return to a previous job. Client and counselor must discuss the potential ways in which disability could affect the previous job/person equilibrium. Changes in personal abilities and needs as well as job demands and reinforcers may result from the person's handicapping condition.

ASSUMING A WORK ROLE

When counselors are knowledgeable about the world of work, they can then move into helping the client select a feasible vocation. This decision-making process has been discussed by many authors. Generally, it consists of steps such as specifying the task, gathering data, identifying alternatives, selecting alternatives, and taking action (Thoresen & Ewart, 1976).

Specifying the Task

The task, of course, is the selection of a vocational goal for the rehabilitation plan. In identifying the vocational goal, counselor and client should realize that they have embarked on a task involving exploration of the world of work and of multiple vocational alternatives. These alternatives must be understood in terms of their relationship to specific client aptitudes and interests in order to select one of these alternatives to pursue in a systematic way. This planned pursuit of the vocational objective requires identification and remediation of client job-seeking skills, vocational skills, and work adjustment deficits. It requires that the counselor support the client by developing jobs in the community and by providing the appropriate level of assistance in the placement process, while recognizing that some clients need more help than others (Rubin & Roessler, 1978).

Gathering Data

The vocational selection process also requires counselor and client to devote considerable time to developing the client's career awareness (Wise et al., 1976). To develop career awareness, the individual must consider information pertinent to work routines, requisites, and returns. Work routines (Wise et al., 1976) can be described in terms of content and function. One way to discuss content and function with the client would be to review the Dictionary of Occupational Titles description of the job (Dictionary of Occupational Titles, 1977), focusing specifically on the job functions that an individual must be able to do within the content areas of data, people, and things.

Work requisites refer to those aspects of work which are related to either the work routine or its setting and serve to "constrain the eligibility of an individual to perform some type of work activity" (Wise et al., 1976, p. 49). For example, requisites that the client must be able to meet include proficiency or skill levels (general education and specific vocational skills) and physical conditions of the work (inside, outside, light work, heavy work, etc.). Social requisites limiting the individual's access to work include the supply and demand of individuals with certain types of skills and patterns of discrimination in hiring and advancement practices in the industry.

Incentives for working have been variously referred to as work returns (Wise et al., 1976) and job reinforcers (Dawis & Lofquist, 1976). Satisfactions from work range from concrete examples of extrinsic satisfaction, such as wage and benefit practices, to more subtle forms of intrinsic satisfaction, such as the opportunity to use and improve one's capacities.

Having helped the individual gather data on these work routines, requisites, and returns, the counselor should then encourage the person to explore personal values and preferences regarding them. Expectations of success and failure as a worker are also important parts of this discussion. By promoting exploration of these factors, the counselor involves the client in an important process of viewing self in the role of work. Of course, other issues are important as well at this stage of gathering data. For example, counselor and client must look at the way in which environmental factors will affect the client if he or she moves into a work role. Important considerations include how the family will react, the long-term economic projections for various jobs, and the availability of certain jobs locally (Eigner & Jackson, 1978).

Identifying Alternatives

Identification of alternatives often does not occur as a result of the previous steps of task specification and data collection. Usually, individuals begin the vocational counseling process with some idea of the job they would like to have. They then consider these alternatives as they gather data about themselves and the world of work. However, being involved in this exploration of self and the world of work will also reveal many new alternatives they might wish to pursue.

Research has shown that expressed vocational preference is a good predictor of the type of job an individual takes at a later date. The importance of initial vocational preferences should therefore not be minimized. An even better prediction of the type of work assumed at a later date can be made from estimates of the individual's level of certainty regarding personal desire to pursue a certain vocational goal and the congruence of that goal with existing vocational interests (Barthing & Hood, 1981; Borgen & Seling, 1978; North & Jepsen, 1981). These vocational preferences then become the basis for the next phase, selecting vocational alternatives.

Selecting Alternatives

Selecting a vocational alternative involves counselor and client in making two types of predictions for each job, namely, probability and utility predictions (Thoresen & Ewart, 1976). To make a probability prediction about a job, the individual must understand the educational and vocational requisites of the job. Utility predictions require the individual to know what are the satisfactions and rewards of different jobs (Eigner & Jackson, 1978). In probability predictions, the individual is essentially asking work-requisite questions: "Can I get the job?" and "Can I do the job?" In utility predictions, the individual is inquiring about work rewards: "Would I like the job if I did get it?" A sound vocational decision reflects consideration of both probability and utility predictions. Once individuals have identified a vocational goal which they feel they can do and want to do, they are ready to move to the next phase, taking action.

Taking Action

Taking action is a complex step incorporating several subphases. First, the counselor and client must establish an action plan. As Crites (1976) pointed out, too often in vocational counseling the counselor overlooks the action plan, and the individual is left with only vague notions of how to proceed. Of course, in rehabilitation, a placement plan (Individualized Written Rehabilitation Plan) is required in the case file. This plan specifies the vocational objective, the necessary intermediate objectives (counseling, restoration, training, and placement), the services the client will need to attain the vocational and intermediate objectives, how to acquire those services, and the placement and follow-up responsibilities of client and counselor.

To increase the probability that they will act on their plans, clients need to participate in selecting a desirable vocational objective and developing a vocational plan that helps them meet employment-related problems. If these two prerequisites are met, the individual can initiate the plan, evaluate outcomes of the steps, and recycle, if necessary, to previous stages of the decision-making model. Careful client and counselor monitoring of results provides the only opportunity for determining whether the problem-solving strategies are working. Unfortunately, problem solving, as taught in a controlled situation, often fails outside of the laboratory because no effort is devoted to monitoring contingencies of action (Dixon, Heppner, Petersen, & Ronning, 1979).

Career development considerations are also often omitted from vocational plans (Crites, 1976). In addition to procedures for securing an entry-level position, the plan should include some suggestions for how the individual might secure more responsible and remunerative positions either through job change or advancement in the firm that first employs the individual (Vandergoot & Swirsky, 1980).

RESUMING A WORK ROLE: MID-LIFE CAREER PLANNING

For some individuals, a thorough review of multiple vocational alternatives may be inconsistent with their vocational counseling needs. These individuals may simply wish to return to a previous job which they enjoyed and felt they could do adequately. The issue before them at this stage of their life is to determine how mid-career disability has affected their functioning in and enjoyment of their past work. Counselor and client, therefore, find themselves involved in a process of mid-life career planning which may involve vocational redevelopment if the individual is to return to work. By integrating several vocational counseling theories, McMahon (1979) provided an excellent model of this redevelopment process which is managed by the rehabilitation counselor.

The central dynamic in McMahon's approach is the individual's need to establish or restore balance or equilibrium between person and job. Based on the Minnesota theory of work adjustment (Lofquist & Dawis, 1969), this fit is defined as congruence within a certain critical range of tolerance between worker competencies and job requirements and worker needs and job reinforcers. As Dawis and Lofquist (1976) noted, this range of tolerance represents the extent to which individuals and environment adjust to each other. Furthermore, individuals quite likely differ in the amount of "discorrespondence" they can tolerate.

In discussing discorrespondence, Dawis and Lofquist (1976) speculated that several individual personality variables come into play. For example, flexibility represents the amount of discorrespondence the individual can tolerate before seeking to change some aspect of self or situation. The individual may then seek to re-establish the balance by changing either his or her work personality (reactive approach) or the work environment (active approach). Most individuals utilize both approaches. Dawis and Lofquist (1976) also referred to a dimension of celerity, or the speed with which an individual seeks to restore equilibrium or correspondence.

Restoring correspondence is of particular concern to the individual who has experienced a mid-life disability. Because they may differ in terms of flexibility, active/reactive approach, and the celerity dimension, these individuals will need to begin a process of career development. To facilitate career redevelopment, counselor and client must carefully consider aspects of both person and job which affect the level of correspondence between person and environment. These dimensions include worker competencies and reinforcer preferences (needs) and job demands and work reinforcers, each of which has a subjective and a more reality-oriented or objective dimension.

The crucial significance of these concepts for vocational rehabilitation counseling focuses on the way in which disability "alters the needs or competencies of the individual or the reinforcers of the job in either the subjective or objective values" (McMahon, 1979, p. 40). As McMahon illustrated, disability may have an impact on any one of these aspects of worker/job fit. For example, objective worker needs may be changed as a result of costs of medical treatment and physical restoration, which increase the individual's expenses and therefore the need for compensation. Obviously, the limitations imposed by the disability may disrupt the objective competencies of the individual. Similarly, objective job demands may change as employers, in response to the individual's disability, reduce their demands for previous levels of productivity. Objective job reinforcers may be disrupted by disability, as in the case in which an employer reduces the worker's opportunity for authority for fear that subordinates will object. Changes in subjective worker needs may occur as the individual attempts to adjust to disability. McMahon provided the example of a worker who exaggerated independence or autonomy needs "in order to prove something to others." Succumbing to the effects of disability, the individual may also experience a change in subjective worker competencies, as when the individual underestimates his or her competency to produce at former levels. Disruption of subjective job reinforcers may occur because the worker believes that he or she is being treated differently by others, that is, being isolated and ignored because of disability. Finally, the worker may experience a disruption of subjective job demands. McMahon (1979, p. 43) gave an example of a worker who believed that job demands were being increased to effect termination.

Through a vocational planning process, the rehabilitation counselor can assist the individual in anticipating and overcoming these disruptions. For example, discussing outcomes of the vocational evaluation process may enable the individual to get a more accurate understanding of the way in which the disability has affected worker needs and worker competencies. Occupational information can enable the individual to gain a realistic understanding of job reinforcers and job demands. Personal counseling with the individual can clarify the relationship of this information to subjective perceptions of worker needs and capacities.

The rehabilitation counselor also has many services that enable the individual to increase need fulfillment and personal competencies (McMahon, 1979). For example, assistance with finances or transportation meets certain objective worker needs. Physical restoration, skill and aptitude training, educational training, tools, equipment, and licenses contribute to the development of objective worker competencies. Again, development of objective worker needs and objective worker competencies enables the individual to adapt successfully to the environment.

Counselors should also allocate time to making environmental changes that facilitate the client's vocational redevelopment. For example, counselors can contribute to increasing objective job reinforcers and changing objective job demands through techniques such as employer education, advocacy efforts, job development, job engineering, job restructuring, job modification, and job placement (McMahon, 1979).

Therefore, the key thrust in vocational redevelopment is to examine the way in which disability has disrupted the equilibrium between the individual and the job. In some cases, services directed at one or several of these aspects of the person or job may enable the person to return to a previous job role. In other cases, the disruption will be so severe that the individual must seek new employment. For the latter individuals the previously discussed model of vocational choice making becomes more appropriate. Indeed, McMahon (1979) emphasized that some clients will need to make a new vocational choice, but they can only do so if they understand themselves and the realities of work; these are key components of the redevelopment process also. From this base of understanding, they can move to the process of decision making in which the basic emphasis is on the use of systematic problem-solving techniques (Gatz, Tyler, & Pargament, 1978) involving goal selection, strategy selection (vocational plan), strategy implementation, and strategy evaluation (Dixon, Heppner, Petersen, & Ronning, 1979; Rubinton, 1980).

IMPLICATIONS FOR PRACTICE

1. Because of the depressed state of the economy and the marginal employment potential of some rehabilitation clients, successful outcomes of vocational planning with rehabilitation clients are achieved with some difficulty. Therefore, the rehabilitation counselor needs a model of the vocational planning process to follow.
2. This model of vocational planning should clarify the special counseling needs of the individual beginning work or changing careers as well as the individual resuming work after mid-life disability.
3. Regardless of whether the individual with a disability is beginning or resuming work, he or she must have assistance with some common employment-related problems. These problems require the counselor to move out of the traditional one-to-one vocational counseling relationship and into the role of a change agent.

4. As a change agent, the counselor operates in the environment to develop new jobs and to modify existing jobs. The counselor functions also as a change agent for the person by helping the individual develop job-seeking skills and overcome key work adjustment deficits.
5. At the same time, the counselor has a significant vocational counseling role. Fundamental competencies of this role include the abilities to a) develop therapeutic relationships with clients, b) structure the evaluation process so that it provides adequate information about the client for exploring potential person/job matches, c) understand the world of work so as to convey accurately to the client the routines, requisites, and rewards of work, and d) identify the proper vocational counseling approach to be employed, for example, the decision-making or the vocational redevelopment model.
6. Clients enter the rehabilitation process with one of two basic vocational counseling needs. Some are seeking to begin work or to change careers, and therefore need to explore multiple vocational alternatives in order to select an appropriate vocational goal. Others wish to return to a previous job, and therefore need to explore the effects of a mid-life disability on their current capacity to be satisfied and satisfactory in their past work.
7. To improve the individual's ability to begin work or to enter a new job, the counselor must help him or her develop a vocational plan. However, before they prepare a vocational plan, counselor and client must complete a series of decision-making steps. The client must be committed to returning to work and be willing to participate in the vocational evaluation process. The client must review evaluation and job information in order to arrive at a list of feasible vocational goals. Each job is then considered in terms of a list of important questions: Can I get the job? Can I do the job? Would I like the job? Depending upon the answers to these questions, the individual makes a tentative vocational choice which becomes the basis for the vocational plan. The vocational plan lists the intermediate objectives and rehabilitation services required to achieve the vocational goal.
8. Returning to a previous job after disability presents a different type of vocational counseling task. The issue is not one of what job to pursue but of how disability has affected the previous level of person/job equilibrium. For example, disability-imposed limitations may have affected the individual's actual or perceived capability to satisfy certain job demands. Disability may have affected the person's need for certain types of rewards from work,

and therefore altered the person's extent of job satisfaction. As a result of disability, the worker may be viewed differently by others. Prejudicial thinking on the part of employers and co-workers may lead to subtle changes in work demands or reinforcers, which have a negative effect on the disabled individual. In the vocational redevelopment process, the counselor's task is to help the individual examine how disability, with its effects on personal capabilities, needs, and social stimulus value, has altered the previous job/person equilibrium.

9. Sometimes the results of the vocational redevelopment analysis reveal that the previous job is no longer suitable. In such cases, client and counselor should initiate the decision-making model. Potential jobs should be explored for their feasibility, following the steps of generating alternatives, gathering pertinent data, identifying feasible alternatives, selecting alternatives, and taking action.

10. Whether they are beginning a working career or returning to a previous job, clients require career development assistance from their counselors. Counselors should help individuals create pathways to more responsible and remunerative jobs through constructive job change or through advancement with a single employer. Vocational planning encompasses more than simply helping a person secure an entry-level position.

chapter 10
VOCATIONAL PLACEMENT STRATEGIES

Reed Greenwood

The rehabilitation system in the United States has proven effective in assisting millions of handicapped persons to enter into and maintain themselves in the mainstream of American society. Many of the programs of the state/federal vocational rehabilitation system have been directed toward vocational adjustment and employment. Vocational rehabilitation has been central to the public rehabilitation program, and placement has been a service objective since the inception of the program in the 1920s. Providing placement assistance seems essential in labor markets characterized by continual change and employer resistance to hiring handicapped persons. However, placement has been a service plagued with controversy and frustration.

    The placement literature has often dealt in admonishments about rehabilitation counselor resistance to placement or inactivity in placement, or a repetition of principles seldom subjected to validation (Zadny & James, 1976). Placement services are similar to other rehabilitation services in terms of the state of evolution of programming. Rehabilitation services have moved from beginnings built upon commitment, dedication, and growth, through a great deal of trial and error, to programs bolstered by continuing commitment but with a thirst and search for sound and proven techniques. Since others have provided a review of the past literature and philosophical positions on placement, the intent of this chapter is to concentrate on a discussion of a) the problems handicapped persons experience in securing employment, b) the role of the rehabilitation counselor in placement, and c) rehabilitation programming techniques that may enhance placement success.

JOB PLACEMENT ISSUES

Before any discussion of placement in current practice, it is necessary to review three major issues, the first of which is the definition of placement that is used in this chapter. Placement as a service title has diverse meanings to rehabilitation practitioners. Also, to some rehabilitation clients placement has a negative connotation, since it suggests a paternalistic approach: "We place you in a job." The phrase chosen for use in this chapter is "job acquisition," and the focus is on job acquisition problems and activities. This phrase directs attention to a stage of the rehabilitation process through which the client must proceed to become employed. Also, this expression is compatible with the vocational development stages presented by Hershenson (1974) and others. Specifically, job acquisition involves what Krantz (1971) referred to as critical vocational behaviors, including seeking work frequently enough, demonstrating appropriate interview behaviors, and using helpful job leads.

A second issue related to job acquisition involves the different problems of individuals with emotional, intellectual, and physical disabilities. Often the literature on placement and job acquisition does not provide for real distinctions in recognition of the variability in needs across different disabilities. Common problems exist across these disabilities (e.g., negative employer attitudes, job acquisition skills deficits), but there are also disability-specific problems that should be considered in the development of job acquisition programs. These variations will likely lead to a need for considerably different programming for clients with different disabilities.

The third issue of concern is the state of the art in job placement as reflected in the literature. Zadny and James summarized the situation as follows:

> What we have come to know about placement derives from the experience and reflections of a limited number of practitioners and educators. Their recommendations, though subjectively appealing, are largely unsubstantiated by evidence of comparative effectiveness for different persons and situations. The literature has proliferated unrestrained by burdens of proof and requirements of synthesis. Therefore, placement remains genuinely an art; each practitioner selecting from the many methods known on the basis of preference and taste (Zadny & James, 1976, p. 3).

Given such an assessment from two investigators who have devoted much time and energy to placement research, what is offered in this chapter are what seem to be, in the opinion of the author, reasonable methods for enhancing job acquisition by handicapped persons.

It should be clear from the outset, therefore, that the operational definition of job placement used here, job acquisition, is more narrow than some definitions. Because of the state of the art, the presentation of a number of proven techniques for job acquisition applicable to a wide variety of settings is not possible at this time. Also, the applicability of these techniques should be verified with each major group of handicapped persons, because different problems occur across disability classifications in the area of job acquisition. It is feasible to review the major job acquisition problems of handicapped persons and the more promising rehabilitation techniques and job acquisition programs.

PROBLEMS IN JOB ACQUISITION

Individuals with disabilities are faced with the same complexities and information problems of the job search as are other potential workers in the labor force. The economic system in the United States provides for freedom and flexibility in the way in which the acquisition of jobs takes place. The economic system also presents problems in understanding and predicting future directions in labor market demands, since ours is essentially a free market. These and other factors should be considered in identifying the problems experienced by handicapped persons in relation to job acquisition. However, the areas reviewed in this chapter are limited to a) client motivation for the job search, b) client knowledge and skill deficits related to job acquisition, c) employer receptivity to hiring handicapped persons, and d) economic factors that influence the job acquisition process.

As Zadny and James concluded, the difficulty in understanding placement and job acquisition activities of handicapped persons "appears to lie in the interplay between the complex nature of the placement task and high variability in client need for assistance" (Zadny & James, 1976, p. 2). There are two areas in which client problems have been widely discussed: client motivation and client job search abilities. The assessment of these areas of client functioning has been assigned to the rehabilitation counselor, who applies diagnostic techniques at varying points in the rehabilitation process, including the stage of job acquisition. If the assessment leads to the conclusion that the client will be reluctant to pursue the job search, the problem may be motivational.

The problems associated with disability are frequently variable across individuals, and this is also the case for motivation to seek a job. The subject of motivation has been dealt with in a number of ways, from an analysis of the economic disincentives faced by some clients when returning to work to intrapsychic factors resulting in a lack of motivation. As Vandergoot, Jacobsen, and Worrall (1979) reported, the costs and benefits of working are important in understanding job search behavior. Vandergoot et al. indicated that such factors include the investment in preparation for work, the costs and benefits from working, the costs of the job search, and imperfect and incomplete knowledge of the labor market. It is important to understand the costs to the individual in terms of security, income maintenance, medical services, food stamps, and other government or charity support in taking a job. The anxiety aroused by potential loss of such benefits can be considerable.

Hershenson (1979) suggested that work motivation is a component of the work personality and that persons who experience problems in motivation may require value clarification counseling to resolve such problems prior to the job search. Client motivation to persevere in the job search is affected by the potential loss of benefits and also the likely fear of rejection. Motivation as a client problem has been one of the major problems perceived by rehabilitation counselors in the delivery of rehabilitation services (Thoreson, Smits, Butler, & Wright, 1968). Also, motivation was one of the factors cited in the Comprehensive Needs Study, a major national research investigation of persons served by vocational rehabilitation agencies.

> Some studies of unemployment indicate that motivation appears extremely important in determining what a person is able to do economically. This observation is even more applicable to the severely handicapped who are confronted with severe psychological barriers to performance. However, although many of these individuals and their families probably have developed negative attitudes about the prospects of becoming employed and about their capabilities, it does not necessarily reflect a lack of interest in becoming employed (Urban Institute, 1975, p. 328).

Therefore, the importance of motivation to seek employment should not be minimized in understanding the behavior of the client who has reached this stage of the rehabilitation process. The lack of active, job-seeking behavior may be quite understandable in the face of the negative reactions anticipated by the person and the possible problems presented by the loss of financial security if government benefits are terminated. As Safilios-Rothschild (1970) suggested, although the meaning of work varies from person to person, occupational categories and social class play significant roles. For workers who have stable, professional employment, a disability may not be as problematic as for workers who have unskilled or semiskilled jobs frequently interrupted by periods of unemployment. For the latter individuals, particularly those who do not see work as central to their lives except for income, the ability to sustain themselves securely through government disability assistance may be the most stable experience of their lives.

Although rehabilitation services are able to provide substantial gains through improved preparation for work roles, clients often complete vocational preparation services with limited knowledge and skills related to job acquisition. This problem is not unique to this population, as demonstrated by the fact that many colleges and universities have found a need for career planning and placement services and provide assistance in areas such as resume preparation and interviewing. Clarcq (1973), reporting on the experience of the National Technical Institute for the Deaf, revealed that many deaf students have limited knowledge and abilities essential for the job search. Similar findings are reported in the Institute on Rehabilitation Issues publication on placement (Rehabilitation Services Administration, 1975). Therefore, it would not be unusual to expect the rehabilitation client to experience problems due to a lack of job search skills.

In addition to concerns about motivation and job search knowledge and abilities, severely handicapped persons may also require modifications through assistive devices and work site engineering. Although this may have been attended to in the vocational preparation phase of the rehabilitation process, such modifications have to be dealt with when faced with the realistic demands of the employment setting. In addition to basic needs such as transportation, barrier-free housing, and work settings, the handicapped person may not have the physical ability to perform the job tasks without assistance. Human and work site engineering represent technical aspects of preparation for and adjustment to work and will gain more importance as more severely handicapped persons are served by rehabilitation programs. Mallik (1979) reported on breakthrough innovations in this area developed through a comprehensive job development laboratory.

As Vandergoot and Worrall (1979) indicated, the demand for labor in the economy is one of the aspects of job acquisition that must be taken into account in understanding the experience of the handicapped person in the labor market. Although there is limited evidence to support the thesis, it is generally assumed that high rates of unemployment affect handicapped persons more adversely than nonhandicapped persons. In reviewing the literature on employer attitudes toward employment of handicapped persons, the Urban Institute (1975, p. 324) concluded that a large proportion of employers do not report favorable attitudes toward employment of handicapped persons, and that these attitudes are "in large part based on nonrational, negative feelings—prejudice in other words—rather than on realistic fears of low productivity, high absenteeism, and high insurance rates." Additionally, the receptivity of employers toward hiring handicapped persons may be no more favorable than that of co-workers and labor unions. The requirements for job modification or bypassing seniority systems to secure a job for a handicapped person may run head-on into the opposition of the work force.

The demand for handicapped persons by the labor market is another factor of importance for the job acquisition process. Although conclusive research evidence is not available, two studies (Tausig, 1972; Wolkowitz, 1973) reported demand for handicapped workers to be less than for workers in general, and that handicapped workers participate chiefly in the secondary labor market, which is characterized by lower wages, less job security, and less full-time employment.

Although the literature and reported experiences of handicapped persons in the job search process are not so conclusive that firm generalizations can be made, the picture that develops shows that handicapped persons are likely to experience job acquisition problems in the areas of motivation for the job search, limited knowledge and skills in executing the job search process, and limited abilities without assistive devices to execute the tasks required of the job. This is in addition to the transportation, housing, and other needs required to sustain employment. Also, there is likely to be less demand for the services of handicapped persons from the labor market, and when available, the demand will likely be for the inferior jobs. This demand is not only affected by the general labor market conditions, but also by unfavorable attitudes on the part of employers and potential coworkers. These problems are some of the job acquisition difficulties faced by handicapped persons and by those rehabilitation practitioners charged with direct client services. One of these practitioners is the rehabilitation counselor, who is usually considered as the practitioner most concerned with job acquisition.

JOB ACQUISITION AND THE REHABILITATION COUNSELOR

Given the problems outlined in the preceding section, assistance in job acquisition is likely to be essential to meet the needs of many handicapped persons. As Zadny and James (1976) indicated, such assistance exists on a continuum from no assistance required to extensive assistance. Therefore, program interventions will also need to vary considerably. The purpose of this review is to address those interventions for clients who need assistance from the perspective of the rehabilitation counselor.

The counselor is the practitioner usually charged with the responsibility of assisting the client in job acquisition, although it is actually an agency responsibility. The work of the counselor begins with an analysis of readiness for employment leading to the provision of or arrangement for services where problems or limitations exist. The method most favored by the present author is the process of co-management (Wright, 1960), which is consistent with efforts to consider the client an equal partner in the rehabilitation process. The rehabilitation counselor should assist the client in an analysis of job acquisition requirements, and client and labor market problems should guide the analysis, with major questions such as the following directing the counseling process: a) What are the client's concerns in the job search? b) What knowledge and abilities does the client possess in the job search? c) Is the client equipped to deal with employer resistance? d) What is the experience the client will likely encounter in contacting and interviewing employers? e) Are there human or site engineering requirements necessary for employment?

The rehabilitation counselor's first activity, therefore, in regard to job acquisition is to apply diagnostic skills in determining the client's readiness to initiate and conduct the job search. The next step is to analyze the services needed to address problems or limitations. The hesitancy of many rehabilitation counselors to provide such direct services in job acquisition has been documented through research studies on counselor role and functions, which consistently reveal that rehabilitation counselors devote little time directly to placement. No doubt the vocational rehabilitation counselor should have considerable expertise in the job acquisition process. However, the counselor most surely has a number of limitations also. The ability of the counselor to intervene directly in the labor market, by performing such tasks as job analysis, public relations, and job development, is limited usually to a segment of one course in graduate school or to in-service training courses which introduce the concepts but usually do not provide the practical experience necessary to fully develop placement skills. Faced with the requirements for success in this area, most counselors not surprisingly spend little time on placement through direct intervention.

The counselor should be active in the job acquisition process within the general counseling role, with the desires and abilities of the client to conduct the job search process a paramount concern. The counselor should be able to assist the client in answering significant questions regarding job acquisition and about local labor market conditions. Also, the counselor should be able to refer the client to or arrange for additional services to provide for remediation of knowledge or skills limitations. Above all, the counselor should maintain a proactive, supportive role with the client during the job search, with periodic conferences to assess progress.

Much of the placement literature is directed toward the involvement of rehabilitation professionals, particularly the counselor, directly with employers on behalf of specific clients. Such direct intervention must be based on the counselor's assessment of the readiness and ability of the client to seek employment and to meet the problems encountered in the labor market. When is such direct intervention required? Some type of direct intervention with the employer may be required if the assessment conducted jointly by the counselor and client reveals such findings as the following: a) a disability severe enough to raise substantial doubt regarding client employability in the mind of the employer; b) a disability that in and of itself creates problems in seeking and interviewing for a job (e.g., some persons with a history of emotional disturbance); c) a requirement for engineering adaptations in order to perform work tasks; d) severely limited work skills on the part of the client; and e) extremely limited work experience or limited experience in interpersonal interaction on the part of the client.

Although there are other circumstances where assistance in job acquisition may be required, these are situations where the counselor should carefully analyze the abilities of the client to conduct the job search. It should be emphasized that such intervention may also have negative consequences by creating doubts in the employer's mind about the abilities of a client who does not seek his or her own job. In such a situation the employer should be informed about the need for assistance and the presentation of information about client skills to offset any possible doubts.

When direct intervention is required, the counselor should have access to specialized assistance to help in the job acquisition process. This assistance can usually be provided by placement specialists skilled in job development, job analysis, employer relations, and rehabilitation engineering. The rehabilitation counselor is best equipped to meet the counseling and case management needs of the client and can work with a placement specialist in accomplishing the difficult tasks associated with direct placement intervention. Thus, the rehabilitation counselor should provide counseling services during the job acquisition process and should be held accountable for the process in relation to overall case management. However, the counselor should not have the responsibility for interventions that call for abilities beyond the skills of most counselors. Placement intervention is an area calling for advanced specialty skills, and placement specialists should be provided by rehabilitation programs to provide this vital service.

REHABILITATION PROGRAMMING FOR JOB ACQUISITION

The rehabilitation agency should address a variety of programming techniques when developing a job acquisition program, particularly if direct placement interventions with employers are to be conducted. In addition to the assistance within the competencies of the counselor, a number of other programming techniques in this area deserve attention. Media and public information campaigns, such as those conducted by the President's Committee on Employment of the Handicapped, are examples of activities used to encourage employers to be more open to the handicapped person as a candidate for employment. Although such campaigns do not seem to have produced significant results (Urban Institute, 1975), they probably contribute to the total rehabilitation and employment effort. Programming has also been developed to provide client assistance in motivation and job seeking, most notably job-seeking skills programs and job-finding clubs. Moving from the client focus to the employer, other programming techniques such as job analysis and modification, job development, concentrated statewide placement systems, and cooperative rehabilitation and employer projects are being used with increasing success.

If the client is limited in the knowledge and skills essential for job acquisition, specific skills training may be required. For some clients the counselor may be able to deal with this problem through role playing and directed search of labor market information sources and related job acquisition information. (This assumes that the counselor can devote the time and effort required for this activity.) In other cases, the counselor and client may identify other needs requiring systematic and formalized training such as that offered through job-seeking skills training. Also, the counselor may refer the client to a job-finding club. In each situation, the client is involved in a program to develop job-seeking skills, with motivation for the job search as a secondary emphasis.

One of the best known job-seeking programs was developed at the Minneapolis Rehabilitation Center (Anderson, 1968). The Minneapolis program is similar to others in basic format, with training provided in a) identifying personal job-related assets, b) presenting assets in an effective manner, c) handling questions about disability or past personal problems, d) accessing helpful labor market information, e) approaching employers for interviews, f) completing applications, g) interviewing, and h) grooming and attire. The more successful programs have used extensive role playing and videotaping for feedback and criticism. Research has shown these programs to have positive effects on job acquisition rates of both disadvantaged and handicapped persons (Anderson, 1968; McClure, 1972; Pumo, Sehl, & Cogan, 1966). Job-seeking skills training has become accepted in a number of rehabilitation facilities and agencies and is now often used prior to the completion of the vocational preparation process.

The job-finding club was developed to address both the motivational and skills deficits of job-seekers. Reports of the success of this approach by Azrin, Flores, and Kaplan (1977) indicate that serious consideration should be given to its use with handicapped persons who are experiencing difficulties in job acquisition. The job-finding club combines training in job-seeking skills with other features similar to group counseling. During the process of the client's participation in the club, counseling is provided in combination with a buddy system and family involvement. The focus of the entire process is a full-time job search. Participants are encouraged to expand their job options and attend to personal attributes related to their attractiveness as potential employees. According to Azrin and Philip (1979, p. 144), the job club method can best be described as "an intensive behavioral counseling program based on the view of job finding as involving interpersonal skills, a social information network, motivational factors and the obvious need for job skills." The results of research by these authors with disadvantaged and disabled persons who were selected on the basis of their desire for a full-time job, attendance at two or more club sessions, and a clear job-finding problem, revealed that 95% of the participants obtained jobs, whereas only 28% of a comparison group did so. Also, the median time to obtain a job through the club was 10 days. These results are quite dramatic, and the authors guard against overgeneralization. However, considering the state of the art, this is a technique that should be helpful for rehabilitation clients who are ready to initiate the job search or who have had difficulty in job acquisition.

Direct intervention with employers through job development is frequently proposed as a technique for dealing with employer resistance. Job development requires both the ability to convince the employer of the benefits to be derived from employing rehabilitation clients and the technical skills to analyze the work setting and understand the employer's operation and concerns. In educating employers about the abilities and needs of rehabilitation clients, the job developer must have knowledge about the client as well as about job analysis, human and work site engineering, and business operations. Rehabilitation counselors, for example, are traditionally trained as counselors first, with an emphasis on counseling skills rather than persuasiveness skills, yet the latter is a critical component of job development. Also, job developers should have substantial knowledge of business operations such as management and economics to understand and work within the private sector. In examining the most effective method of job development and the history of rehabilitation counselor involvement in such activities, a major emphasis should be placed on job development through the use of placement specialists working with rehabilitation counselors. Such placement specialists are now being trained at the graduate level in several universities, and others have been prepared through placement institutes such as the one at Southern Illinois University.

The placement specialist should be well trained in job analysis techniques. Job analysis involves the ability to identify the functions and tasks of a job and the modifications required for specific rehabilitation clients. Techniques from industrial engineering have been applied to human and work site engineering problems to make job performance possible for rehabilitation clients. As defined by Engelkes (1979, p. 130), job analysis is an "organized, intensive, and direct method of obtaining the pertinent facts about jobs." Engelkes identified the basic components of job analysis as a thorough description of the job, job tasks, and requirements made upon the worker. Although this sounds simple in concept, such analyses involve both the study of physical performance factors and equipment as well as interpersonal and emotional requirements. In the opinion of the present author, the specialized skills required for job analysis require extensive training beyond that provided for most rehabilitation counselors.

Job analysis, when performed by a skilled placement specialist, contributes to the client's and the counselor's understanding of the requirements of a job. On a general level, job analysis data are also available from the *Dictionary of Occupational Titles,* published periodically by the U.S. Department of Labor. The placement specialist can provide job analysis information to a number of counselors, who can use the information in planning with clients.

In addition to the use of specific programming techniques such as job development, some rehabilitation agencies have recognized the problems of job acquisition and have developed concentrated placement programs. These agencies are moving toward systematic, agency-wide placement services to improve the job acquisition rates of their clients. Other programs such as Projects with Industry have been initiated to develop a partnership relationship between rehabilitation agencies and employers.

Molinaro (1977) described a placement system being used in the Michigan Division of Vocational Rehabilitation. This system includes the following components: a) an account system in which counselors and placement specialists develop relationships with large employers much as sales personnel develop sales accounts; b) a skill bank registry of job-ready clients; c) a job bank of openings throughout the state; d) job-seeking skills clinics and job-finding clubs; e) staff development training and direct joint efforts by placement specialists and counselors;

f) labor market projections; g) sheltered-shop placements to develop competitive work skills; h) group vocational counseling; and i) employer services in areas such as worker compensation, affirmative action, awareness training, selective placement, and troubled employee assistance. Molinaro reviewed the problems and successes of this program, although few data have been made available on the system. However, the fact that the agency has a systematic, concentrated approach to the problems of job acquisition, with a strong emphasis on employer relations and job acquisition skills training, reveals a commitment to overcoming major job acquisition problems encountered by handicapped persons.

Projects with Industry is another innovation directed toward job acquisition. Puleo and Davis (1976) described this program as an initiative to establish a liaison between the employer and the rehabilitation program, with dual and coequal responsibility in the provision of services leading to employment. Client selection, training, and employment are conducted jointly. Morgan and Owens (1979) reported on two such projects operated by the Vocational Guidance and Rehabilitation Service of Cleveland, Ohio, and the Arkansas Enterprises for the Blind in Little Rock, Arkansas. The Cleveland program includes the use of trial employment of a group of rehabilitation clients, with a rehabilitation counselor assigned on site to assist with client and employer adjustment. At the end of the trial, clients are either employed at the site or referred to another opportunity. The Little Rock project involves a partnership between a facility serving blind clients and the federal government and seeks to prepare information specialists for a variety of agencies including the Internal Revenue Service and the Civil Service Commission. According to the reports on both programs, each has been successful in preparing persons for employment and in job acquisition at the completion of the program. Although these projects include more than job acquisition activities, the linkage between rehabilitation and employers in attacking the job acquisition problems of handicapped persons offers a promising vehicle for future experimentation.

The rehabilitation programming techniques discussed here are directed toward the development of a favorable employment climate for the rehabilitation client and are critical to meeting the employment needs and problems of this population. Improvement of the employment climate requires an active program involving rehabilitation professionals and handicapped persons. Rehabilitation specialists who can work directly with employers through job development are a significant part of this effort. The ability of specialists to conduct job development, job analyses, and job modification is critical to improved job acquisition, particularly for the severely handicapped client. Programs like the one developed in Michigan call for the use of job development specialists working on a team with rehabilitation counselors and other agency staff. Continuing to place the placement task in the hands of rehabilitation counselors while giving them little assistance is not accomplishing much to remedy the extensive problems rehabilitation clients experience in the labor market. It is refreshing to see a statewide effort toward this problem with participation at all levels of program operation.

Also, projects in which employers and rehabilitation programs jointly prepare clients for employment should be studied carefully for application on a broader basis. This represents a departure from the tradition of vocational preparation for a variety of jobs followed by placement in an entry job. However, the collaborative effort between employers and rehabilitation programs to address the employment problems of rehabilitation clients is a major step in the resolution of the problem of employer receptivity.

SUMMARY AND IMPLICATIONS

This has been a brief review of some of the job acquisition problems experienced by handicapped persons and rehabilitation programming techniques for remediation of these problems. The employment problems should be viewed from the perspective of job acquisition being a stage in the rehabilitation process, rather than as placement problems. This provides a guide for rehabilitation practitioners and administrators to understand the client within the context of rehabilitation services and the labor market environment. Job acquisition calls for a variety of abilities which are likely to be deficient in both handicapped and nonhandicapped persons. However, the labor market provides more limited opportunities for handicapped persons and offers considerably less receptivity to their entry into the work force.

We have learned little about the effectiveness of rehabilitation programs designed to address job acquisition problems. Placement as a service has been investigated through a limited number of studies, and little advancement seems to have been made in this area during the history of vocational rehabilitation. However, there now appears to be a concern across the system for controlled studies as well as for concentrated rehabilitation program development in the area of job acquisition.

Some of the lessons learned along the way have been reviewed and discussed in this chapter. The significance of job acquisition becomes even more apparent during stressful economic circumstances.

This situation calls for heightened attention to the employment problems of handicapped persons and also to the use of the best rehabilitation technology available to remedy the problems. The major implications for consideration at this time appear to be as follows:

1. Many rehabilitation clients face problems in job acquisition, both in terms of personal characteristics involving motivation to seek employment, ability deficits in job-seeking skills, and personal financial disincentives, as well as environmental problems such as employer resistance and limited labor market demand.
2. Although rehabilitation counselors have been charged with placement, they have not devoted much time to this area and often are not skilled in the techniques required to intervene directly on behalf of clients.
3. Placement specialists can fill the void in the placement area in part and should be used on a more extensive basis operating as a team with the rehabilitation counselor. Such specialists can provide expertise in such areas as job analysis, job development, and rehabilitation engineering.
4. Job-seeking skills training and job-finding clubs have been proven effective for a variety of persons and should be made available to clients with deficits in these areas.
5. Job acquisition should be viewed as a rehabilitation agency responsibility with agency-wide emphasis, services, and programs.
6. Continued efforts to link employers and rehabilitation programs such as Projects with Industry should be undertaken to overcome many of the environmental problems experienced by handicapped persons, including employer resistance.

chapter 11
EMPLOYMENT DECISIONS REGARDING HANDICAPPED PERSONS

Gerald L. Rose

Employment decisions based upon physical or mental handicaps unrelated to job performance are economically wasteful (Becker, 1971). They also discourage the handicapped from disclosing their condition and from seeking training or employment, even though data frequently show them to be at least as effective as normal workers in most jobs (Bressler & Lacy, 1980; Pennsylvania State Bureau of Rehabilitation, 1955). Public recognition of these considerations resulted in the Vocational Rehabilitation Act of 1973 and at least 20 state laws prohibiting discrimination against the handicapped in employment decisions (Schlei & Grossman, 1976).

The Vocational Rehabilitation Act of 1973 defines the handicapped person as any individual who has a disabling physical or mental condition, or a history of such a condition, or who is perceived or regarded as impaired. Under amendments to the Act passed in 1978, qualified handicapped are defined as those who could perform a job with no more than reasonable accommodations by the employer. Under these definitions, estimates of the number of handicapped range from 15 to 65 million members of the labor force.

Because of the vagueness of the definitions of handicap in the federal law, and the limited progress made under both the federal and the state laws, many of the handicapped do not currently enjoy the degree of protection from discrimination that has been extended to the aged, minorities, and women.

However, recent legal trends may accelerate employment opportunities for the handicapped. The criteria that have been applied to employment testing are increasingly being extended to all employment decision-making systems. Thus, interviewers or evaluators whose judgments adversely affect a disproportionate number of society's outgroup members (e.g., aged, black, female, and handicapped persons) may create legal risks for their employer (Schlei & Grossman, 1976; Latham & Wexley, 1981). The sources of adverse and unequal treatment of outgroup members are frequently subtle and unknown to the evaluator or to the employer (Cohen & Bunker, 1975). There is good reason to believe that those who discriminate, those who are the victims of discrimination, and those who provide rehabilitation aid do not accurately comprehend the number or nature of the causes of discriminatory judgments (e.g., Dawes, 1979; Slovic, Fischhoff, & Lichtenstein, 1977; Einhorn & Hogarth, 1981).

Hence, following Mayfield's (1964) perspectives, experiments to identify causes of discrimination against the handicapped have begun in very recent years. Nonexperimental methods were rejected because of their inability to confirm causal linkages between variables (Campbell & Stanley, 1966) and because of their reliance on self-report data. Appropriately, because a) employers are relying increasingly on interviews (Bureau of National Affairs, 1976), and b) interviews are notoriously unreliable evaluation mechanisms (Guion, 1976), most research focuses on interviewer decisions rather than on the decisions produced by all the other components of a selection system. This chapter describes the major research findings and their implications for employment practices by handicapped persons, employers, and rehabilitation agencies.

POTENTIAL CAUSES OF DISCRIMINATION AGAINST HANDICAPPED PERSONS

Although negative stereotypes of handicapped persons are often observed (Green, Kappes, & Parish, 1979) in other contexts, in employment settings there is no compelling basis for expecting that handicapped applicants will always experience unfavorable treatment. Instead, the degree of discrimination will probably depend on an interaction between handicap status and other variables (Rose & Brief, 1979).

Four classes of variables may be related to the propensity to discriminate. These are a) the nature of the handicap, b) other personal attributes of the applicant or worker, c) the nature of the job(s) or occupation(s) being considered, and d) the characteristics of the potential employing organization, particularly the characteristics of the hiring and assessment procedures used by the organization.

Handicaps can be characterized in several ways: on the basis of their source (e.g., disease versus accident), their visibility, their present state (active or under remission), their frequency and/or duration, and their effects on various criteria of job performance in different jobs. Some dimensions are probably more important than others. For example, visibility is probably a more potent basis for discrimination than source (because of visibility's immediate impact on the interviewer, and because of the interviewer's concern for the reactions of co-workers, customers, and others, if the applicant is hired). It is also likely that the current status of the handicap is more important than the frequency of remission, and so on. Comments and data from interviewers, rehabilitation specialists, and the handicapped could provide useful research priorities for these dimensions (Newman & Krzystofiak, 1979).

Research on sex discrimination suggests that other personal qualities of the applicant may interact with handicap to affect an employer's willingness to hire the applicant (e.g., Rosen & Jerdee, 1974a,b). For example, an employer who would normally refuse to hire a paraplegic as a salesperson might do so given evidence of outstanding past educational or job performance by the applicant. It seems likely that the degree of discrimination would also be affected by the applicant's age, race, sex, work history, intelligence, motivation, and similar personal variables interacting with the disability dimensions discussed in the preceding paragraph.

The job factors that seem to be most relevant are degree of supervisory responsibility, degree of interaction with co-workers, degree of contact with the public, amount and type of physical competence required, amount and type of mental abilities needed, job status, and relationship of immediate job to subsequent jobs within or outside the organization (career path). These job characteristics probably interact with the organizational characteristics in the next paragraph to affect personnel evaluations (Landy & Farr, 1980).

Many organizational variables have been related to job performance and satisfaction for nonhandicapped employees. However, only a few organizational factors may interact with handicap. Organizational size is one possibility. Large firms may be more frequent targets of government enforcement agencies and of interest groups advocating handicap causes. Large organizations may also find it profitable to conduct selection research aimed at identifying hiring and promotion criteria that are not related to job performance. Thus, for several reasons it might be expected that small firms would discriminate against the handicapped more than large ones. Similarly, organizational stability, rate of growth, technological sophistication, age, and degree of bureaucratization may affect the amount of discrimination. Already, some organizational policies and practices are known to affect personnel decisions in unplanned ways (cf. Bolster & Springbett, 1961;

Carlson, 1967; Hakel, Ohnesorge, & Dunnette, 1970; Hollman, 1972; London & Hakel, 1974; Miller & Rowe, 1967; Webster, 1964).

The relative importance of each of these variables, and of their interactive or joint effects, has not yet been clearly established by researchers. Survey research has been useful for identifying potentially important variables and relationships (e.g., Florian, 1978), but efficient remedial programs require more precise information. For example, if the appearance of a worker is affected by some handicaps, it is vital to know which performance criteria, which occupations, and which organizational characteristics induce the most serious barriers to those whose handicaps are readily observed.

Explicit evidence regarding the importance of various factors and the potential value of alternative remedies can only be generated by experimental studies. Although direct experimental evidence needs to be extended, it already provides a basis for remedial policies and programs. The next three sections summarize the implications of the most relevant research.

GENERAL RESULTS FROM STUDIES OF HANDICAPPED PERSONS

Not surprisingly, results have been fragmented. The most frequent finding is that evaluators do *not* discriminate. This result was reported at least 15 times in the studies that directly compared nonhandicapped and handicapped persons. No significant differences were found in evaluations with respect to expected job performance (Hastorf, Northcraft, & Picciotto, 1979; Krefting & Brief, 1976; Rose & Brief, 1979), probable absenteeism or tardiness (Krefting & Brief, 1976), ability to benefit from training (Rose & Brief, 1979), skill as an interviewee, recommendations to hire (Stone & Sawatzki, 1980), or seven of nine semantic differential items (Hastorf, Wildfogel, & Cassman, 1979). Some studies have reported no discrimination in specific contexts and evaluations even when it was reported in other parts of the same study. For example, no discrimination was reported in evaluations of salary and hiring propensities (Rose & Brief, 1979; Stone & Sawatzki, 1980), perceived job qualifications (Krefting & Brief, 1976; Johnson & Heal, 1976), expected effort (Hastorf, Wildfogel, & Cassman, 1979; Rose & Brief, 1979), promotion prospects (Krefting & Brief, 1976; Rose & Brief, 1979), anticipations of health problems affecting sick leave (Krefting & Brief, 1976; Rose & Brief, 1979), and expected interpersonal relationships with clients and customers (Rose & Brief, 1979).

Discrimination against handicapped persons was the second most frequent result. Discrimination was reported in a total of eight evaluations. Four were found only in limited circumstances: promotion prospects, health prospects (Krefting & Brief, 1976), hiring recommendations (Johnson & Heal, 1976), and salary (epileptic and nonhandicapped applicants received significantly higher salary recommendations than did amputees in Rose and Brief's 1979 study). The interviewer's comfort (Hastorf, Wildfogel, & Cassman, 1979) and the interviewee's number of offers (Johnson & Heal, 1976) and opportunity to interact with others (Snyder, Kleck, Strenta, & Mentzer, 1979) were higher with nonhandicapped than with handicapped applicants.

Reverse discrimination favoring handicapped persons was rarely observed. Evaluations favoring handicapped persons included job qualifications (Johnson & Heal, 1976), feedback on past performance (Hastorf, Northcraft, & Picciotto, 1979), and probable tenure (Krefting & Brief, 1976). Three additional evaluations also favored handicapped persons in specific settings: motivation (Krefting & Brief, 1976), ability to work well with co-workers, and ability to deal effectively with customers and clients (Rose & Brief, 1979).

It is important to note that in both studies with more than one kind of handicapped applicant (Rose & Brief, 1979; Stone & Sawatzki, 1980), significant differences in evaluations between nonhandicapped applicants and one kind of handicap were not observed when the other kind of handicap was considered. Furthermore, both studies found that differences that were significant for one evaluation (e.g., hiring recommendation) usually did not generalize to another evaluation (e.g., skill of interviewee in the interview). Interaction effects were reported in every study that examined two or more independent variables even though the number and nature of possible interactions were very limited because of the extensive use of designs involving no more than three independent variables, most of which had only two levels. The frequent interactions indicate that discrimination tends to hinge on complex combinations of factors, making generalizations risky.

Despite these problems, the research results are provocative. The following two sets of propositions are drawn from experimental studies of the effects of handicap and related characteristics in the interview decision processes.

PROPOSITIONS BASED ON SPECIFIC EXPERIMENTAL RESULTS

Several of the following conclusions may receive additional support as more results become available. On the basis of available studies, and ignoring their limitations, the following propositions can be advanced.

    1. Handicapped applicants who have work experience will be more optimistic about their prospects than nonhandicapped or inexperienced handicapped applicants. Hastorf, Northcraft, and Picciotto (1979) reported that low performing handicapped workers received more favorable task feedback than did comparably performing nonhandicapped workers. If this tendency to overstate the past performance of handicapped employees is pervasive, then experienced handicapped applicants should expect more favorable consideration from subsequent potential employers than do inexperienced handicapped applicants who have not received the inflated feedback. If the favorable consideration is not forthcoming, the experienced handicapped worker may falsely blame the potential employer rather than past leniency. Bitterness and cynicism about employment opportunities and relationships may also evolve from excessive expectations based on past leniency.

2. Interviewers will receive more favorable recommendations for handicapped than for nonhandicapped applicants with comparable previous employment records. This proposition is also consistent with the findings of Hastorf, Northcraft, and Picciotto (1979). It may also be a basis for "reverse discrimination" in a limited form.

3. Handicapped applicants will be less optimistic about their prospects than nonhandicapped applicants. Johnson and Heal (1976) discovered that, even though interviewers evaluated their qualifications more favorably than those of comparable nonhandicapped applicants, handicapped workers who relied on private placement agencies received significantly less favorable forecasts regarding their employment prospects than did comparable nonhandicapped workers. If potential employers and public employment agencies exhibit the same tendency, both experienced and inexperienced handicapped applicants would anticipate less success than nonhandicapped applicants, the difference being largest for inexperienced handicapped applicants (because of proposition 1).

Also due to the combined effects of the first two propositions, it might be anticipated that experienced handicapped applicants would be more confused about their prospects with an employer than would either inexperienced handicapped or nonhandicapped applicants. Conceivably the feeling of experienced handicapped applicants will be one of tension or anger rather than confusion, depending how long they have experienced the conflicting signals regarding their employability.

If, as has been suggested (Hastorf, Wildfogel, & Cassman, 1979), the presence of handicapped applicants causes discomfort for interviewers, the confusion, tension, or anger felt by an experienced handicapped applicant might cause stress for the interviewer. Assuming that the interviewer is already highly motivated to make valid selection decisions, the additional tension would be unlikely to benefit the qualified handicapped applicant, because excessive arousal tends to reduce performance in mental tasks.

4. Discrimination against handicapped applicants will be lower for those who openly acknowledge and show a willingness to frankly discuss their handicap (including its probable performance impact) than for those who do not do so. This proposition is suggested by the study reported by Hastorf, Wildfogel, and Cassman (1979). They found their subjects much more favorably disposed toward, and willing to work with, handicapped others who acknowledged their disability than they were vis-à-vis handicapped who either did not disclose or who disclosed some other highly personal confidence. This proposition deserves serious consideration, because it is the only one in the studies of handicapped persons to receive support in replications.

5. Handicapped applicants will be perceived as more motivated to achieve high performance, and will be viewed as better prospects for long tenure than nonhandicapped applicants. Krefting and Brief (1976) obtained significantly more favorable evaluations of motivation and tenure among applicants for typing positions who were confined to a wheelchair due to an accident than were obtained for nonhandicapped applicants. However, as noted below, they also found less favorable evaluations of the handicapped than of nonhandicapped applicants on other attributes. Thus, the net impact on the probability of selecting handicapped rather than nonhandicapped was not determined.

6. Nonhandicapped applicants will receive more favorable evaluations of their prospects for promotion and adequate health than will handicapped applicants. These are the only other significantly different evaluations Krefting and Brief (1976) obtained. Data from Bressler & Lacy's (1980) survey did indicate that some handicapped workers take more sick leave than do nonhandicapped employees. Krefting and Brief also found that handicapped and nonhandicapped applicants were viewed as equal in ability, potential for high levels of performance (in terms of both quantity and quality), absenteeism, tardiness, interpersonal competence, and overall desirability as employees. Thus, their overall results suggest that very little differentiation will be made between nonhandicapped and handicapped applicants except on a few attributes. When differential judgments are made, some will favor nonhandicapped applicants; others will favor handicapped applicants.

7. Handicapped applicants will be favored over comparable nonhandicapped applicants if the job stresses interpersonal competence. In a study relating two forms of handicap, epilepsy and amputation, to nonhandicapped applicants in four types of job settings, Rose and Brief (1979) reported very significant differences between epileptic and nonhandicapped applicants consistent with this proposition. However,

their amputees were not favored to a significant degree over nonhandicapped applicants. These results are different from those reported by Krefting and Brief (1976). Several major differences between the two experiments could account for the differences in results. For example, the earlier study considered a typing task, whereas the latter involved either sales or computer programming work (at either the supervisory or the nonsupervisory level, depending on experimental condition). Furthermore, the failure to find significant differences in the earlier study could be due to insensitive measures, differences in the same direction which failed to achieve conventional levels of significance, or many other factors. The tendency for more favorable evaluations of interpersonal skills for handicapped than for nonhandicapped applicants in the data of Rose and Brief masks an interaction between type of handicap and degree of public contact in the job. This interaction is the basis for the next proposition.

8. If the job involves minimal public contact, applicants with some forms of disability will be preferred to nonhandicapped applicants and to those with different handicaps. In their research, Rose and Brief (1979) found that epileptics were preferred over both amputees and nonhandicapped applicants for "internal" jobs.

9. If a decision to hire is made, the salary recommended will depend on the type of handicap. Rose and Brief (1979) report that nonhandicapped and epileptic applicants were recommended to receive significantly higher salaries than amputees regardless of the job characteristics they considered.

10. Among the handicapped, the higher their verbosity, intelligibility, and responsiveness during the interview, the higher the interviewer's overall rating of the applicant, and the greater the probability of hiring the applicant. This proposition is a direct interpretation of the results reported by Sigelman, Elias, and Danker-Brown (1980). In their (nonexperimental) study, videotapes of interviews with mentally retarded adults were viewed by four male and two female undergraduates in a personnel interviewing course. The six rated each interviewee on eight semantic differential items which were summed to the overall score, and also indicated whether or not they recommended hiring the interviewee. Based on earlier work by Imada and Hakel (1977) and by Sterrett (1978), 10 predictor measures were obtained for each interviewee. IQ as well as ratings of complexity of language use, amounts of smiling, gazing, fidgeting, obstruction of one's face, and physical attractiveness failed to affect either the overall ratings or the hiring recommendations. Verbosity, intelligibility, and responsiveness all had significant pairwise correlations of at least 0.60, and the overall rating correlated significantly with the hiring recommendations.

11. When differences between handicapped and nonhandicapped applicants closely parallel other differences, discrimination will be masked by preferences for nonhandicapped applicants expressed in terms of the other differences. Snyder, Kleck, Strenta, and Mentzer (1979) demonstrated in two studies that, if subjects could avoid interaction with the handicapped by engaging in one activity, but could not avoid interaction by engaging in a second activity, the first activity would be preferred or chosen significantly more often than the second.

12. Psychiatrically handicapped applicants are less likely to be hired than are physically handicapped or nonhandicapped applicants. This proposition was advanced by Florian (1978) on the basis of survey data. Stone and Sawatzki (1980) obtained some experimental results consistent with this proposition when their subjects made hiring judgments. However, their subjects did not exhibit significantly different evaluations of nonhandicapped and handicapped applicants in ratings of 12 unspecified applicant characteristics.

These 12 propositions are not adequate to provide comprehensive guidance to employers, employment agencies, counselors, or handicapped persons. Consequently, guidance was also sought from the experimental literature on employment interviewing processes.

PROPOSITIONS FROM STUDIES OF
THE INTERVIEW DECISION PROCESS

Perhaps the strongest implicit evidence regarding discrimination has been generated in experiments on the interviewer's decision process (Wagner, 1949; Mayfield, 1964; Ulrich & Trumbo, 1965; Wright, 1969; Carlson, Thayer, Mayfield, & Peterson, 1971; Schmitt, 1976). Extrapolations from these results suggest that the handicapped will suffer discrimination to the extent that:

1. Interviewers have accepted stereotypes about handicapped persons. Where the dominant negative stereotype (Florian, 1978) has been seriously challenged by training, personal experience, or legal pressure, the handicapped applicant may find reverse discrimination in his or her favor if past performance or other qualifications are comparable to nonhandicapped applicants (Larrance, Pavelich, Storer, Polizzi, Baron, Jordan, & Reis, 1979; Wexley, Sanders, & Yukl, 1973).

2. The disability is readily observed. Handicaps affecting appearance may cause more discrimination than those affecting speech (Washburn & Hakel, 1973). If the impairment is difficult to observe, appearance may not adversely affect the handicapped applicant (Carlson, 1967b), and the primacy effects noted in the next point will be reduced.

3. The handicap is discovered before other information is obtained by the interviewer, or very early in the interview. Early revelation can cause gating, or the restructuring of questions to focus on areas supporting the initial impression, as well as provide a dominant negative impression that prevails early in the process when the decision is actually made (Webster, 1964). These temporal effects can be attenuated by relying on highly trained and experienced interviewers (Johns, 1975), or by providing a large amount of information about the job to the interviewer (Peters & Terborg, 1975).

4. Unfavorable information (other than handicap status) is obtained. Usually such information will tend to bias the subsequent questions and interviewer interpretations of answers against a favorable evaluation. This bias will be reduced to the extent that it is normally encountered in similar contexts (Constantin, 1976), and/or the interviewer expects the interviewee to be of "high quality" (London & Hakel, 1974).

5. The interviewer frequently encounters handicapped applicants. If nonhandicapped applicants are the rule, the contrasting status of the handicap will focus more attention on the handicap than it would otherwise receive (Hakel, Ohnesorge, & Dunnette, 1970; Wexley, Sanders, & Yukl, 1973). Because the dominant stereotype is that handicapped persons are less capable of satisfactory performance than are nonhandicapped workers (Florian, 1978), only very substantial positive evidence could reverse the negative impression (cf. Bolster & Springbett, 1961; Constantin, 1976; Hollman, 1972; Miller & Rowe, 1967; Shaw, 1972).

6. Interviewer and interviewee attitudes are not similar (Peters & Terborg, 1975; Rand & Wexley, 1975; Wexley & Nemeroff, 1974). However, some evidence indicates that attitudinal agreement is less important the more experienced the interviewer (Frank & Hackman, 1975).

7. Handicapped applicants have not received training in interview skills (Barbee & Keil, 1973; Venardos & Harris, 1973).

8. Interviewers do not have a clear idea of the specific factors required for satisfactory performance on the job (Carlson, Thayer, Mayfield, & Peterson, 1971) or they have very limited information about the job (Wiener & Schneiderman, 1974).

9. Structured interviews are not used (cf. Schwab & Heneman, 1969). The benefits of structured interviews include higher inter-rater reliability and a barrier to gating (Webster, 1964), as well as restricting the focus to performance-relevant factors (assuming the structure is validated against specific jobs).

10. Assessments of interviewer performance provide stronger incentives for them to make false rejection rather than false acceptance errors (Webster, 1964).
11. The selection system's or the interviewer's predictive validity has not been established (Dunnette & Borman, 1979).
12. Employment decisions rely exclusively or heavily on interviewer judgments rather than upon extensive data from many sources (e.g., validated biographical histories, tests, assessment center results; Dunnette & Borman, 1979).
13. Selection decisions rely on human judgment rather than actuarial models or heuristics. Rarely are human judges able to outperform the models (Dawes, 1979; Sawyer, 1966; Wagner, 1949).

These propositions from the interview decision process literature are not exhaustive. However, they convincingly demonstrate that factors which have not yet been raised by experiments on sources of discrimination on the basis of handicap should be considered when designing employment programs for handicapped persons. They also provide additional bases for tentative recommendations to the parties involved in employing handicapped persons.

RECOMMENDATIONS

The evidence reviewed to this point provides the main basis for the recommendations that follow. Rehabilitation specialists should view the first two of the following three sets of recommendations as implicit recommendations for rehabilitation programs. Recommendations that apply primarily to specialists are reserved for the third set.

Recommendations for Employers

1. Explore the productivity benefits that could be captured by employing more handicapped persons and advancing them more rapidly. In most jobs it will be discovered that most handicaps do not reduce performance, and in some jobs performance may improve. New technologies and occupations frequently facilitate use of handicapped workers with only minimal costs required to accommodate the workplace to their handicaps. For example, computer programmers can work at home with inexpensive communications links to the office (Labor Letter, 1980).
2. Determine applicant qualities that are job-related for each job. This requires sophisticated job analyses rather than simple job descriptions or vague statements of jobholder responsibilities (Latham & Wexley, 1981).

3. Use interviews to collect information on applicant qualities only if interviewing is the least expensive method for obtaining the data, or if the interview process satisfies organizational purposes other than personnel selection which otherwise would not be achieved (Darlington, 1976).

4. If interviewers must be used, train them regarding sources of bias and error in the interview process and how to avoid them (Wexley, Sanders, & Yukl, 1973). Keep interviewers aware of tendencies like those cited in the three sets of propositions above. Also, give them complete information about the job-related or predictor data needed for *each* job (Schmitt, 1976).

5. Use structured interviews if possible (Dunnette & Borman, 1979).

6. Integrate information collected by interviewers with data from other sources; do not permit interviewers to make the decision, and do not rely exclusively on interview data (Dawes, 1979; Slovic, Fischhoff, & Lichtenstein, 1977; Einhorn & Hogarth, 1981).

7. Evaluate the predictive performance of all components of the selection system periodically (Dunnette & Borman, 1979). Provide interviewers with data regarding the career progress of applicants, both those accepted and those rejected (if possible).

8. Hire interviewers who have demonstrated their predictive ability, who have positive conceptions about handicapped workers, and who are not highly authoritarian.

Recommendations for Handicapped Persons

1. Be certain you have marketable skills. If you do not, check before beginning a training program to be sure it develops a skill that will be in demand when you finish training.

2. Develop and practice interpersonal skills on a daily basis. Technical skills may suffice for some entry jobs, but not for those that require teamwork or the exercise of supervision over others.

3. If possible, avoid interviews by making your qualifications known to employers via personal letters, resumes, and letters of recommendation.

4. Because interviews, however informal, are usually inevitable, be certain that the interviewer has reviewed your written information before meeting you for the interview.

5. Do not schedule an interview that will last for less than one-half hour. You will want enough time to present all your positive qualities, as well as to discuss frankly any issues raised by the interviewer. Interviewers will also use less information and rely more on

negative information the less time they have to consider your credentials (Wright, 1974).

6. Before you go to the interview, be sure you know all the applicable affirmative action laws, both state and federal, as well as the employer's affirmative action policies.

7. Also before the interview, verify the accuracy of any feedback you have received from past employers about your prior performance. It is probable that you have been treated leniently compared to workers without handicaps who performed at the same level you did. You should have a realistic sense of your own abilities and past record before the interview begins.

8. If you can control who interviews you, try to find an interviewer who is: a) well informed about specific jobs and specific job requirements, b) trained in interviewing skills, c) experienced in the conduct of interviews, d) comfortable with a wide variety of people, e) has favorable conceptions of handicapped workers, f) uses a structured interview form and sticks to it, g) does not have a quota of interviews which must be conducted or placements which must be made (Carlson, 1967a), h) is not very authoritarian, and i) has a record of valid selection judgements.

9. Do not expect handicapped interviewers to give you more favorable consideration than nonhandicapped interviewers. Evidence of favored treatment due to matching personal characteristics (such as sex or race) is rare (but see Schwab & Heneman, 1978), particularly when past performance data are available to the interviewer. However, you might obtain more accurate interpretations of the information acquired by the interviewer to the extent that the interviewer shares many characteristics in common with you (Landy & Farr, 1980).

10. Try to discover the interviewer's conception of an ideal applicant for the job, and then see if you can match it. If not, attempt to obtain a probationary appointment to prove your ability to do the job.

11. Be certain that your strengths are presented in detail before the interview is over, preferably early in the interview if you can control the topics.

12. If or when the question of health or handicap arises, acknowledge it frankly, openly discuss its relationship to job performance, and clearly convey a willingness to discuss any related issues as fully as the interviewer wishes. Even if this makes you nervous, it is better than not clearing the air.

13. Give accurate answers, not those you think the interviewer wants to hear. Handicapped applicants have tended to report shorter times since last being employed, and less reliance on aid from service agencies than they actually experienced (Weiss & Dawis, 1980; Weiss, Dawis, Englund, & Lofquist, 1961). Incorrect answers reduce your credibility and provide or enhance a negative image.

14. Be as attentive as possible throughout the interview. Be certain that your body language, dress, and all other nonverbal behaviors are consistent with what you say, and with the requirements of the job.

15. If the interviewer is doing little talking, you have probably been rejected—even before the interview is over (Anderson, 1960). Attempt to obtain a trial employment period long enough to demonstrate your competence.

16. Avoid jobs that have been stereotyped as jobs for the handicapped. Good performance in such jobs is expected and will not attract the same degree of favorable attention that it would in jobs that are not stereotyped as jobs for the handicapped.

17. Ask how personnel decisions are made in the organization. Avoid employers who rely heavily on interviews and unstructured judgments to make hiring, promotion, transfer, training, and similar decisions. If the interviewer is unable to answer these questions, particularly specific questions about the evidence of reliability and validity of interview procedures, performance appraisal systems, and similar formal programs for making personnel decisions, the employer may be liable for violations of affirmative action laws or regulations (Latham & Wexley, 1981).

Recommendations for Rehabilitation Specialists

Most of the implications for rehabilitation specialists are implicit in the preceding recommendations. Clearly, the results discussed in this review can be of little practical value if they are not used in conjunction with the following propositions.

1. Competent forecasts of the composition of labor skill needs and supplies must be obtained before specific vocational training programs are begun. Employers who refuse to hire applicants who lack appropriate skills are not unlawfully discriminating. If they refuse to hire qualified handicapped applicants because of an excess supply of the skills held by handicapped persons, they may also be acting in a nondiscriminatory manner. If handicapped persons are hired in excess supply conditions, their pay will be constrained by the market. More subtle considerations affecting discrimination are often swamped by these labor market conditions. Only when handicapped persons have been provided with skills that are in demand are most of the sources of discrimination considered in this chapter likely to become relatively important.

2. Help handicapped job-seekers become aware of the bases of discrimination revealed by research. They cannot take initiatives to counter subtle barriers to career progress if they have not heard of them. These biases may be particularly strong in backlash situations, that is, where employers have recently experienced pressure or costs imposed by government regulation of employment practices (affirmative action, OSHA, etc.).

3. Instruct handicapped job-seekers on symptoms of unlawful actions by employers, unions, and employment agencies. For example, handicapped persons should realize that if they inquire about job requirements and receive general answers relating to personal traits such as honesty, friendliness, and good work habits, they may be able to question the validity of the employer's selection system.

4. Urge experimentally oriented social scientists to investigate factors that your experience tells you are important, but are frequently overlooked sources of discrimination. There can be no assurance that the most common or the most difficult sources of discrimination against handicapped applicants have been identified. In addition, the importance of those sources that have been identified typically varies depending on the context, i.e., on what other factors are also varied. Also suggest alternative remedies to be experimentally evaluated. The dialogue should be mutually useful, and should increase the relevance and acceptance of social science findings.

5. Work closely with the National Organization for Women (NOW), the Grey Panthers, the Congress of Racial Equality (CORE), and other groups that are also concerned with reducing employment discrimination. Both the sources of discrimination, such as the employer's workforce composition, and the remedies used to reduce it may be common concerns of several interest groups.

6. Select employers who have good performance appraisal systems as your targets for affirmative action campaigns. Those employers have already demonstrated more than the usual concern for obtaining high productivity from people and may be most receptive to your efforts. Be certain that your clients can achieve the performance standards of the employer, show your reasons, and seek at least a minimum probationary employment period. If you have judged the situation correctly, your clients should perform as well as normal workers. Even more important is the fact that the performance will be highly visible and convincing since the performance appraisal system is good. On the other hand, if performance is below the employer's standards, you obtain valuable information regarding the limitations of your rehabilitation programs. In either event, the results should assist you and

your organization in providing better service to your clients. Placing equally competent clients in work situations where their high performance is obscured by inept performance appraisal systems produces minimal results for you and for your clients.

7. Recognize that the judgments about the performance of your clients will probably be subjected to all the discriminatory biases that were present in the interview whenever personnel decisions (e.g., transfers, promotions, raises) are made (Landy & Farr, 1980). The impact of these biases will be diminished to the extent that your clients achieve good performance which is noted by a good appraisal system. Nevertheless, biases will probably remain. Thus, your training for clients needs to continue after the probationary employment period, throughout their careers. Competent career management by handicapped employees will become increasingly important as initial employment barriers weaken. Programs will need to address far more, and far more complex, causes of discrimination than are implied in many postemployment programs (e.g., the program suggested by Shrey, 1980).

8. Some of your clients may be hired under quota systems or as tokens rather than because of their productive potential. Whether or not this is true, some clients may sense that it is. In either case it is important that clients recognize that the job is an opportunity to educate the employer regarding their personal potential, as well as the potential of all handicapped persons. If progress on the job, promotions and raises, recognition, and other evidence of job success do not come as rapidly as your clients believe is warranted, they may attribute the pace to discrimination. Help them to ascertain the validity of such beliefs. If the belief is valid, pressure or legal recourse may be necessary. If not, clients will need help in distinguishing discriminatory from equal treatment of all workers.

9. Concentrate on regular employment opportunities. Sheltered employment may be worse than unemployment as a method of preparing handicapped persons to cope. In sheltered employment they may be exploited, have no access to career ladders, be unable to compare their own performance to that of the nonhandicapped workers, and consequently lose both the knowledge and aspirations necessary to obtain better employment. Practices used to manage handicapped workers in sheltered employment are not at all similar to those used in most employment relationships. Hence, in sheltered employment, handicapped persons adjust to a system which may bear very little similarity to those used by most employers. Rather than a transitional halfway house, sheltered workshops may be an additional barrier to vocational adjustment. They may simply constitute settings in

which handicapped workers acquire attitudes and behaviors which trigger discrimination in competitive employment settings.

10. Once your clients are employed, encourage the development and use of less discriminatory, more productive evaluation systems by seeking to have both evaluators and handicapped employees a) involved in the design and revision of evaluation systems (Friedman & Cornelius, 1976), and b) intensively trained in their use (Latham & Wexley, 1981).

CONCLUSION

Each of these sets of recommendations will be modified or extended by the results of further research. Implementation of these recommendations cannot be expected to eliminate all employment discrimination. However, it can increase productive efficiency and human satisfaction significantly. The amount of improvement will depend upon the extent to which social scientists, rehabilitation specialists, employers, and handicapped persons collaborate on continuing research and implementation of research results. Particular emphasis should be given to the areas of job analysis and task design as necessary complements to the recommendations in this chapter. Poorly designed jobs and vague job analyses make it very difficult for research to validate selection systems, locate and estimate the impact of sources of discrimination, or evaluate remedial efforts. By clearly establishing critical job elements and the sufficient human capacities required to perform them adequately, real but unsuspected and unnecessary barriers to employment opportunities can be eliminated.

appendix A
REVISED SCALE OF EMPLOYABILITY

WI. ATTITUDINAL CONFORMITY TO WORK ROLE

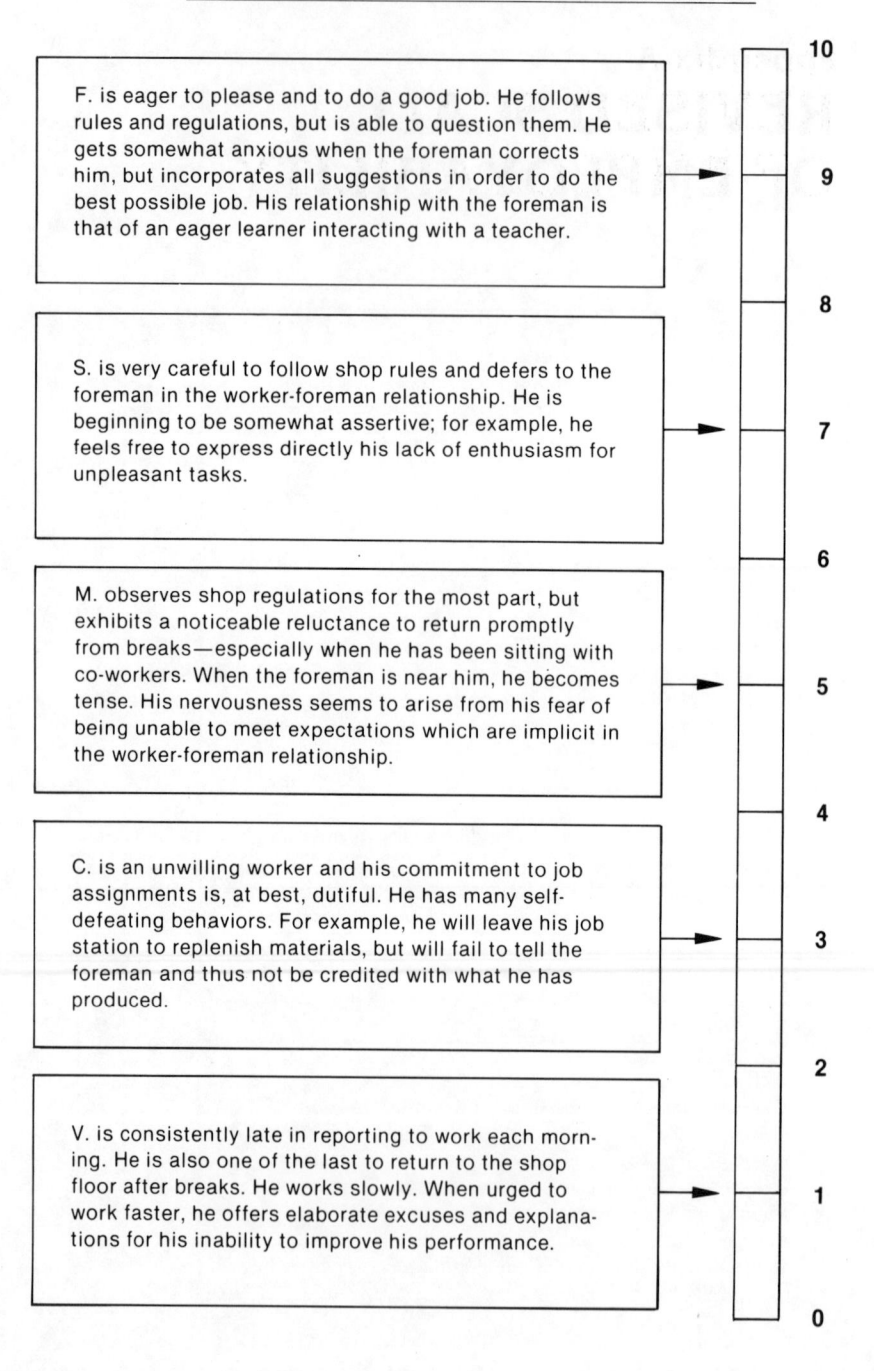

F. is eager to please and to do a good job. He follows rules and regulations, but is able to question them. He gets somewhat anxious when the foreman corrects him, but incorporates all suggestions in order to do the best possible job. His relationship with the foreman is that of an eager learner interacting with a teacher. → 9

S. is very careful to follow shop rules and defers to the foreman in the worker-foreman relationship. He is beginning to be somewhat assertive; for example, he feels free to express directly his lack of enthusiasm for unpleasant tasks. → 7

M. observes shop regulations for the most part, but exhibits a noticeable reluctance to return promptly from breaks—especially when he has been sitting with co-workers. When the foreman is near him, he becomes tense. His nervousness seems to arise from his fear of being unable to meet expectations which are implicit in the worker-foreman relationship. → 5

C. is an unwilling worker and his commitment to job assignments is, at best, dutiful. He has many self-defeating behaviors. For example, he will leave his job station to replenish materials, but will fail to tell the foreman and thus not be credited with what he has produced. → 3

V. is consistently late in reporting to work each morning. He is also one of the last to return to the shop floor after breaks. He works slowly. When urged to work faster, he offers elaborate excuses and explanations for his inability to improve his performance. → 1

WII. **MAINTENANCE OF QUALITY**

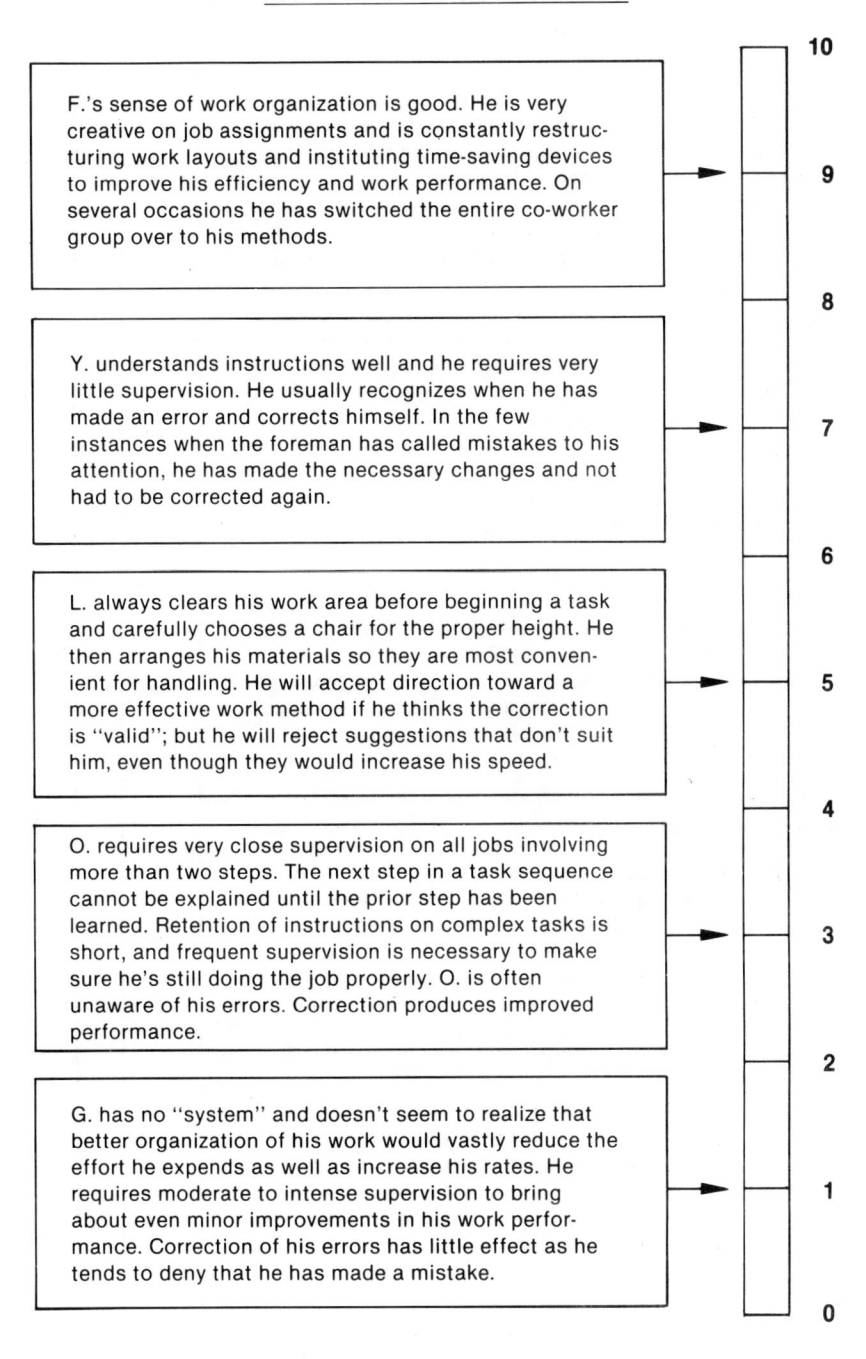

— 10

F.'s sense of work organization is good. He is very creative on job assignments and is constantly restructuring work layouts and instituting time-saving devices to improve his efficiency and work performance. On several occasions he has switched the entire co-worker group over to his methods. → 9

— 8

Y. understands instructions well and he requires very little supervision. He usually recognizes when he has made an error and corrects himself. In the few instances when the foreman has called mistakes to his attention, he has made the necessary changes and not had to be corrected again. → 7

— 6

L. always clears his work area before beginning a task and carefully chooses a chair for the proper height. He then arranges his materials so they are most convenient for handling. He will accept direction toward a more effective work method if he thinks the correction is "valid"; but he will reject suggestions that don't suit him, even though they would increase his speed. → 5

— 4

O. requires very close supervision on all jobs involving more than two steps. The next step in a task sequence cannot be explained until the prior step has been learned. Retention of instructions on complex tasks is short, and frequent supervision is necessary to make sure he's still doing the job properly. O. is often unaware of his errors. Correction produces improved performance. → 3

— 2

G. has no "system" and doesn't seem to realize that better organization of his work would vastly reduce the effort he expends as well as increase his rates. He requires moderate to intense supervision to bring about even minor improvements in his work performance. Correction of his errors has little effect as he tends to deny that he has made a mistake. → 1

— 0

WIII. ACCEPTANCE OF WORK DEMANDS

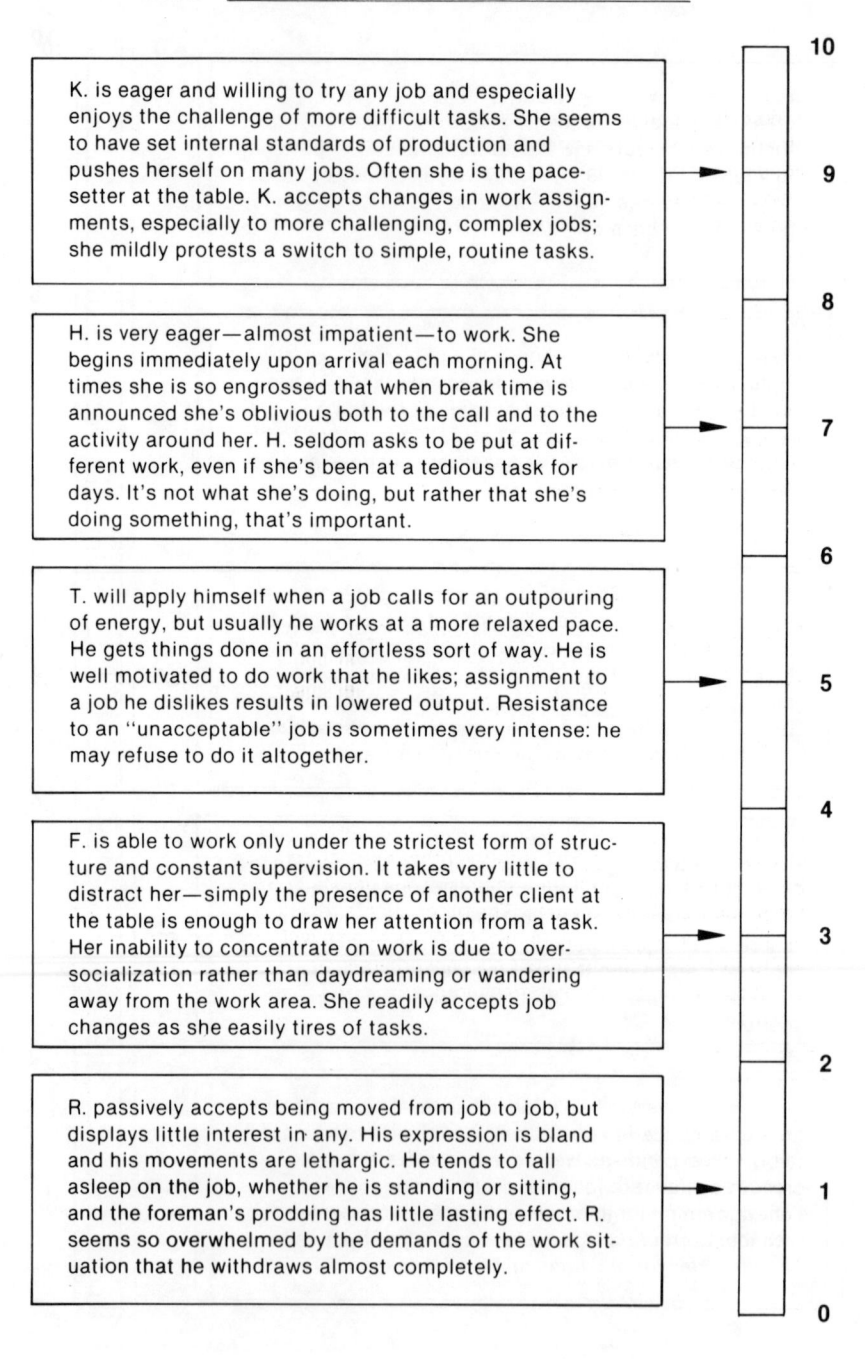

K. is eager and willing to try any job and especially enjoys the challenge of more difficult tasks. She seems to have set internal standards of production and pushes herself on many jobs. Often she is the pacesetter at the table. K. accepts changes in work assignments, especially to more challenging, complex jobs; she mildly protests a switch to simple, routine tasks. → 9

H. is very eager—almost impatient—to work. She begins immediately upon arrival each morning. At times she is so engrossed that when break time is announced she's oblivious both to the call and to the activity around her. H. seldom asks to be put at different work, even if she's been at a tedious task for days. It's not what she's doing, but rather that she's doing something, that's important. → 7

T. will apply himself when a job calls for an outpouring of energy, but usually he works at a more relaxed pace. He gets things done in an effortless sort of way. He is well motivated to do work that he likes; assignment to a job he dislikes results in lowered output. Resistance to an "unacceptable" job is sometimes very intense: he may refuse to do it altogether. → 5

F. is able to work only under the strictest form of structure and constant supervision. It takes very little to distract her—simply the presence of another client at the table is enough to draw her attention from a task. Her inability to concentrate on work is due to oversocialization rather than daydreaming or wandering away from the work area. She readily accepts job changes as she easily tires of tasks. → 3

R. passively accepts being moved from job to job, but displays little interest in any. His expression is bland and his movements are lethargic. He tends to fall asleep on the job, whether he is standing or sitting, and the foreman's prodding has little lasting effect. R. seems so overwhelmed by the demands of the work situation that he withdraws almost completely. → 1

WIV. **INTERPERSONAL SECURITY**

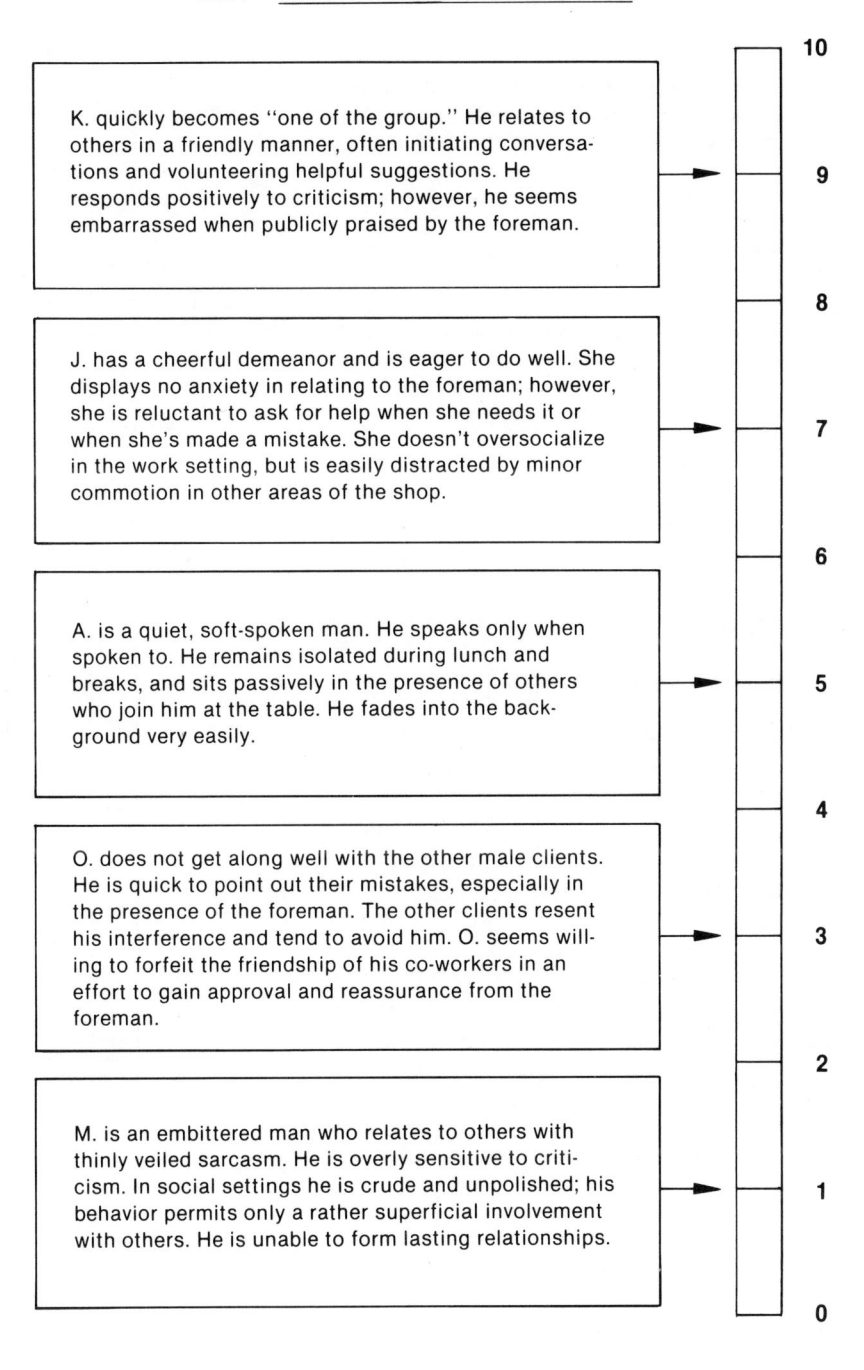

K. quickly becomes "one of the group." He relates to others in a friendly manner, often initiating conversations and volunteering helpful suggestions. He responds positively to criticism; however, he seems embarrassed when publicly praised by the foreman. → 9

J. has a cheerful demeanor and is eager to do well. She displays no anxiety in relating to the foreman; however, she is reluctant to ask for help when she needs it or when she's made a mistake. She doesn't oversocialize in the work setting, but is easily distracted by minor commotion in other areas of the shop. → 7

A. is a quiet, soft-spoken man. He speaks only when spoken to. He remains isolated during lunch and breaks, and sits passively in the presence of others who join him at the table. He fades into the background very easily. → 5

O. does not get along well with the other male clients. He is quick to point out their mistakes, especially in the presence of the foreman. The other clients resent his interference and tend to avoid him. O. seems willing to forfeit the friendship of his co-workers in an effort to gain approval and reassurance from the foreman. → 3

M. is an embittered man who relates to others with thinly veiled sarcasm. He is overly sensitive to criticism. In social settings he is crude and unpolished; his behavior permits only a rather superficial involvement with others. He is unable to form lasting relationships. → 1

Appendix A

WV. SPEED OF PRODUCTION

A. **Production Tasks** (jobs for which objective performance standards are available, e.g., percent of industrial minimum, raw count of items completed)

　　Estimated Average Rate: _____

　　Comments:

B. **Nonproduction Tasks** (jobs which require a judgment of performance, e.g., messenger, custodial, shop helper, clerical)

　　Specify Job: _____

　　Overall Performance Rating:

　　　　_____ Excellent
　　　　_____ Very Good
　　　　_____ Good
　　　　_____ Fair
　　　　_____ Poor

　　Comments:

CI. ADEQUACY OF WORK HISTORY

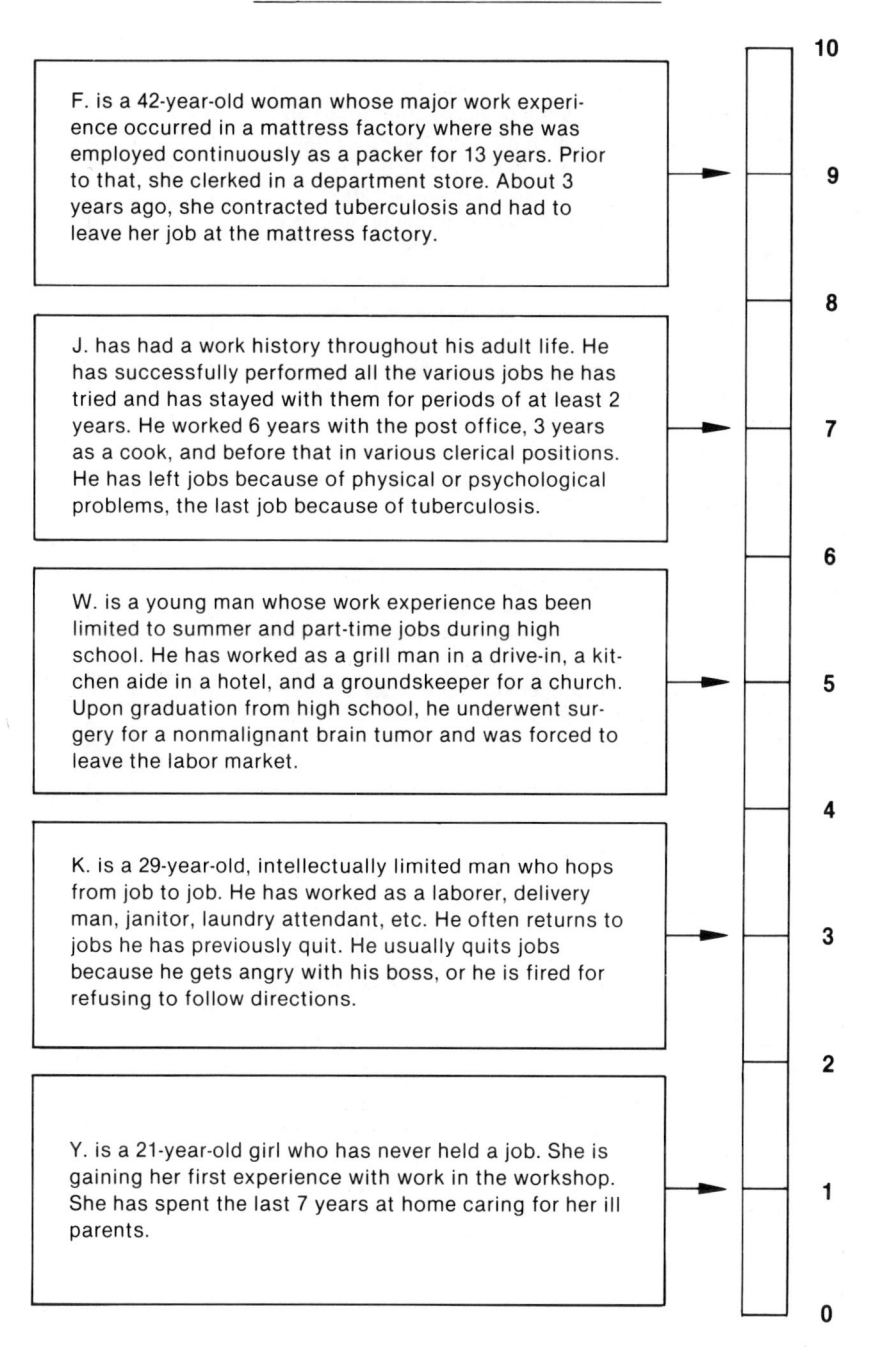

F. is a 42-year-old woman whose major work experience occurred in a mattress factory where she was employed continuously as a packer for 13 years. Prior to that, she clerked in a department store. About 3 years ago, she contracted tuberculosis and had to leave her job at the mattress factory. → 9

J. has had a work history throughout his adult life. He has successfully performed all the various jobs he has tried and has stayed with them for periods of at least 2 years. He worked 6 years with the post office, 3 years as a cook, and before that in various clerical positions. He has left jobs because of physical or psychological problems, the last job because of tuberculosis. → 7

W. is a young man whose work experience has been limited to summer and part-time jobs during high school. He has worked as a grill man in a drive-in, a kitchen aide in a hotel, and a groundskeeper for a church. Upon graduation from high school, he underwent surgery for a nonmalignant brain tumor and was forced to leave the labor market. → 5

K. is a 29-year-old, intellectually limited man who hops from job to job. He has worked as a laborer, delivery man, janitor, laundry attendant, etc. He often returns to jobs he has previously quit. He usually quits jobs because he gets angry with his boss, or he is fired for refusing to follow directions. → 3

Y. is a 21-year-old girl who has never held a job. She is gaining her first experience with work in the workshop. She has spent the last 7 years at home caring for her ill parents. → 1

CII. **APPROPRIATENESS OF JOB DEMANDS**

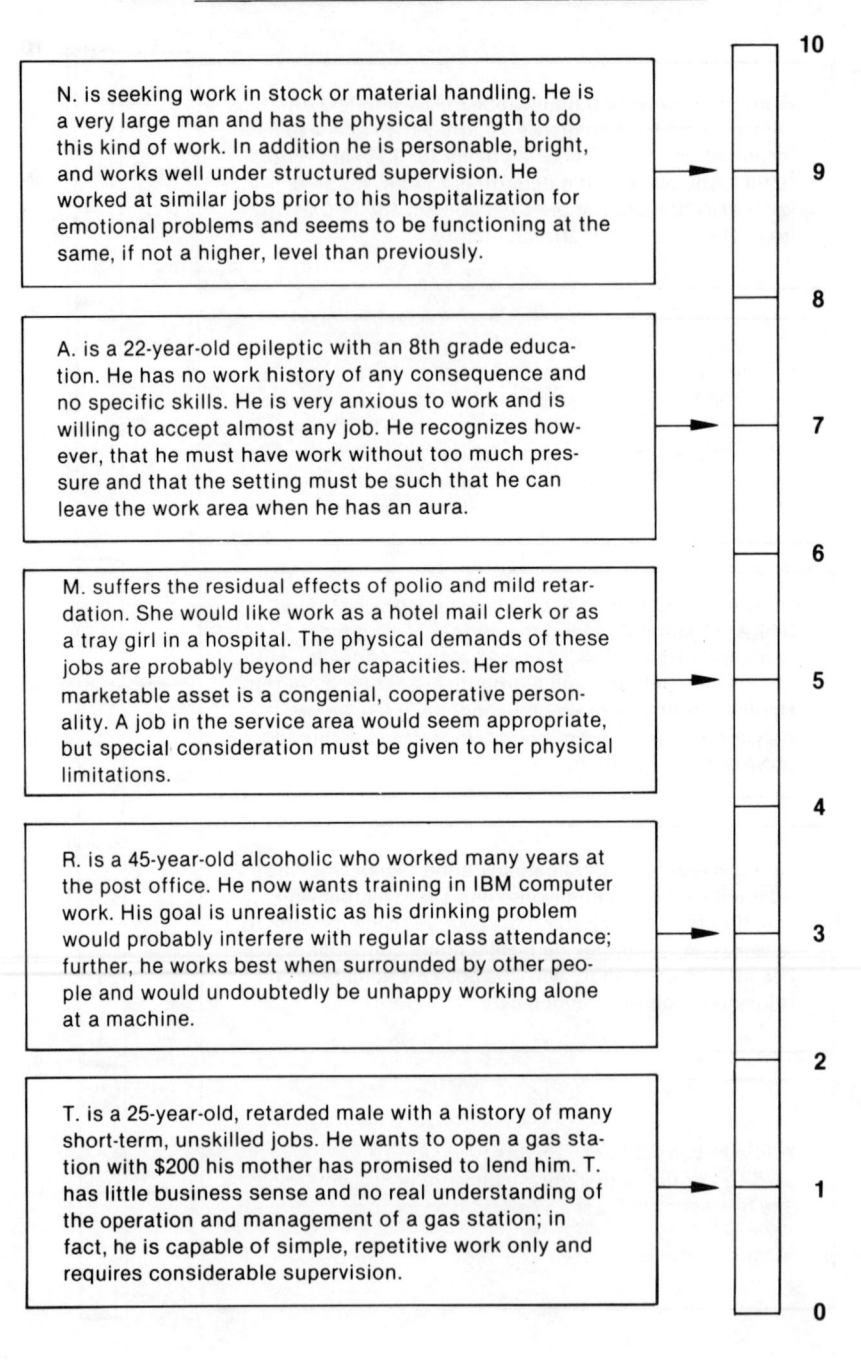

N. is seeking work in stock or material handling. He is a very large man and has the physical strength to do this kind of work. In addition he is personable, bright, and works well under structured supervision. He worked at similar jobs prior to his hospitalization for emotional problems and seems to be functioning at the same, if not a higher, level than previously. → 9

A. is a 22-year-old epileptic with an 8th grade education. He has no work history of any consequence and no specific skills. He is very anxious to work and is willing to accept almost any job. He recognizes however, that he must have work without too much pressure and that the setting must be such that he can leave the work area when he has an aura. → 7

M. suffers the residual effects of polio and mild retardation. She would like work as a hotel mail clerk or as a tray girl in a hospital. The physical demands of these jobs are probably beyond her capacities. Her most marketable asset is a congenial, cooperative personality. A job in the service area would seem appropriate, but special consideration must be given to her physical limitations. → 5

R. is a 45-year-old alcoholic who worked many years at the post office. He now wants training in IBM computer work. His goal is unrealistic as his drinking problem would probably interfere with regular class attendance; further, he works best when surrounded by other people and would undoubtedly be unhappy working alone at a machine. → 3

T. is a 25-year-old, retarded male with a history of many short-term, unskilled jobs. He wants to open a gas station with $200 his mother has promised to lend him. T. has little business sense and no real understanding of the operation and management of a gas station; in fact, he is capable of simple, repetitive work only and requires considerable supervision. → 1

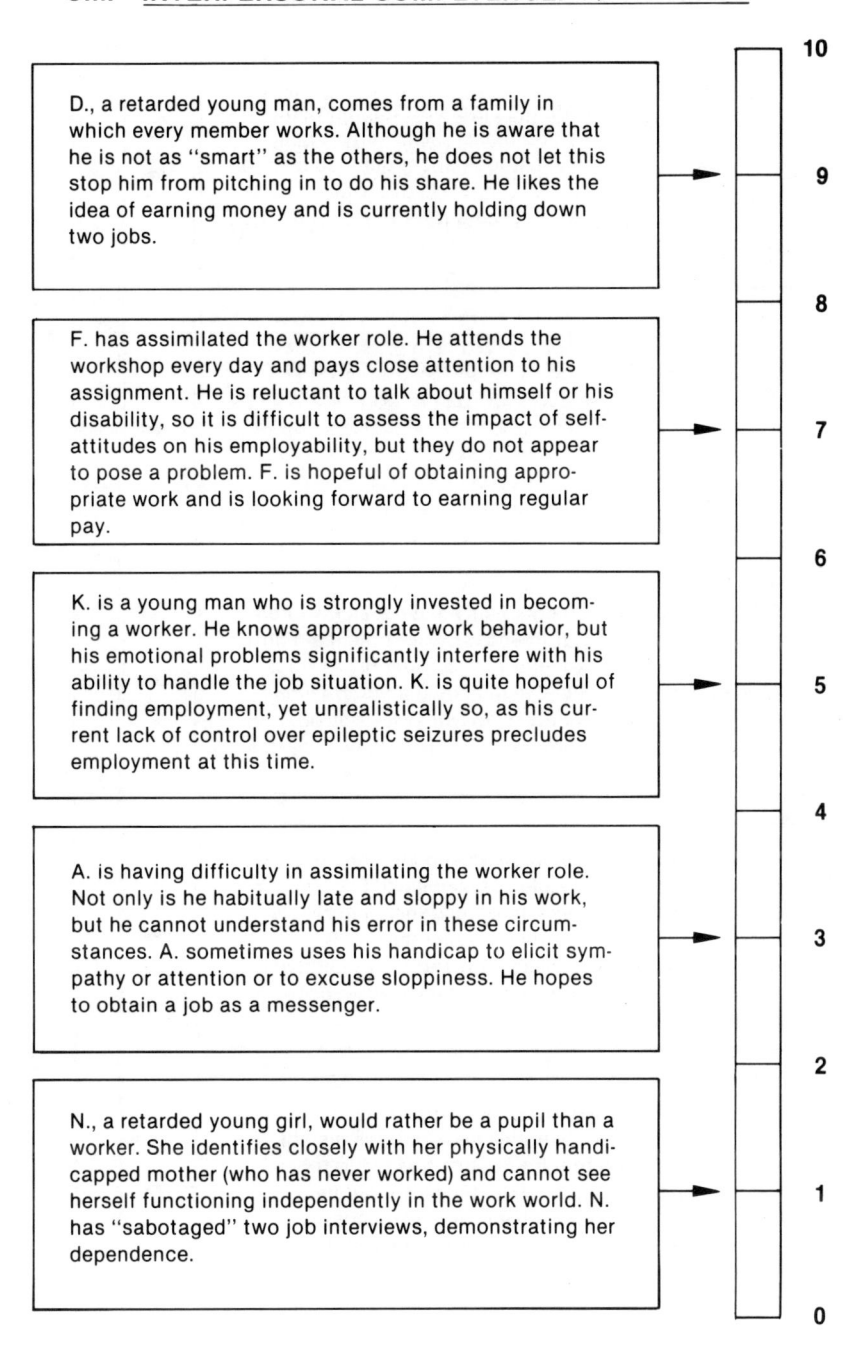

CIII. **INTERPERSONAL COMPETENCE: VOCATIONAL**

D., a retarded young man, comes from a family in which every member works. Although he is aware that he is not as "smart" as the others, he does not let this stop him from pitching in to do his share. He likes the idea of earning money and is currently holding down two jobs.	→ 9
F. has assimilated the worker role. He attends the workshop every day and pays close attention to his assignment. He is reluctant to talk about himself or his disability, so it is difficult to assess the impact of self-attitudes on his employability, but they do not appear to pose a problem. F. is hopeful of obtaining appropriate work and is looking forward to earning regular pay.	→ 7
K. is a young man who is strongly invested in becoming a worker. He knows appropriate work behavior, but his emotional problems significantly interfere with his ability to handle the job situation. K. is quite hopeful of finding employment, yet unrealistically so, as his current lack of control over epileptic seizures precludes employment at this time.	→ 5
A. is having difficulty in assimilating the worker role. Not only is he habitually late and sloppy in his work, but he cannot understand his error in these circumstances. A. sometimes uses his handicap to elicit sympathy or attention or to excuse sloppiness. He hopes to obtain a job as a messenger.	→ 3
N., a retarded young girl, would rather be a pupil than a worker. She identifies closely with her physically handicapped mother (who has never worked) and cannot see herself functioning independently in the work world. N. has "sabotaged" two job interviews, demonstrating her dependence.	→ 1

CIV. **INTERPERSONAL COMPETENCE: SOCIAL**

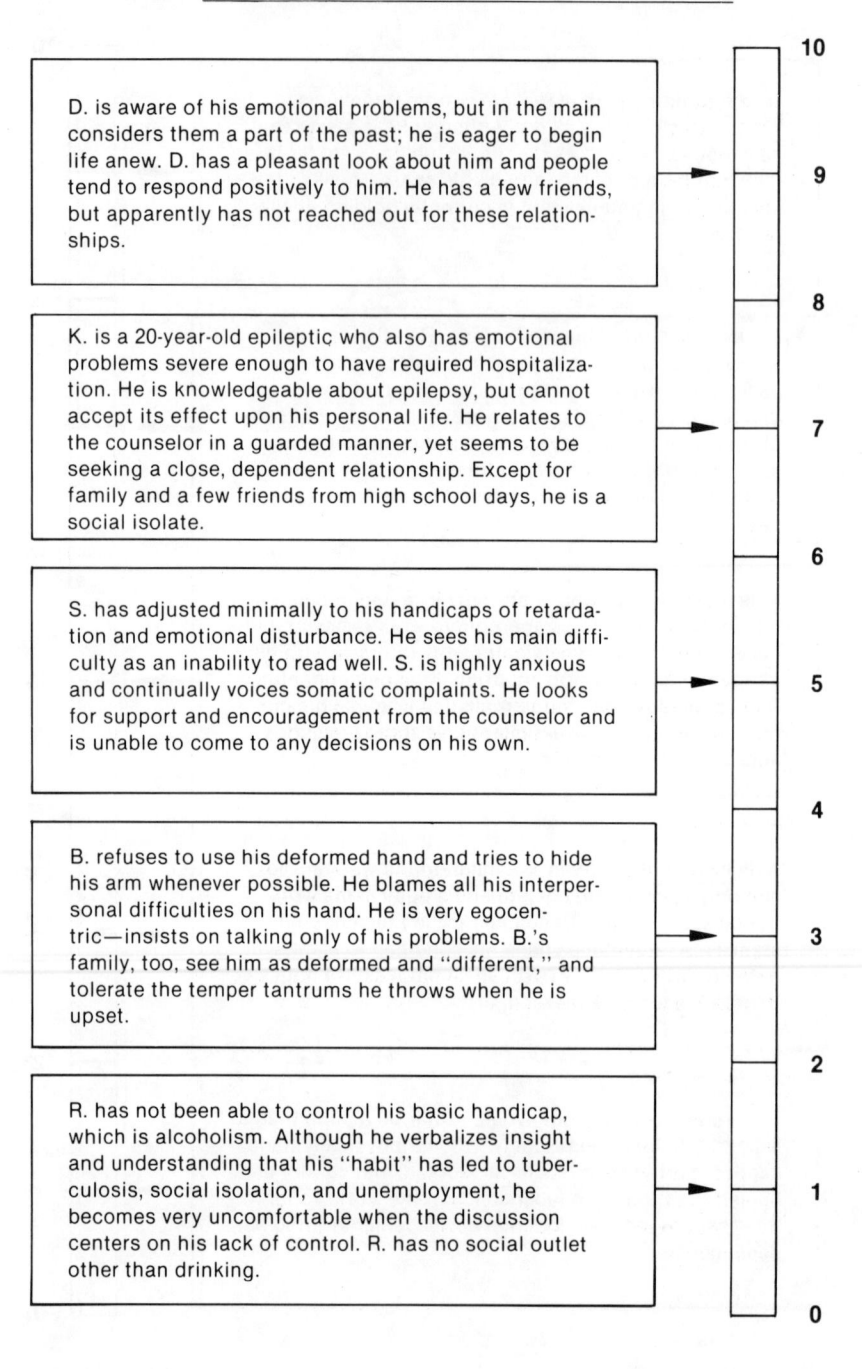

Description	Rating
D. is aware of his emotional problems, but in the main considers them a part of the past; he is eager to begin life anew. D. has a pleasant look about him and people tend to respond positively to him. He has a few friends, but apparently has not reached out for these relationships.	9
K. is a 20-year-old epileptic who also has emotional problems severe enough to have required hospitalization. He is knowledgeable about epilepsy, but cannot accept its effect upon his personal life. He relates to the counselor in a guarded manner, yet seems to be seeking a close, dependent relationship. Except for family and a few friends from high school days, he is a social isolate.	7
S. has adjusted minimally to his handicaps of retardation and emotional disturbance. He sees his main difficulty as an inability to read well. S. is highly anxious and continually voices somatic complaints. He looks for support and encouragement from the counselor and is unable to come to any decisions on his own.	5
B. refuses to use his deformed hand and tries to hide his arm whenever possible. He blames all his interpersonal difficulties on his hand. He is very egocentric—insists on talking only of his problems. B.'s family, too, see him as deformed and "different," and tolerate the temper tantrums he throws when he is upset.	3
R. has not been able to control his basic handicap, which is alcoholism. Although he verbalizes insight and understanding that his "habit" has led to tuberculosis, social isolation, and unemployment, he becomes very uncomfortable when the discussion centers on his lack of control. R. has no social outlet other than drinking.	1

CV. **LANGUAGE FACILITY**

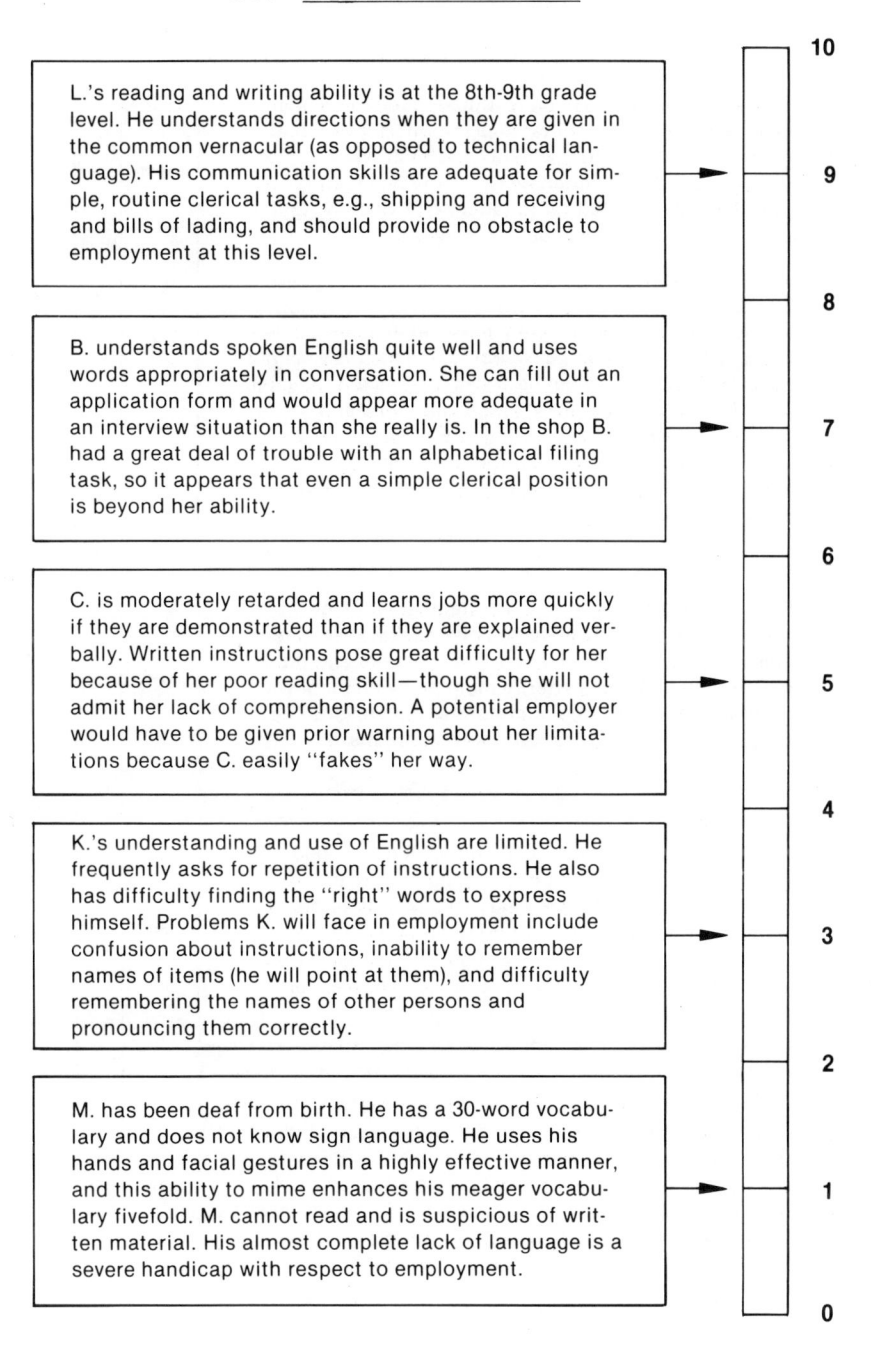

L.'s reading and writing ability is at the 8th-9th grade level. He understands directions when they are given in the common vernacular (as opposed to technical language). His communication skills are adequate for simple, routine clerical tasks, e.g., shipping and receiving and bills of lading, and should provide no obstacle to employment at this level. → 9

B. understands spoken English quite well and uses words appropriately in conversation. She can fill out an application form and would appear more adequate in an interview situation than she really is. In the shop B. had a great deal of trouble with an alphabetical filing task, so it appears that even a simple clerical position is beyond her ability. → 7

C. is moderately retarded and learns jobs more quickly if they are demonstrated than if they are explained verbally. Written instructions pose great difficulty for her because of her poor reading skill—though she will not admit her lack of comprehension. A potential employer would have to be given prior warning about her limitations because C. easily "fakes" her way. → 5

K.'s understanding and use of English are limited. He frequently asks for repetition of instructions. He also has difficulty finding the "right" words to express himself. Problems K. will face in employment include confusion about instructions, inability to remember names of items (he will point at them), and difficulty remembering the names of other persons and pronouncing them correctly. → 3

M. has been deaf from birth. He has a 30-word vocabulary and does not know sign language. He uses his hands and facial gestures in a highly effective manner, and this ability to mime enhances his meager vocabulary fivefold. M. cannot read and is suspicious of written material. His almost complete lack of language is a severe handicap with respect to employment. → 1

CVI.   PROMINENCE OF HANDICAP

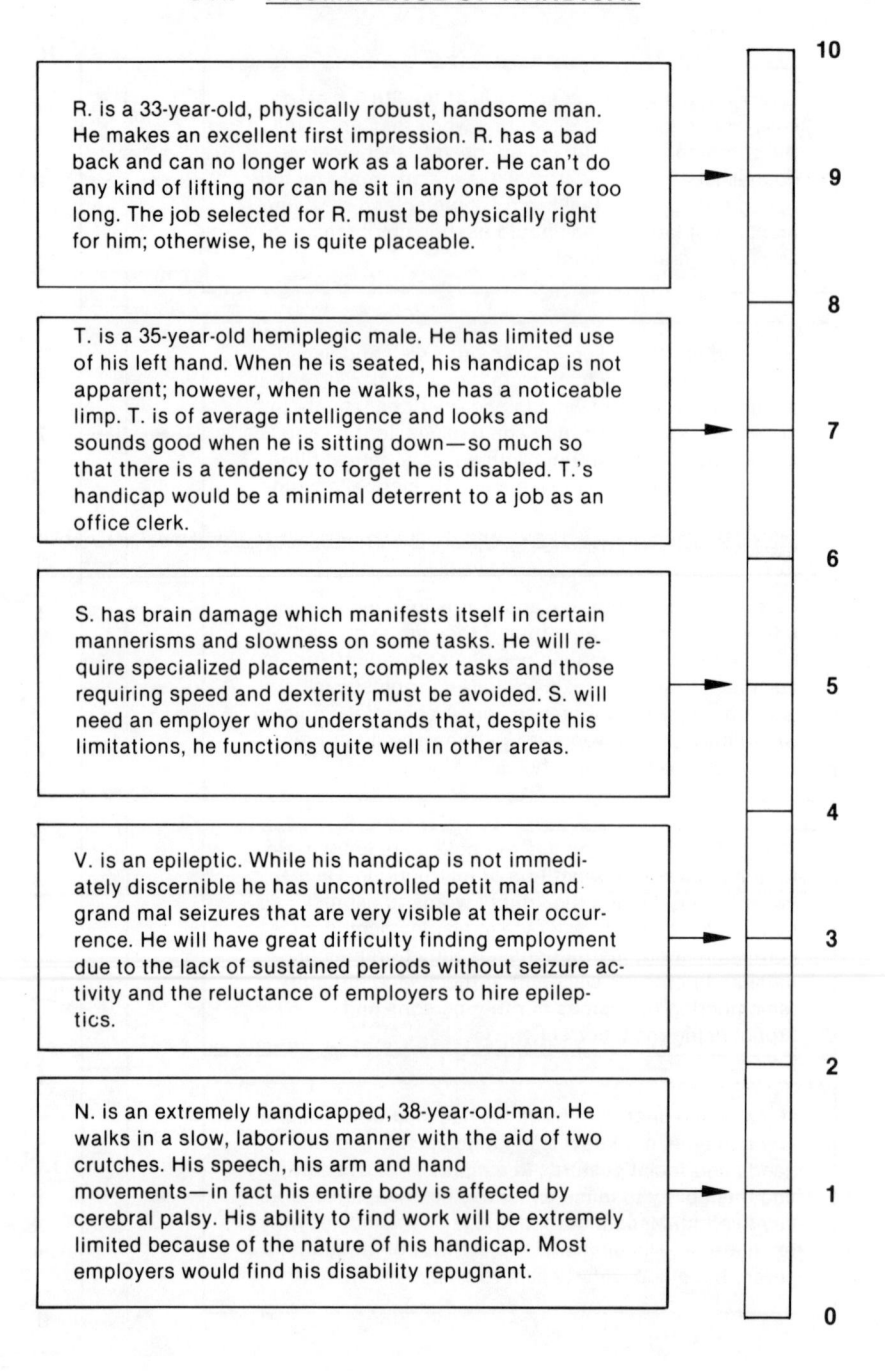

R. is a 33-year-old, physically robust, handsome man. He makes an excellent first impression. R. has a bad back and can no longer work as a laborer. He can't do any kind of lifting nor can he sit in any one spot for too long. The job selected for R. must be physically right for him; otherwise, he is quite placeable.   → 9

T. is a 35-year-old hemiplegic male. He has limited use of his left hand. When he is seated, his handicap is not apparent; however, when he walks, he has a noticeable limp. T. is of average intelligence and looks and sounds good when he is sitting down—so much so that there is a tendency to forget he is disabled. T.'s handicap would be a minimal deterrent to a job as an office clerk.   → 7

S. has brain damage which manifests itself in certain mannerisms and slowness on some tasks. He will require specialized placement; complex tasks and those requiring speed and dexterity must be avoided. S. will need an employer who understands that, despite his limitations, he functions quite well in other areas.   → 5

V. is an epileptic. While his handicap is not immediately discernible he has uncontrolled petit mal and grand mal seizures that are very visible at their occurrence. He will have great difficulty finding employment due to the lack of sustained periods without seizure activity and the reluctance of employers to hire epileptics.   → 3

N. is an extremely handicapped, 38-year-old-man. He walks in a slow, laborious manner with the aid of two crutches. His speech, his arm and hand movements—in fact his entire body is affected by cerebral palsy. His ability to find work will be extremely limited because of the nature of his handicap. Most employers would find his disability repugnant.   → 1

appendix B
WORK ATTITUDES SCALE

WHAT I THINK ABOUT WORK

People have a lot of different ideas about work and not everybody thinks the same thing. We would like to know what *you* think.

Below is a list of the different things people have said about work. There's nothing right or wrong about them. They are simply different ways that people have answered the question: "What do you think about work?"

Each of the statements about work has a space next to it, like this...( ). You can show us what you think about each of them by putting any *one* of the numbers 1 to 5 in the space. This is what the numbers mean:

5 means you agree with it, and are pretty sure about it.
4 means you agree but you're not so sure.
3 means you don't know or you can't make up your mind.
2 means you disagree but you're not so sure.
1 means you disagree and are pretty sure about it.

Remember! You only put *one* of these numbers in each of the spaces. This will give us an idea of how much you agree and how much you disagree. Use number 3 only when you really can't tell.

One thing more. It doesn't matter whether you have ever had a job or not, because some of the people we asked had never worked either.

Be sure to fill all the spaces!

---

1. The main thing about working is that it fills your day ....( )
2. If you don't work, there may be no money to take care of you when you're old ....( )
3. What I dislike about working is the people you meet ....( )
4. The trouble with working is that it keeps me from doing things with the people I meet ....( )
5. Working just means carrying out someone else's ideas ....( )
6. When you're not working, the time passes very slowly ....( )
7. Working means you're pulling your weight along with others ....( )
8. You can't trust the people you have to work with ....( )
9. I don't see why you have to work to be considered part of the human race ....( )
10. If you're not able to work, you can't really feel grown up ....( )

11. I work hard enough for my money, without having to support a bunch of other people.....................................( )
12. People respect you if you have a job ....( )
13. Working is just something you have to do....................( )
14. Life can get very boring, without some work to do ....( )
15. People don't think much of you unless you can hold a job.......( )
16. Working keeps you tied down................................( )
17. Working just makes me feel like a cog in a machine............( )
18. When you work they make you give up your own ideas ....( )
19. It makes me feel important when people think I'm doing a good job...( )
20. Without the money you can get from working, there would be very little to make life worthwhile........................( )
21. If you have a job, you can raise a family......................( )
22. The people you work with make the time pass faster than the work you do ....( )
23. I find when I'm working I get all sorts of new ideas from the people I work with ....( )
24. The trouble with working is that I can't do the things I really want to do ....( )
25. I'd rather not raise a family, if I had to work all my life to do it..( )
26. To have to work is to be forced to do what you don't want to do..( )
27. Working just makes me feel I'm on the bottom of the heap ......( )
28. With the money you get from working, you can help support those dear to you...( )
29. Working means just doing the same things over and over again..( )
30. The important thing about working is the pay.................( )
31. You can't expect people to support you all your life. You have to do something for them, too ....( )
32. The trouble with working is that you have to be with people who care nothing about you ....( )
33. Work just means you're pleasing other people................( )
34. The really lucky people are those who can live without working...( )

Appendix B

35. When you work, you have to spend time with a lot of boring people ....( )
36. What I like about working is the people you meet ....( )
37. The important thing about working is the friends you can make on the job ....( )
38. If I didn't work, I would feel I am creating nothing ....( )
39. It's a bad feeling to be completely dependent on others ....( )
40. Working just puts you in contact with people who give you a hard time ....( )
41. The big thing about working is that it puts you in contact with other people ....( )
42. The money you get from working enables you to do things for people ....( )
43. It's tough to have to depend on the opinion of people you work for ....( )
44. When you're not working, you get very lonely ....( )
45. Work is exciting because of the new ideas people have ....( )
46. If you have to work, you just have to give up thinking ....( )
47. To work means to be forced into a rut made up by other people ....( )
48. Working just dulls the imagination ....( )
49. I find work satisfying because it makes me feel creative ....( )
50. I'm not interested in working just because other people want me to ....( )
51. I have to be working in order to get new ideas from people ......( )
52. Work gives me a chance to develop new ideas ....( )
53. If somebody gave you the same amount of money as you could make, there would be no point working ....( )
54. Working means that you help others and they help you ....( )
55. If you aren't able to work, people really do not treat you as an equal ....( )
56. Having a job makes you feel you're worth something ....( )
57. Working doesn't give you enough time to be by yourself ....( )
58. Work is boring ....( )
59. I wouldn't mind working if it wasn't for the people you have to work with ....( )
60. If I could make a living without working, I'd grab the chance .....( )

Scoring Key for the Work Attitudes Scale

Gratification	Focus	Needs	Items
Satisfaction	On Self	Material	2, 20, 30
		Activity	1, 6, 14
		Self-Esteem	10, 39, 56
		Esteem by Others	12, 37, 55
		Creativity	38, 49, 52
	On Others	Material	21, 28, 42
		Activity	22, 41, 44
		Self-Esteem	15, 19, 36
		Esteem by Others	7, 31, 54
		Creativity	23, 45, 51
Dissatisfaction	On Self	Material	34, 53, 60
		Activity	16, 24, 58
		Self-Esteem	13, 17, 26
		Esteem by Others	8, 32, 43
		Creativity	29, 46, 48
	On Others	Material	11, 25, 50
		Activity	4, 35, 57
		Self-Esteem	3, 27, 40
		Esteem by Others	9, 33, 59
		Creativity	5, 18, 47

REFERENCES

Adams, J. S. 1963. Toward an understanding of inequity. Journal of Abnormal and Social Psychology 3:9–16.
Advisory Committee on the Status of Women. 1969. California women. State of California, Documents Section, Sacramento, Calif.
Akridge, R. L. 1979. The Psychosocial Development Matrix: A taxonomy of intermediate objectives in the psychosocial domain. Psychosocial Rehabilitation Journal 3(1):27–37.
Akridge, R. L. 1981. Psychosocial Development Matrix User's Manual. Arkansas Rehabilitation Research and Training Center, Fayetteville, Ark.
Anderson, C. 1960. The relationship between speaking times and decisions in the employment interview. Journal of Applied Psychology 44:267–268.
Anderson, J. 1968. Job Seeking Skills Project. Minneapolis Rehabilitation Center, Minneapolis, Minn.
Anthony, P. D. 1980. Work and the loss of meaning. International Social Science Journal 32(3):416–426.
Anthony, W. A., Pierce, R. M., Cohen, M. R., and Cannon, J. R. 1980. The Skills of Diagnostic Planning (Psychiatric Rehabilitation Practice Series, Book 1). University Park Press, Baltimore.
Arendt, H. 1958. The Human Condition. Chicago Press, Chicago.
Arkansas Rehabilitation Services Operating Procedures Manual. 1981. Department of Human Services, Little Rock, Ark.
Astin, A. W. 1980. The American Freshman: National Norms for Fall, 1980. American Council on Education and the University of California, Los Angeles.
Authier, J., Gustafson, K., Guerney, B., Jr., and Kasdorf, J. A. 1975. The psychological practitioner as a teacher: A theoretical-historical and practical review. The Counseling Psychologist 5:31–50.
Ayllon, T., and Azrin, N. H. 1968. The Token Economy: A Motivational System for Therapy and Rehabilitation. Appleton, New York.
Azrin, N. H., Flores, T., and Kaplan, S. J. 1977. Job-finding club: A group-assisted program for obtaining employment. Rehabilitation Counseling Bulletin 2:130–140.
Azrin, N. H., and Philip, R. A. 1979. The job club method for the job handicapped: A comparative outcome study. Rehabilitation Counseling Bulletin 2:144–155.
Bailey, J. D. A Survey of Rehabilitation Follow-up Studies. 1965. Pennsylvania Bureau of Vocational Rehabilitation, Harrisburg, Pa.
Bandura, A. 1977a. Self-efficacy: Toward a unifying theory of behavioral change. Psychological Review 84:181–215.
Bandura, A. 1977b. Social Learning Theory. Prentice-Hall, Englewood Cliffs, N.J.
Bandura, A., and Walters, R. H. 1963. Social Learning and Personality Development. Holt, Rinehart & Winston, New York.
Barbee, J., and Keil, E. 1973. Experimental techniques of job interview training for the disadvantaged and advantaged clerical employee. Journal of Applied Psychology 58:209–213.

Barry, J. R., and Malinovsky, M. R. 1965. Client Motivation for Rehabilitation: A Review. (Rehabilitation Research Series, No. 1). University of Florida, Gainesville, Fla.

Barthing, H., and Hood, A. 1981. An 11-year follow-up of measured interest and vocational choice. Journal of Counseling Psychology 28(1):27–35.

Becker, G. 1971. The Economics of Discrimination, Second Edition. University of Chicago Press, Chicago.

Bellack, A. S., and Hersen, M. 1977. Self-report inventories in behavioral assessment. In J. D. Crone and R. P. Hawkins (Eds.), Behavioral Assessment: New Directions in Clinical Psychology. Bruner/Mazel, New York.

Better, S. R. 1979. Overcoming Disincentives to Rehabilitation of SSI and SSDI Beneficiaries. Monograph No. 5. Alabama Rehabilitation Research and Training Center, Birmingham, Ala.

Bitter, J. A., and Bolanovich, D. J. 1970. WARF: A scale for measuring job-readiness behaviors. American Journal of Mental Deficiency 74:616–621.

Bolster, B., and Springbett, B. 1961. The reactions of interviewers to favorable and unfavorable information. Journal of Applied Psychology 45:97–103.

Bolton, B. 1970. The Revised Scale of Employability: An application of Taylor's rating scale construction technique. APA Experimental Publication System, No. 7 (Ms No. 261-346).

Bolton, B. (Ed.). 1976. Handbook of Measurement and Evaluation in Rehabilitation. University Park Press, Baltimore.

Bolton, B. 1979. Rehabilitation Counseling Research. University Park Press, Baltimore.

Bolton, B. 1981. Follow-up studies in vocational rehabilitation. In T. Backer et al. (Eds.), Annual Review of Rehabilitation, Vol. 2. Springer, New York.

Bolton, B. 1982. Measurement in rehabilitation. In T. Backer et al. (Eds.), Annual Review of Rehabilitation, Vol. 3. Springer, New York.

Bolton, B., and Cook, D. W. (Eds.). 1980. Rehabilitation Client Assessment. University Park Press, Baltimore.

Bolton, B., and Davis, S. 1979. Rehabilitation counselors' uses of an experimental RIDAC unit. Journal of Rehabilitation 45:41–44.

Bolton, B., Rowland, P., Brookings, J., Cook, D., Taperek, P., and Short, H. 1980. Twelve years later: The vocational and psychosocial adjustment of former rehabilitation clients. Journal of Applied Rehabilitation Counseling 11:113–123.

Bolton, B., and Soloff, A. 1973. To what extent is research utilized? A ten-year follow-up study. Rehabilitation Research and Practice Review 4(2):75–79.

Borgen, F., and Seling, M. 1978. Expressed and inventoried interests revisited: Perspicacity in the person. Journal of Counseling Psychology 26(2):133–139.

Borgen, F. H., Weiss, D. J., Tinsley, H. E. A., Dawis, R. V., and Lofquist, L. H. 1968. The measurement of occupational reinforcer patterns. Minnesota Studies in Vocational Rehabilitation, No. 25. University of Minnesota, Minneapolis, Minn.

Boring, E. G. 1950. A History of Experimental Psychology. Appleton-Century-Crofts, New York.

Botterbusch, K. F. 1976. The Use of Psychological Tests with Individuals Who Are Severely Disabled. Materials Development Center, Menomonie, Wisc.

Botterbusch, K. F. 1980. A Comparison of Commercial Vocational Evaluation Systems. Materials Development Center, Menomonie, Wisc.

Bregman, M. 1979. Some components in vocational evaluation. Paper presented at the National Rehabilitation Association Annual Conference, New York, November, 1979.

Bressler, R., and Lacy, A. 1980. An analysis of the relative job progression of the perceptibly physically handicapped. Academy of Management Journal 23:132–143.

Brown, M., Diller, L., Fordyce, W., Jacobs, D., and Gordon, W. 1980. Rehabilitation indicators: Their nature and uses for assessment. *In* B. Bolton and D. Cook (Eds.), Rehabilitation Client Assessment. University Park Press, Baltimore.

Bureau of National Affairs. 1976. Personnel Policies Forum (Survey No. 114). Bureau of National Affairs, Washington, D.C.

Campbell, D., and Stanley, J. 1966. Experimental and Quasi-experimental Designs for Research. Rand McNally, Chicago.

Campbell, J. P., and Pritchard, R. D. 1976. Motivation theory in industrial and organizational psychology. *In* M. D. Dunnette (Ed.), Handbook of Industrial and Organizational Psychology. Rand McNally, Chicago.

Carkhuff, R. R. 1971. The Development of Human Resources. Holt, Rinehart & Winston, New York.

Carlson, R. 1967a. Selection interview decisions: The effect of interviewer experience, relative quota situation, and applicant sample on interviewer decisions. Personnel Psychology 20:259–290.

Carlson, R. 1967b. Selection interview decisions: The relative influence of appearance and factual written information on an interviewer's final rating. Journal of Applied Psychology 51:461–464.

Carlson, R., Thayer, P., Mayfield, E., and Peterson, T. 1971. Improvements in the selection interview. Personnel Journal 50:268–275ff.

Carroll, T. E. 1965. The ideology of work. Journal of Rehabilitation 31(4):26.

Caseload Statistics: State Vocational Rehabilitation Agencies. 1978. U.S. Department of Health, Education and Welfare, Washington, D.C.

Cautela, J. R., and Kastenbaum, R. 1967. A reinforcement survey schedule for use in therapy, training, and research. Psychological Reports 20:1115–1120.

Clarcq, J. R. 1973. Placement planning—No room for chance. Journal of Rehabilitation 39:26–30.

Cohen, S., and Bunker, K. 1975. Subtle effects of sex role stereotypes on recruiters' hiring decisions. Journal of Applied Psychology 60:566–572.

Constantin, S. 1976. An investigation of information favorability in the employment interview. Journal of Applied Psychology 61:743–749.

Cook, D. W. 1981. A multivariate analysis of motivational attributes among spinal cord injured rehabilitation clients. International Journal of Rehabilitation Research 4:5–15.

Cook, D., Bolton, B., and Taperek, P. 1980. Adjustment to Spinal Cord Injury. Research Report. Arkansas Rehabilitation Research and Training Center, Fayetteville, Ark.

Craighead, W., Kazdin, A. E., and Mahoney, M. J. 1981. Behavior Modification: Principles, Issues and Applications. Houghton Mifflin, Boston.

Crewe, N. M., and Athelstan, G. T. 1978. Functional Assessment Inventory. University of Minnesota Department of Physical Medicine and Rehabilitation, Minneapolis, Minn. (Reprinted in B. Bolton and D. W. Cook (Eds.), Rehabilitation Client Assessment. University Park Press, Baltimore, pp. 389–399.)

Crewe, N. M., and Athelstan, G. T. 1980. The Functional Assessment Inventory: Field-testing results and further development. Paper presented to the Conference on Functional Assessment in Independent Living in Washington, D.C., April 8, 1980.

Crites, J. 1976. Career counseling: A comprehensive approach. The Counseling Psychologist 6(3):2–12.

Crone, J. D., and Hawkins, R. P. (Eds.). 1977. Behavioral Assessment. Bruner/Mazel, New York.

Crowne, D. P., and Marlowe, D. 1964. The Approval Motive. Wiley, New York.

Darlington, R. 1976. Another look at "culture fairness." Journal of Educational Measurement 13:48–82.

Dawes, R. 1979. The robust beauty of improper linear models in decision making. American Psychologist 34:571–582.

Dawis, R. V. 1976. The Minnesota theory of work adjustment. In B. Bolton (Ed.), Handbook of Measurement and Evaluation in Rehabilitation. University Park Press, Baltimore.

Dawis, R., and Lofquist, L. 1976. Personality styles and the process of work adjustment. Journal of Counseling Psychology 23(1):55–59.

Dawis, R. V., Lofquist, L. H., and Weiss, D. J. 1968. A theory of work adjustment. (A revision). Minnesota Studies in Vocational Rehabilitation, Vol. XXIII. University of Minnesota, Minneapolis, Minn.

Dentan, R. 1968. The Semai: A Non-violent People of Malaya. Holt, Rinehart & Winston, New York.

Dickson, M. B. 1976. Work Sample Evaluation of Blind Clients: Criteria for Administration and Development. Materials Development Center, Menomonie, Wisc.

Dictionary of Occupational Titles, Fourth Edition. 1977. U.S. Department of Labor, Washington, D.C.

Diller, L., Fordyce, W., Jacobs, D., and Brown, M. 1979. Rehabilitation Indicators: Overview and Forms. Institute of Rehabilitation Medicine, New York.

Dixon, D., Heppner, P., Petersen, C., and Ronning, R. 1979. Problem solving workshop training. Journal of Counseling Psychology 26(2):133–139.

Dubin, R. 1956. Industrial workers' worlds: A study of central life interests of industrial workers. Social Problems 3:131–142.

Dunnette, M., and Borman, W. 1979. Personnel selection and classification systems. Annual Review of Psychology 30:477–525.

Eigner, J., and Jackson, D. 1978. Effectiveness of a counseling intervention program for teaching career decision-making skills. Journal of Counseling Psychology 25(1):45–52.

Einhorn, H., and Hogarth, R. 1981. Behavioral decision theory: Processes of judgment and choice. Annual Review of Psychology 32:53–88.

Engelkes, J. 1979. Job analysis in vocational rehabilitation. In D. Vandergoot and J. D. Worrall (Eds.), Placement in Rehabilitation: A Career Development Perspective. University Park Press, Baltimore. pp. 127–141.

Esser, T. J. 1980. Gathering Information for Evaluation Planning. Materials Development Center, Menomonie, Wisc.

Fink, S. L., Fantz, R., and Zinker, J. C. 1963. The relevance of Maslow's hierarchy to rehabilitation. Rehabilitation Counseling Bulletin 6:41–48.

Florian, V. 1978. Employers' opinions of the disabled person as a worker. Rehabilitation Counseling Bulletin 22:38–43.

Fordyce, W. E. 1971. Behavioral methods in rehabilitation. In W. S. Neff

(Ed.), Rehabilitation Psychology. American Psychological Association, Washington, D.C.

Fordyce, W. E. 1976. A behavioral perspective on rehabilitation. *In* G. L. Albrecht (Ed.), The Sociology of Physical Disability and Rehabilitation. Feffer and Simons, London.

Foxx, R. M., and Martin, P. L. 1971. A reliable portable timer. Journal of Applied Behavioral Analysis 4:60.

Frank, L., and Hackman, J. 1975. Effects of interviewer-interviewee similarity on interviewer objectivity in college admission interviews. Journal of Applied Psychology 60:356–360.

Friedman, B., and Cornelius, E. 1979. Effect of rater participation in scale construction on the psychometric characteristics of two rating scale formats. Journal of Applied Psychology 61:210–216.

Gay, E. G., Weiss, D. J., Hendel, D. D., Dawis, R. V., and Lofquist, L. H. 1971. Manual for the Minnesota Importance Questionnaire. Monograph No. 28. University of Minnesota Industrial Relations Center, Minneapolis, Minn.

Gatz, M., Tyler, F., and Pargament, K. 1978. Goal attainment, locus of control, a coping style in adolescent group counseling. Journal of Counseling Psychology 25(4):310–319.

Gellman, W. 1953. Components of vocational adjustment. Personnel and Guidance Journal 31:536–539.

Gellman, W., Gendel, H., Glaser, N. M., Friedman, S. B., and Neff, W. S. 1957. Adjusting People to Work. Chicago Jewish Vocational Service, Chicago.

Gellman, W., Stern, D., and Soloff, A. 1963. A scale of employability for handicapped persons (Chicago Jewish Vocational Monograph No. 4). Chicago Jewish Vocational Services, Chicago.

Goldberg, R. T., and Satow, K. L. 1972. Vocational development of adults with congenital heart disease. Rehabilitation Psychology 19:159–168.

Goldstein, A. P., Gershaw, J. M., and Sprafkin, R. P. 1976. Skill Training for Community Living. Pergamon, New York.

Goldstein, A. P., Sprafkin, R. P., Gershaw, N. J., and Klein, P. 1979. Skill Streaming the Adolescent: A Structured Learning Approach to Teaching Prosocial Skills Training Package. Research Press, Champaign, Ill.

Goodyear, D., and Stude, E. 1975. Work performances: A comparison of severely disabled and non-disabled employees. Journal of Applied Rehabilitation Counseling 6(4):210–216.

Green, S., Kappes, B., and Parish, T. 1979. Attitudes of educators toward handicapped and nonhandicapped children. Psychological Reports 44:829–833.

Greene, R. R., and Hoots, D. L. 1969. Reinforcing capabilities of television distortion. Journal of Applied Behavioral Analysis 2:139–142.

Guion, R. 1976. Recruiting, selection, and job placement. *In* M. Dunnette (Ed.), Handbook of Industrial and Organizational Psychology. Rand McNally, Chicago, pp. 777–828.

Hakel, M., Ohnesorge, J., and Dunnette, M. 1970. Interviewer evaluations of job applicants' resumés as a function of the qualifications of the immediately preceding applicants. Journal of Applied Psychology 54:27–30.

Halpern, A. S., Raffeld, P., Irwin, L., and Link, R. 1975a. Measuring social and prevocational awareness of mildly retarded adolescents. American Journal of Mental Deficiency 80:81–90.

Halpern, A. S., Raffeld, P., Irwin, L., and Link, R. 1975b. Social and Prevocational Information Battery (Examiner's Manual). CTB/McGraw-Hill, Monterey, Calif.

Halpern, A. S., Raffeld, P., Irwin, L., and Link, R. 1975c. Social and Prevocational Information Battery (User's Guide). CTB/McGraw-Hill, Monterey, Calif.

Halpern, A. S., Irwin, L., and Landman, J. 1980. Tests for Everyday Living. CTB/McGraw-Hill, Monterey, Calif.

Hamilton, L. S., and Muthard, J. E. 1973. Reducing Economic Dependency among Welfare Recipients: A Review of Vocational Rehabilitation and Manpower Training Research. University of Florida Regional Rehabilitation Research Institute, Gainesville, Fla.

Harris, M. 1980. Culture, People, Nature: An Introduction to General Anthropology, Third Edition, Harper & Row, New York.

Hastorf, A., Northcraft, G., and Picciotto, S. 1979. Helping the handicapped: How realistic is the performance feedback received by the physically handicapped? Personality and Social Psychology Bulletin 5:373–376.

Hastorf, A., Wildfogel, J., and Cassman, T. 1979. Acknowledgement of handicap as a tactic in social interaction. Journal of Personality and Social Psychology 37:1790–1797.

Hershenson, D. B. 1974. Vocational guidance and the handicapped. In E. L. Herr (Ed.), Vocational Guidance and Human Development. Houghton Mifflin, Boston, pp. 478–501.

Hershenson, D. B. 1977. A three-dimensional model for client evaluation. Rehabilitation Counseling Bulletin 20:308–310.

Hershenson, D. B. 1979. Work behavior development and placement. In D. Vandergoot and J. D. Worrall (Eds.), Placement in Rehabilitation: A Career Development Perspective. University Park Press, Baltimore, pp. 59–70.

Hershenson, D. B. 1981. Work adjustment, disability, and the three R's of vocational rehabilitation: A conceptual model. Rehabilitation Counseling Bulletin 25:91–97.

Hinman, S., and Marr, J. N. 1982. Cases in behavioral consultation in rehabilitation. Research Report. Arkansas Rehabilitation Research and Training Center, Fayetteville, Ark.

Hoffman, P. R. 1971. History of the vocational evaluation and work adjustment association. Vocational Evaluation and Work Adjustment Bulletin 4(3):6–16.

Hoffman, P. R. 1973. Work evaluation: An overview. In R. E. Hardy and J. D. Cull (Eds.), Vocational Evaluation for Rehabilitation Services. Charles C Thomas, Springfield, Ill.

Hollman, T. 1972. Employment interviewers' errors in processing positive and negative information. Journal of Applied Psychology 56:130–134.

Imada, A., and Hakel, M. 1977. Influence of non-verbal communication and rater proximity on impressions and decisions in simulated employment interviews. Journal of Applied Psychology 62:295–300.

Ince, L. P. 1976. Behavior Modification in Rehabilitation Medicine. Charles C Thomas, Springfield, Ill.

Irwin, L. K., Halpern, A. S., and Reynolds, W. M. 1977. Assessing social and prevocational awareness in mildly and moderately retarded individuals. American Journal of Mental Deficiency 82:266–272.

Irwin, L. K., Halpern, A. S., and Reynolds, W. M. 1979. Social and Prevocational Battery, Form T. CTB/McGraw-Hill, Monterey, Calif.

Ivey, A. E., and Authier, J. 1978. Microcounseling: Innovations in Interviewing, Counseling, Psychotherapy, and Psychoeducation. Charles C Thomas, Springfield, Ill.

Iwata, B. A., Bailey, J. S., Brown, K. M., Foshee, T. J., and Alpern, M.

1976. A performance based lottery to improve residential care and training by institutional staff. Journal of Applied Behavioral Analysis 9:417–432.
Jaques, M., & Hershenson, D. 1970. Culture, work, and deviance: Implications for rehabilitation counselors. Rehabilitation Counseling Bulletin 14:49–56. (Reprinted in B. Bolton (Ed.), The Rehabilitation Client. University Park Press, Baltimore, pp. 23–29.)
Johns, G. 1975. Effects of informational order and frequency of applicant evaluation upon linear information-processing competence of interviewers. Journal of Applied Psychology 60:427–433.
Johnson, R., and Heal, L. 1976. Private employment agency responses to the physically handicapped applicant in a wheelchair. Journal of Applied Rehabilitation Counseling 7:12–21.
Jones, R. J., and Azrin, N. H. 1973. An experimental application of social reinforcement approach to the problem of job finding. Journal of Applied Rehabilitation Analysis 6:345–353.
Kahn, R. 1980. Faltering economy takes a toll on America's mental health. Institute of Social Research Newsletter 12:3–4.
Kazdin, A. E. 1977. The Token Economy. Plenum, New York.
Kelly, H. H. 1967. Attribution theory in social psychology. Nebraska Symposium on Motivation 15:192–210.
Kelly, G. A. 1955. The Psychology of Personal Constructs. A Theory of Personality (Vol. 1), Clinical Diagnosis and Psychology (Vol. 2). Norton, New York.
Koorland, M. A., and Martin, M. B. 1975. Principles and Procedures of the Standard Behavior Chart, Third Edition. Learning Environments, Inc., Gainesville, Fla.
Krantz, G. 1971. Critical vocational behaviors. Journal of Rehabilitation 36:14–16.
Kravetz, S. 1973. Rehabilitation need and status: Substance, structure, and process. Unpublished doctoral thesis, University of Wisconsin.
Krefting, L., and Brief, A. 1976. The impact of applicant disability on evaluative judgments in the selection process. Academy of Management Journal 19:675–680.
Labor Letter. 1980. Wall Street Journal, September 9, p. 1.
Landman, J., Irwin, L. K., and Halpern, A. S. 1980. Measuring life skills of adolescents: Tests for everday living. Measurement and Evaluation in Guidance 13:95–106.
Landy, F., and Farr, J. 1980. Performance ratings. Psychological Bulletin 87:72–107.
Landy, F. J., and Trumbo, D. A. 1980. Psychology of Work Behavior, Second Edition. The Dorsey Press, Homewood, Ill.
Larrance, D., Pavelich, S., Storer, P., Polizzi, M., Baron, B., Sloan, S., Jordan, R., and Reis, H. 1979. Competencies and incompetencies: Asymmetric responses to women and men in a sex-linked task. Personality and Social Psychology Bulletin 5:363, 366.
Latham, G., and Wexley, K. 1981. Increasing Productivity through Performance Appraisal. Addison-Wesley, Reading, Mass.
Lazarus, A. A. 1973. Multimodal behavior therapy: Treating the "Basic ID." Journal of Nervous and Mental Disease, 156:404–411.
Lee, R. 1979. The !Kung San: Men, Women, and Work in a Foraging Society. Cambridge University Press, New York.
Lewin, K. 1935. A Dynamic Theory of Personality. McGraw-Hill, New York.

References

Likert, R. 1961. New Patterns of Management. McGraw-Hill, New York.
Locke, E. A., Shaw, K. N., Saari, C. M., and Latham, G. P. 1981. Goal setting and task performance: 1969–1980. Psychological Bulletin 90:125–152.
Lofquist, L., and Dawis, R. 1969. Adjustment to Work. Meredith Corporation, New York.
London, M., and Hakel, M. 1974. Effects of applicant stereotypes, order and information on interviewer impressions. Journal of Applied Psychology 59:157–162.
Lutzker, J. R., and Martin, J. A. 1981. Behavior Change. Brooks/Cole, Monterey, Calif.
MacDonald, M. L. 1978. Measuring assertion: A model and method. Behavior Therapy 9:889–899.
Mahoney, M. J. 1979. Self-Change: Strategies for Solving Personal Problems. Norton, New York.
Mallik, K. 1979. Job accommodation through job restructuring and environmental modification. In D. Vandergoot and J. D. Worrall (Eds.), Placement in Rehabilitation: A Career Development Perspective. University Park Press, Baltimore, pp. 143–165.
Marr, J. N., and Means, B. 1980. Behavior Management Manual: Procedures for Psychological Problems in Rehabilitation. Arkansas Rehabilitation Research and Training Center, Fayetteville, Ark.
Marsh, S. K., Konar, V., Langton, M. S., and LaRue, A. J. 1980. The Functional Asssessment Profile: A rehabilitation model. Journal of Applied Rehabilitation Counseling 11:140–144.
Martin, G., and Pear, G. 1978. Behavioral Modification: What It Is and How to Do It. Prentice-Hall, Englewood Cliffs, N.J.
Maslow, A. H. 1954. Motivation and Personality. Harper, New York.
Maslow, A. H. 1970. Motivation and Personality, Second Edition. Harper and Row, New York.
Materials Development Center. 1974. MDC Behavior Identification Format. Materials Development Center, Menomonie, Wisc.
Matkin, R. 1980. Vocational rehabilitation during economic recession. Journal of Applied Rehabilitation Counseling 11(3):149–155.
Mayfield, E. 1964. The selection interview: A reevaluation of published research. Personnel Psychology 17:239–260.
McClure, D. P. 1972. Placement through improvement of clients job-seeking skills. Journal of Applied Rehabilitation Counseling 3:188–196.
McCray, P. 1978. The Individual Evaluation Plan. Materials Development Center, Menomonie, Wisc.
McDaniel, J. W. 1976. Physical Disability and Human Behavior, Second Edition. Pergamon Press, New York.
McGregor, D. 1960. The Human Side of Enterprise. McGraw-Hill, New York.
McMahon, B. 1979. A model of vocational redevelopment for the midcareer physically disabled. Rehabilitation Counseling Bulletin 23(1):35–47.
Means, B. L. 1980. Personal Adjustment Skills Self-Assessment Instrument (unpublished research scale). Arkansas Rehabilitation Research and Training Center, Fayetteville, Ark.
Means, B. L., and Roessler, R. T. 1976. Personal Achievement Skills Training: A Structured Group Personal Adjustment Training Package. Arkansas Rehabilitation Research and Training Center, Fayetteville, Ark.
Meichenbaum, D. 1977. Cognitive-Behavior Modification. Plenum, New York.
Miller, J., and Rowe, P. 1967. Influence of favorable and unfavorable infor-

mation upon the assessment decision. Journal of Applied Psychology 51:432–435.

Mills, C. W. 1951. White Collar. Oxford University Press, London.

Molinaro, D. 1977. A placement system develops and settles: The Michigan model. Rehabilitation Counseling Bulletin 2:121–130.

Morgan, C., and Owens, T. W. 1979. Job Placement of the Severely Handicapped: Seminar Proceeding. Arkansas Rehabilitation Research and Training Center, Fayetteville, Ark.

Morse, N. C., and Weiss, R. S. 1955. The function and meaning of work and the job. American Sociological Review 20(2):191–199.

Myers, J. 1980. Counseling the disabled older person for the world of work. Journal of Employment Counseling 17(1):37–48.

Nadler, E. B., and Shontz, F. C. 1959. A factor analytic study of motivational patterns in a sheltered workshop. Personnel and Guidance Journal 37:444–450.

Nagi, S., and Hadley, L. 1972. Disability behavior: Income change and motivation to work. Industrial and Labor Relations Review 25:223–233.

Neff, W. S. 1966. Problems of work evaluation. Personnel and Guidance Journal 44(7):682–688.

Neff, W. S. 1971. Rehabilitation and work. *In* W. S. Neff (Ed.), Rehabilitation Psychology. American Psychological Association, Washington, D.C.

Neff, W. S. 1977. Work and Human Behavior, Second Edition. Aldine Press, Chicago.

Neff, W. S., and Helfand, A. 1963. A Q-sort instrument to assess the meaning of work. Journal of Counseling Psychology 10:139–145.

Newman, J., and Krzystofiak, F. 1979. Self-reports versus unobtrusive measures: Balancing method variance and ethical concerns in employment discrimination research. Journal of Applied Psychology 64:82–85.

North, R., and Jepsen, D. 1981. Predicting field of job entry from expressed vocational choice and certainty level. Journal of Counseling Psychology 28(1):22–26.

Overs, R. P. 1971. Employment and Other Outcomes after a Vocational Program in a Rehabilitation Center. Curative Workshop of Milwaukee, Milwaukee.

Peacock, J., and Kirsch, A. T. 1970. The Human Direction: An Evolutionary Approach to Social and Cultural Anthropology. Appleton-Century-Crofts, New York.

Pennsylvania State Bureau of Rehabilitation. 1955. Report of Handicapped Workers. Harrisburg, Pa.

Peters, L., and Terborg, J. 1975. The effects of temporal placement of favorable information and of attitude similarity on personnel selection decisions. Organizational Behavior and Human Performance 13:279–293.

Petrak, N. 1971. The Token Economy (unpublished manual). Veterans Administration Hospital, St. Cloud, Minn.

Phillips, D., Fischer, S. C., and Singh, R. A. 1977. A children's reinforcement survey schedule. Journal of Behavior Therapy and Experimental Psychiatry 8:131–134.

Poor, C. R. 1975. Vocational rehabilitation of persons with spinal cord injury. Rehabilitation Counseling Bulletin 18:264–272.

Prazak, J. A. 1969. Learning job-seeking interview skills. *In* J. D. Krumboltz and R. E. Thoresen (Eds.), Behavioral Counseling. Holt, Rinehart & Winston, New York.

Pruitt, W. A. 1977. Vocational (Work) Evaluation. Walt Pruitt Associates, Menomonie, Wisc.

References

Puleo, C. V., and Davis, J. E. 1976. Business and rehabilitation: New partners. American Rehabilitation 1:11–13.

Pumo, B., Sehl, R., and Cogan, R. 1966. Job readiness: Key to placement. Journal of Rehabilitation 32:18–19.

Rand, T., and Wexley, K. 1975. A demonstration of the Byrne similarity hypothesis in simulated employment interviews. Psychological Reports 36:535–544.

Rappaport, R. 1968. Pigs for the Ancestors: Ritual in the Ecology of a New Guinea People. Yale University Press, New Haven.

Reagles, K. W., and Butler, A. J. 1976. The Human Service Scale: A new measure for evaluation. Journal of Rehabilitation 42:34–38.

Rehabilitation Services Administration. 1975. Placement of the Severely Handicapped: A Counselor's Guide. Second Institute on Rehabilitation Issues. West Virginia Rehabilitation Research and Training Center, Institute, W. Va.

Rice, B. D. 1972a. Prescriptive vocational evaluation. Vocational Evaluation and Work Adjustment Bulletin 5(1):8–11.

Rice, B. D. 1972b. Considerations for improved counselor-evaluator relationships. Vocational Evaluation and Work Adjustment Bulletin 5(4):24–27.

Rice, B. D., and Roessler, R. T. 1980. Introduction to Independent Living Rehabilitation Services. Arkansas Rehabilitation Research and Training Center, Fayetteville, Ark.

Rice, B. D., and Thornton, C. L. 1972. Utilization of a prescriptive vocational evaluation to increase counselor effectiveness. Rehabilitation Research and Practice Review 4(1):59–63.

Roessler, R., and Bolton, B. 1978. Psychosocial Adjustment to Disability. University Park Press, Baltimore.

Roessler, R., and Rubin, S. 1979. Knowledge of the world of work: A necessity for rehabilitation counselors. Journal of Rehabilitation 45(4):55–58.

Roessler, R., and Rubin, S. 1980. Goal-setting: Guidelines for Diagnosis and Program Development. Arkansas Rehabilitation Research and Training Center, Fayetteville, Ark.

Rose, G., and Brief, A. 1979. Effects of handicap and job characteristics on selection evaluations. Personnel Psychology 32:385–392.

Rosen, B., and Jerdee, T. 1974a. Influence of sex role stereotypes on personnel decisions. Journal of Applied Psychology 59:9–14.

Rosen, B., and Jerdee, T. 1974b. Effects of applicant's sex and job difficulty on evaluations of candidates for managerial positions. Journal of Applied Psychology 59:511–512.

Rosen, S. D., Weiss, D. J., Hendel, D. D., Dawis, R. V., and Lofquist, L. H. 1972. Occupational Reinforcer Patterns, Vol. 2. Monograph No. 29. University of Minnesota Industrial Relations Center, Minneapolis.

Rosenberg, B. 1969. Development of the TOWER system. Vocational Evaluation and Work Adjustment Bulletin 2:9–11.

Rubin, S. E., and Farley, R. C. 1980. Intake Interview Skills for Rehabilitation Counselors. Akansas Rehabilitation Research and Training Center, Fayetteville, Ark.

Rubin, S., and Roessler, R. 1978. Foundations of the Vocational Rehabilitation Process. University Park Press, Baltimore.

Rubinton, N. 1980. Instruction in career decision-making styles. Journal of Counseling Psychology 27(6):581–588.

Safilios-Rothschild, C. 1970. The Sociology and Social Psychology of Disability and Rehabilitation. Random House, New York.

Sahlins, M. 1972. Stone Age Economics. Aldine, Chicago.
Sawyer, J. 1966. Measurement and prediction: Clinical and statistical. Psychological Bulletin 66:178-200.
Sax, A. B., and Allen, T. C. 1973. The Materials Development Center: A national resource for materials on work evaluation and adjustment. *In* R. E. Hardy and J. G. Cull (Eds.), Vocational Evaluation for Rehabilitation Services. Charles C Thomas, Springfield, Ill.
Schaefer, H. H., and Martin, P. L. 1969. Behavior Therapy. McGraw-Hill, New York.
Schlei, B., and Grossman, P. 1976. Employment Discrimination Law. Bureau of National Affairs, Washington, D.C.
Schmitt, N. 1976. Social and situational determinants of interview decisions: Implications for the employment interview. Personnel Psychology 29:79-101.
Schwab, D., and Heneman, H. 1978. Age stereotyping in performance appraisal. Journal of Applied Psychology 63:573-578.
Schwimmer, E. 1979. The self and the product: Concepts of work in comparative perspective. *In* S. Wallman (Ed.), Social Anthropology of Work. Academic Press. New York.
Shaw, E. 1972. Differential impact of negative stereotyping in employee selection. Personnel Psychology 25:333-338.
Shontz, F. C. 1957. Concept of motivation in physical medicine. Archives of Physical Medicine and Rehabilitation 38:635-639.
Shostrom, E. L. 1963. Personal Orientation Inventory. EDITS/Educational and Industrial Testing Service, San Diego.
Shrey, D. 1980. Postemployment needs of the rehabilitated client: A skilled assessment approach. Rehabilitation Counseling Bulletin 23:266-272.
Shulman, L. S. 1967. The Vocational Development of Mentally Handicapped Adolescents: An Experimental and Longitudinal Study. Chicago Jewish Vocational Service, Chicago.
Sigelman, C., Elias, S., and Danker-Brown, P. 1980. Interview behaviors of mentally retarded adults as predictors of employability. Journal of Applied Psychology 65:67-73.
Skinner, B. F. 1953. Science and Human Behavior. Macmillan, New York.
Skinner, B. F. 1974. About Behaviorism. Knopf, New York.
Skouholt, T. 1977. Issues in psychological education. Personnel and Guidance Journal 55:472-476.
Slovic, P., Fischloff, B., and Lichtenstein, S. 1977. Behavioral decision theory. Annual Review of Psychology 28:1-39.
Snyder, M., Kleck, R., Strenta, A., and Mentzer, S. 1979. Avoidance of the handicapped: An attributional ambiguity analysis. Journal of Personality and Social Psychology 37:2297-2306.
Social Security Administration. 1981. 1980 disability amendments: A training aid for vocational rehabilitation counselors. (SSA Publ. No. 64-015). Office of Operational Policy & Procedure, Washington, D.C.
Soloff, A. 1967. A Work Therapy Research Center. Chicago Jewish Vocational Service, Chicago.
Sterrett, J. 1978. The job interview: Body language and perceptions of potential effectiveness. Journal of Applied Psychology 63:388-390.
Stone, C., and Sawatzki, B. 1980. Hiring bias and the disabled interviewee: Effects of manipulating work history and disability information of the disabled applicant. Journal of Vocational Behavior 16:96-104.
Sulzer-Azaroff, B., and Mayer, G. R. 1977. Applying Behavioral Analyses Pro-

cedures with Children and Youth. Holt, Rinehart & Winston, New York.
Super, D. E., 1957. The Psychology of Careers. Harper & Row, New York.
Tausig, D. 1972. The participation by the disabled in the secondary labor markets (unpublished paper). Institute for Urban and Regional Planning. University of California, Berkeley. (Cited in the Comprehensive Needs Study, Urban Institute, 1975, p. 297.)
Taylor, O. B., and Rice, B. D. 1976. Postemployment Services in Rehabilitation. Arkansas Rehabilitation Research and Training Center, Fayetteville, Ark.
Tenth Institute on Rehabilitation Services. 1972. Vocational Evaluation and Work Adjustment Services in Vocational Rehabilitation. U.S. Department of Health, Education and Welfare, Washington, D.C.
Terkel, S. 1974. Working. Pantheon Books, New York.
Thoresen, C., and Ewart, C. 1976. Behavioral self-control and career development. The Counseling Psychologist 6(3):29–43.
Thoreson, R., Smits, S., Butler, A., and Wright, G. 1968. Counselor problems associated with client characteristics. Wisconsin Studies in Vocational Rehabilitation, Monograph No. 3. Regional Rehabilitation Research Institute, Madison, Wisc.
Tichenor, D., Thomas, K., and Kravetz, S. 1975. Client-counselor congruence in perceiving handicapping problems. Rehabilitation Counseling Bulletin 19(1):299–304.
Tilgher, A. 1930. Work: What It Has Meant to Men through the Ages. Harcourt Brace, New York.
Treitel, R. 1979. Recovery of disabled beneficiaries: A 1975 follow-up of 1972 allowances. Social Security Bulletin 42(4):whole issue.
Ulrich, L., and Trumbo, D. 1965. The selection interview since 1949. Psychological Bulletin 63:100–116.
Upper, D., and Ross, S. M. (Eds.). 1980. Behavioral group therapy. An Annual Review. Research Press, Champaign, Ill.
Urban Institute. 1975. Report of the Comprehensive Needs Study. The Urban Institute, Washington, D.C.
U.S. Senate Committee on Labor and Public Welfare. 1973. Work in America. U.S. Government Printing Office, Washington, D.C.
Usdane, W. M. 1972. Rehabilitation initial diagnostic assessment center. Focus 3(2):1–2.
Vandergoot, D., Jacobsen, R., and Worrall, J. D. 1979. New directions for placement practice in vocational rehabilitation. *In* D. Vandergoot and J. D. Worral (Eds.), Placement in Rehabilitation: A Career Development Perspective. University Park Press, Baltimore, pp. 1–41.
Vandergoot, D., and Swirsky, J. 1980. Applying a systems view to placement and career services in rehabilitation: A survey. Journal of Applied Rehabilitation Counseling, 11(3):149–155.
Vandergoot, D., and Worrall, J. D. (Eds.). 1979. Placement in Rehabilitation: A Career Development Perspective. University Park Press, Baltimore.
Venardos, M., and Harris, M. 1973. Job interview training with rehabilitation clients: A comparison of videotape and role playing procedures. Journal of Applied Psychology 58:365–367.
Vinacke, E. 1962. Motivation as a complex problem. Nebraska Symposium on Motivation 10:1–45.
Vroom, V. 1964. Work and Motivation. Wiley, New York.

Wagner, R. 1949. The employment interview: A critical summary. Personnel Psychology 2:17-46.
Walker, R., Anderson, J., and Hutchins, R. 1968. Job Seeking Skills Project. Minneapolis Rehabilitation Center, Minneapolis, Minn.
Walls, R. 1969. Behavior modification and rehabilitation. Rehabilitation Counseling Bulletin 13:173-183.
Walls, R. T., Masson, C., and Werner, T. J. 1977. Negative incentives to voca—tional rehabilitation. Rehabilitation Literature 38:143-150.
Walls, R. T., Zane, T., and Thvedt, J. E. 1979. The Independent Living Behavior Checklist (Experimental Edition). West Virginia Research and Training Center, Morgantown, W. Va.
Walls, R. T., Zane, T., and Werner, T. J. 1979. The Vocational Behavior Checklist (Experimental Edition, Second Printing). West Virginia Research and Training Center, Dunbar, W. Va.
Wallman, S. (Ed.) 1979. Social Anthropology of Work. Academic Press, New York.
Washburn, P., and Hakel, M. 1973. Visual cues and verbal content as influences on impressions after simulated employment interviews. Journal of Applied Psychology 58:137-140.
Watson, J. B. 1919. Psychology from the Standpoint of a Behaviorist. J. B. Lippincott, Philadelphia.
Webster, B. 1964. Decision-Making in the Employment Interview. Industrial Relations Centre, McGill University, Montreal.
Weiss, D., and Dawis, R. 1960. An objective validation of factual interview data. Journal of Applied Psychology 44:381-385.
Weiss, D., Dawis, R., Englund, G., and Lofquist, L. 1961. Validity of Work Histories Obtained by Interview. Minnesota Studies in Vocational Rehabilitation, Number 12. University of Minnesota, Minneapolis.
Wessman, H. 1965. Absenteeism, accidents of rehabilitated workers. Rehabilitation Record 6(3):15-18.
Westerheide, W. J., and Lenhart, L. 1973. Development and reliability of pretest-posttest rehabilitation services outcome measure. Rehabilitation Research and Practice Review 4(3):15-24.
Westerheide, W. J., Lenhart, L., and Miller, M. C. 1974. Field test of a services outcome measurement form. Monograph No. 2, Case difficulty. Department of Institutions, Social and Rehabilitation Services, Oklahoma City, Okla.
Westerheide, W. J., Lenhart, J., and Miller, M. C. 1975. Field test of a services outcome measurement form. Monograph No. 3, Client change. Department of Institutions, Social and Rehabilitation Services, Oklahoma City, Okla.
Wexley, K., and Nemeroff, W. 1974. Effects of racial prejudice, race of applicant, and biographical similarity on interviewer evaluations of job applicants. Journal of Social and Behavioral Science 20:66-78.
Wexley, K., Sanders, R., and Yukl, G. 1973. Training interviewers to eliminate contrast effects in employment interviews. Jounal of Applied Psychology 57:233-236.
Weiner, Y., and Schneiderman, M. 1974. Use of job information as a criterion in employment decisions of interviewers. Journal of Applied Psychology 59:699-704.
Wilkinson, M. 1975. Leisure: An alternative to the meaning of work. Journal of Applied Rehabilitation Counseling 6(2):73-77.

Williams, R. M. 1959. American Society: A Sociological Interpretation. Knopf, New York.

Wise, R., Charner, I., and Randour, M. 1976. A conceptual framework for career awareness in career decision-making. The Counseling Psychologist 6(3):47-52.

Wolkowitz, B. 1973. Characteristics of the demand for disabled workers (working paper). The Urban Institute, Washington, D.C. (Cited in the Comprehensive Needs Study, Urban Institute, 1975, p. 297).

Wright, B. A. 1960. Physical Disability—A Psychological Approach. Harper and Row, New York.

Wright, G. 1980. Total Rehabilitation. Little, Brown, Boston.

Wright, G. N., and Remmers, H. H. 1960. Manual for the Handicapped Problems Inventory. Purdue Research Foundation, Lafayette, Ind.

Wright, O. 1969. Summary of research on the selection interview since 1964. Personnel Psychology 22:391-413.

Wright, P. 1974. The harried decision maker: Time pressures, distractions, and the use of evidence. Journal of Applied Psychology 59:555-561.

Yankelovich, D. 1974. The meaning of work. *In* J. Rosow (Ed.), The Worker and the Job: Coping with Change. Prentice-Hall, Englewood Cliffs, N.J.

Yankelovich, D. 1981. New Rules: Searching for Self-fulfillment in a World Turned Upside Down. Random House, New York.

Zadny, J. J., and James, L. F. 1976. Another View of Placement: State of the Art 1976. Studies in Placement Monograph No. 1. Portland State University Regional Research Institute, Portland Ore.

Zadny, J., and James, L. 1978. A survey of job search patterns among state vocational rehabilitation clients. Rehabilitation Counseling Bulletin 22(1):60-65.

Zadny, J., and James, L. 1979a. The problem with placement. Rehabilitation Counseling Bulletin 22(5):439-442.

Zadny, J., and James, L. 1979b. Job placement in state vocational rehabilitation agencies: A survey of technique. Rehabilitation Counseling Bulletin 22(4):361-378.

AUTHOR INDEX

Adams, J. S., 40
Akridge, R. L., 149, 155, 156, 163, 164
Alger, H., 32
Allen, T. C., 73
Alpern, M., 147
Anderson, C., 208
Anderson, J., 129, 189
Anthony, P. D., 32
Anthony, W. A., 77
Arendt, H., 30
Astin, A. W., 34
Athelstan, G. T., 55
Authier, J., 152
Ayllon, T., 141, 143
Azrin, N. H., 141, 143, 145, 190

Bailey, J. D., 17
Bailey, J. S., 147
Bandura, A., 143, 144
Barbee, J., 204
Baron, B., 203
Barry, J. R., 41, 42
Barthing, H., 174
Becker, G., 195
Bellack, A. S., 164
Better, S. R., 51
Bitter, J. A., 56
Bolanovich, D. J., 56
Bolster, B., 197, 204
Bolton, B., 1, 14, 17, 19, 51, 53, 55, 60, 61, 65, 67, 68
Borgen, F. H., 57, 59, 174
Boring, E. H., 72
Borman, W., 205, 206
Botterbusch, K. F., 93, 94, 95, 125
Bregman, M., 72
Bressler, R., 195, 201
Brief, A., 196, 198, 199, 201, 202
Brookings, J., 14
Brown, K. M., 147
Brown, M., 57
Bunker, K., 196
Butler, A. J., 39, 41, 59, 161, 184

Calvin, J., 30
Campbell, D., 196
Campbell, J. P., 40
Cannon, J. R., 77
Carkhuff, R. R., 152
Carlson, R., 198, 203, 204, 207
Carroll, T. E., 33, 35
Cassman, T., 198, 199, 200, 201
Cautela, J. R., 135
Charner, I., 172
Clarcq, J. R., 185
Cogan, R., 189
Cohen, M. R., 77
Cohen, S., 196
Constantin, S., 204
Cook, D. W., 14, 39, 46, 50, 60, 61
Cornelius, E., 211
Craighead, W., 128
Crewe, N. W., 55
Crites, J., 175
Crites, N. W., 175
Crone, J. D., 162, 163

Danker-Brown, P., 202
Darlington, R., 206
Davis, J. E., 65, 192
Dawes, R., 196, 205, 206, 208
Dawis, R. V., 2, 5, 49, 57, 59, 170, 174, 176
Dentan, R., 26
Dickson, M. B., 94, 175, 178
Diller, L., 57
Dubin, R., 33
Dunnette, M., 198, 204, 205, 206

Eigner, J., 174, 175
Einhorn, J., 196, 206
Elias, S., 202
Engelkes, J., 191
Englund, G., 208
Esser, T. J., 76
Ewart, C., 173, 175

Fantz, R., 41
Farley, R. C., 77
Farr, J., 197, 207, 210
Ferritor, D. E., 21
Fink, S. L., 41
Fischhoff, B., 196, 206
Fisher, S. C., 135
Flores, T., 190
Florian, V., 198, 203, 204
Fordyce, W. E., 47, 48, 57, 127, 128
Foshee, T. J., 147
Foxx, R. M., 133
Frank, L., 204
Friedman, B., 211
Friedman, S. B., 9

Gatz, M., 178
Gay, E. G., 57
Gellman, W., 2, 3, 9, 13, 56, 67, 68
Gendel, H., 9
Gershaw, J. M., 163
Gershaw, N. J., 152
Glaser, N. M., 9
Goldberg, R. T., 2
Goldstein, A. P., 152, 163
Goodyear, D., 35
Gordon, W., 57
Green, S., 196
Greene, R. R., 135
Greenwood, R., 181
Grossman, P., 195, 196
Guerney, J. B., 152
Guion, R., 196
Gustafson, K., 152

Hackman, J., 204
Hadley, L., 51
Hakel, M., 198, 202, 203, 204
Halpern, A. S., 56, 57, 59
Hamilton, L. S., 17
Harris, M., 26, 204
Hastorf, A., 198, 199, 200, 201
Hawkins, R. P., 162, 163
Heal, L., 198, 199, 200
Helfand, A., 69
Hendel, D. D., 57
Heneman, H., 204, 207
Heppner, P., 175, 178
Hersen, M., 164

Hershenson, D. B., 2, 6, 7, 8, 153, 155, 161, 169, 172, 182, 184
Hinman, S., 136, 137, 139
Hoffman, P. R., 79
Hogarth, R., 196, 206
Hollman, T., 198, 204
Hood, A., 174
Hoots, D. L., 135
Hutchins, R., 129

Imada, A., 202
Ince, L. P., 127
Irwin, L., 56, 57, 59
Ivey, A. E., 152
Iwata, B. A., 147

Jackson, D., 174, 175
Jacobs, D., 57
Jacobsen, R., 183
James, L. F., 39, 170, 171, 181, 182, 183, 186
Jaques, M., 169, 172
Jepsen, D., 174
Jerdee, T., 197
Johns, G., 204
Johnson, R., 198, 199, 200
Jones, R. J., 145
Jordan, R., 203

Kahn, R., 32
Kaplan, S. J., 190
Kappes, B., 196
Kasdorf, J. A., 152
Kastenbaum, R., 135
Kazdin, A. E., 128, 141
Keil, E., 204
Kelly, H. H., 152
Kirsch, A. T., 26
Kleck, R., 199, 203
Klein, P., 152
Konar, V., 163
Koorland, M. A., 133
Krantz, G., 182
Kravetz, S., 58, 171
Krefting, L., 198, 199, 201, 202
Krzystofiak, F., 197

Lacy, A., 195, 201
Landman, J., 57
Landy, F. J., 40, 197, 207, 210
Larrance, D., 203
LaRue, A. J., 163
Lasch, C., 33
Latham, G., 46, 196, 205, 208, 211
Layton, M. S., 163
Lazarus, A. A., 152
Lee, R., 26
Leland, M., 71
Lenhart, L., 58, 163
Lewin, K., 46
Lichtenstein, S., 196, 206
Likert, R., 40, 69
Link, R., 56, 59
Locke, E. A., 46
Lofquist, L. H., 49, 57, 170, 174, 176, 208
London, M., 198, 204
Luther, M., 30
Lutzker, J. R., 128

MacDonald, M. L., 163
Mahoney, M. J., 128, 152
Malinovsky, M. R., 41, 42
Mallik, K., 185
Marr, J. N., 127, 130, 133, 134, 136, 137, 138, 139, 143, 144, 147
Martin, G., 133, 145
Martin, J. A., 128
Martin, M. B., 133
Martin, P. L., 133, 143
Marsh, S. K., 163
Marx, K., 33
Maslow, A. H., 40, 41, 58, 161
Masson, C., 50
Matkin, R., 168, 172
Mayer, G. R., 143
Mayfield, E., 196, 203, 204
McClure, D. P., 189
McCray, P., 77
McDaniel, J. W., 42, 45
McGregor, D., 40
McMahon, B., 2, 8, 176, 177, 178
Means, B. L., 127, 130, 133, 134, 138, 143, 144, 147, 149, 151, 164
Meichenbaum, D., 152
Mentzer, S., 199, 203
Miller, J., 198, 204

Miller, M. C., 58
Mills, C. W., 24
Molinaro, D., 191, 192
Morgan, C., 192
Morse, N. C., 32
Muthard, J. E., 17
Myers, J., 172

Nadler, E. B., 45
Nagi, S., 51
Neff, W. S., 2, 8, 9, 30, 32, 42, 43, 44, 50, 68, 69, 72, 78, 79
Nemeroff, W., 204
Newman, J., 197
North, R., 174
Northcraft, G., 198, 199, 200

Ohnesorge, J., 198, 204
Overs, R. P., 17
Owens, T. W., 192

Pargament, K., 178
Parish, T., 196
Pavelich, S., 203
Peacock, J., 26
Pear, G., 133, 145
Peters, L., 204
Petersen, C., 175, 178
Peterson, T., 203, 204
Petrak, N., 143
Philip, R. A., 190
Phillips, D., 135
Picciotto, S., 198, 199, 200
Pierce, R. M., 77
Pietsch, S., 195
Polizzi, M., 203
Poor, C. R., 42
Prazak, J. A., 145
Pritchard, R. D., 40
Pruitt, W. A., 72, 79
Puleo, C. V., 192
Pumo, B., 189

Raffeld, P., 56, 59
Rand, T., 204
Randour, M., 172
Rappaport, R., 27

Reagles, K. W., 41, 59, 161
Reis, H., 203
Remmers, H. H., 58
Reynolds, W. M., 56
Rice, B. D., 1, 19, 71, 73, 74, 80
Roessler, R. T., 1, 151, 167, 172, 173
Ronning, R., 175, 178
Rose, G. L., 195, 196, 198, 199, 201, 202
Rosen, B., 57, 59, 197
Rosenberg, B., 72
Ross, S. M., 151
Rowe, P., 198, 204
Rowland, P., 14
Rubin, S. E., 77, 172, 173
Rubinton, N., 178

Saari, C. M., 46
Safilios-Rothschild, C., 35, 36, 39, 184
Sahlins, M., 26
Sanders, R., 203, 204, 206
Satow, K. L., 2
Sawatzki, B., 198, 199, 203
Sawyer, J., 205
Sax, A. B., 73
Schaefer, H. H., 143
Schlei, B., 195, 196
Schmitt, N., 203, 206
Schneider, M. J., 21
Schneiderman, M., 204
Schwab, D., 204, 207
Schwimmer, E., 24
Sehl, R., 189
Seling, M., 174
Shaw, E., 46, 204
Shontz, F. C., 44, 45
Short, H., 14
Shostrom, E. L., 161
Shrey, D., 210
Shulman, L. S., 13
Sigelman, C., 202
Singh, R. A., 135
Skinner, B. F., 47, 127, 128
Skouholt, T., 152
Slovic, P., 196, 206
Smith, S., 39
Smits, S., 184
Snyder, M., 199, 203

Soloff, A., 13, 56, 67
Sprafkin, R. P., 152, 163
Springbett, B., 197, 204
Stanley, J., 196
Stern, D., 56, 67
Sterrett, J., 202
Stone, C., 198, 199, 203
Storer, P., 203
Strenta, A., 199, 203
Stude, E., 35
Sulzer-Azaroff, B., 143
Swirsky, J., 168, 175

Taperek, P., 14, 50
Tausig, D., 186
Taylor, O. B., 19
Terborg, J., 204
Terkel, S., 34
Thayer, P., 203, 204
Thomas, K., 171
Thoreson, C, 39, 42, 50, 173, 175, 184
Thornton, C. L., 73, 80
Thvedt, J. E., 163
Tichenor, D., 171
Tilgher, A., 30
Treitel, R., 51
Trumbo, D., 40, 203
Tyler, F., 178

Ulrich, L., 203
Upper, D., 151
Usdane, W. M., 60

Vandergoot, D., 168, 175, 183, 185
Venardos, M., 204
Vinacke, E., 40
Vroom, V., 40, 41, 42, 45, 46

Wagner, R., 203, 205
Walker, R., 129
Wallman, S., 24
Walls, R. T., 50, 54, 55, 59, 127, 163
Walters, R. H., 143
Washburn, P., 203
Watson, J. B., 127
Weber, M., 30

Webster, B., 198, 204, 205
Weiss, D. J., 32, 49, 57, 208
Werner, T. J., 50, 54, 55, 59, 163
Wessman, H., 35
Westerheide, W. J., 58, 163
Wexley, K., 196, 203, 204, 205, 206, 208, 211
Wiener, Y., 204
Wildfogel, J., 198, 199, 200, 201
Wilkinson, M., 35
Williams, R. M., 33
Wise, R., 172, 173, 174
Wolfe, T., 33
Wolkowitz, B., 186
Worrall, J. D., 183, 185

Wright, B. A., 39, 40, 46, 47, 187
Wright, G., 8, 13, 184
Wright, G. H., 58
Wright, O., 203
Wright, P., 207

Yankelovich, D., 32, 34
Yukl, G., 203, 204, 206

Zadny, T., 39, 170, 171, 181, 182, 183, 186
Zane, T., 54, 55, 59, 163
Zinker, J. C., 41

SUBJECT INDEX

Adjustment, 1
   Chicago Jewish Vocational model, 2, 3–5, 8
   Hershenson's developmental model, 2, 6–7, 8
   Minnesota Theory of Work Adjustment, 2, 5–6, 8
   occupational acculturation, 11–12
   therapeutic workshop, 8–13
Agricultural societies, 26–30
Applied behavioral analysis, 127, 128
Assessment, 78–80
   follow-up, 81
   Prescriptive Evaluation Report, 80
   staff conference, 80
Assessment instruments and procedures, 163–166
   behavioral observation, 165
   behavioral rating scales, 163
   personal skills self-assessment instrument, 164
   Psychosocial Development Matrix Questionnaire, 164
Assessment of the handicapped, 53

Back-up reinforcements, 141, 142
Behavioral interventions, 134–147
   aversive consequences, 138–140
   extinction, 138
   fading, 137, 138
   modeling, 143–145
   negative practice, 139
   overcorrection, 139, 140
   positive practice, 140
   positive reinforcement, 134–137
   response cost, 140
   restitution, 139
   shaping, 135, 136
   time-out, 138–140
   token economies, 141–143
Behavior modification, 127–147
Behavioral rating scales, 163

Chaining, 145, 146
Chicago Jewish Vocational Service, 2
Client assessment, 60–67
Commercial vocational evaluation, 94, 95
   client population, 94, 95
   purpose of, 94, 95
   selection, 94, 95
Comprehensive Occupational Assessment Training (COATS), 95–98
   method of instruction, 97
   organization, 95
   utility, 97, 98
   work evaluation process, 97

Data-People-Things (DPT), 98
Deaf, 185
Diagnostic evaluation, 172
Discrimination against handicapped, 196–198

Economic disincentives, 49–51
Emotional disabilities, 182
Employability, 67–68
Employability Attitudes System, 96
Employers, 205–206
   recommendations for hiring the handicapped, 205, 206
Employment potential, 53, 54
Employment problems, 170, 171
   employer reception, 170
   experience, 170
   job availability, 170
   job-seeking skills, 170, 171
   motivation, lack of, 170
   vocational training, 170
Evaluation interview, 77

Fading, 137, 138
Follow-up, 15–20

Subject Index

Fordyce's Behavioral Model, 47, 48
Functional Assessment Inventory, 55

Generalization, 158
Goal identification, 167
Group cohesion, 157, 158

Handicap Problems Inventory, 58
Hershenson's developmental model, 6–8, 153–154, 161
History of work, 25–32
Human Service Scale, 41, 58, 161

Inappropriate vocational patterns, 12, 13
Incentives, 174
Individualized Written Rehabilitation Program (IWRP), 59, 65, 73
Institute for Crippled and Disabled (ICD), 72
Intellectual disabilities, 182
Interpersonal relations, 12
Interview skills, 206–208

Job acquisition, 182–193
Job analysis, 79, 169
Job club, 190
Job development, 169, 171
Job matching system, 95–96
Job modification, 169
Job performance, 4
Job satisfaction, 3, 5
Job-seeking skills, 54
Job skills, 54
Job tryout, 80

Living skills system, 96–97
Long-term vocational adjustment, 2

Maslow's need hierarchy, 40–41
McCarron-Dial Work Evaluation System (MDWES), 101–103
  instruction giving, 102
  organization, 101
  utility, 103
  work evaluation process, 101–102

McDaniel's decision-making model, 45–46
Meaning attribution, 152
Measurement of work behaviors, 131–134
  baseline, 133
  behavior products, 131
  fixed interval counts, 132
  frequency count, 131
  intervention data, 134
Micro-TOWER, 103–106
  instruction giving, 107
  organization, 103
  utility, 107
  work evaluation process, 103–104
Mid-life career planning, 176–178
Mid-life disability, 176
Minnesota Importance Questionnaire, 57
  Dimensions of vocational need, 57
Minnesota Rehabilitation Center, 189
Minnesota Theory of Work Adjustment, 5–6, 48–49
Modeling, 143–145
  attention, 144
  job club, 145
  job-seeking behaviors, 145
  motivation, 144
  motoric reproduction, 144
  retention, 144
Motivation, 39
Motivational Occupational Vocational Evaluation (MOVE), 98–101
  instruction giving, 100
  organization, 98–99
  utility, 100
  work evaluation process, 99–100

Neff's work personality model, 42–44
Negative practice, 139

Occupational acculturation, 11–12
Overcorrection, 139–140

Personal Achievement Skills Training package, 151
Personal Orientation Inventory, 161
Personal Skills Self-Assessment Instrument, 164–165

Philadelphia Jewish Employment and Vocational Service work sample (JEVS), 106–107
  instruction giving, 107
  organization, 106
  utility, 107
  work evaluation process, 106–107
Physical disabilities, 182
Placement, definition of, 181
Placement services, 181
Positive practice, 140
Positive reinforcement, 134–135
Preliminary screening, 97
Prescriptive approach, 73–81
  client information, 76
  components of, 76–81
  evaluation plan, 77
  evaluation team, 74–76
  vocational evaluation plan, 77
  vocational exploration, 77–78
Pre-vocational Readiness Battery, 108–111
  instruction giving, 109
  organization of, 108
  utility of, 109
  work evaluation process, 108–109
Prevocational skills, 54
Psychometric testing, 78
Psychosocial adjustment instruments, 57–58
  vocational subscales, 57–58
Psychosocial adjustment skills training, 153–157
  description of, 150
Psychosocial Development Matrix Questionnaire, 155

Rehabilitation counselor, 186–188
Rehabilitation indicators, 57
  activity planning indicators, 57
  environmental indicators, 57
  skill indicators, 57
  status indicators, 57
Rehabilitation Initial Diagnosis and Assessment of Clients (RIDAC), 60–67
  components, 61–63
  evaluation of, 64–65
  objective, 60–61
Rehabilitation models of motivation, 42–51

Rehabilitation programming, 88–93
Rehabilitation specialist, 205
  recommendations for, 205–206
Response cost, 140
Revised Scale of Employability, 53, 67–68
  counseling scales, 68
  workshop scales, 68

Self-report measures, 163–165
Service Outcome Measurement form, 58
Shaping, 135–136
Shontz's trait model, 44–45
Situational assessment, 78–79
Skill indicators, 57
Social and Prevocational Information Battery, 56–57
Staff training, 147
Status indicators, 57

Talent assessment programs, 110–111
Target behaviors, 141
Therapeutic workshops, 8–13
  occupational acculturation, 11–12
  interpersonal relations, 12
  inappropriate vocational patterns, 12–13
Time-out, 138–139
Tokens, 141
Token economies, 141–143
TOWER System, 111–113
Training groups, 158–159

Union and financial security skills, 54

Valpar Component Work Sample Series, 113–115
Vocational adjustment, 1–20
Vocational adjustment scales, 55–57
Vocational alternatives, 174
Vocational assessment, 53, 78–80
  job analysis, 79
  job tryout, 80
  prescriptive evaluation report, 80
  psychometric testing, 78
  situational assessment, 79–80
  work sample testing, 78

Vocational Behavior Checklist, 54
  interview skills, 54
  job-related skills, 54
  job seeking skills, 54
  on-the-job social skills, 54
  prevocational skills, 54
  union and financial security skills, 54
  work performance skills, 54
Vocational counseling, 167
Vocational counselor, 169–170
  job analysis, 169
  job development, 169–170
  job modification, 169
  problem solving, 169
Vocational evaluation plan, 77
Vocational evaluation system, 115–117
Vocational exploration, 77–78
Vocational information evaluation, 117–119
Vocational Interest Temperament and Aptitude System (VITAS), 119-121
Vocational measurement in rehabilitation, 54–60
Vocational measurement instruments, 58
  uses of, 58–60
Vocational rehabilitation, 1
Vocational Rehabilitation Act of 1973, 1
Vocational Skills Assessment and Development program, 121–123
Vroom's cognitive model, 41–42

Wide Range Employability Sample Test (WREST), 123–125

Work Adjustment Rating Form, 56
Work Attitude Scale, 53
Work behaviors, 128–129
  deficits, 129–130
  surpluses, 129–130
Work competencies, 6
Work, definition of, 24
Work evaluation process, 97
Work for disabled, 33–36
  rehabilitation, 34–36
Work goals, 6
Work history, 25–32
  agricultural and pastoral societies, 26–30
  hunting-gathering societies, 25–26
  industrial societies, 30–31
Work in American society, 32–34
Work motivation, definition of, 39
Work motivation models, 39–51
  Fordyce's behavioral model, 47–48
  Human Service Scale, 41, 58, 161
  Maslow's need hierarchy, 40–41
  McDaniel's decision-making model, 45–46
  Minnesota work adjustment model, 48–49
  Neff's work personality model, 42–44
  Shontz's trait model, 44–45
  Wright's goal-setting model, 46–47
Work personality, 6
Work role, 173–175
  data collection, 173–174
  task specification, 173
Work samples, 94
Work sample administration, 97
Work sample system, 96
Workshop Scale of Employability, 56